A MODERN TOMBOY

A Story for Girls

MRS. L. T. MEADE

1st WORLD
LIBRARY
Literary Society

A Modern Tomboy

L. T. Meade

© 1st World Library, 2009
PO Box 2211
Fairfield, IA 52556
www.1stworldlibrary.com
First Edition

LCCN: 2009923471

Softcover ISBN: 978-1-4218-8860-6
Hardcover ISBN: 978-1-4218-8959-7
eBook ISBN: 978-1-4218-8761-6

Purchase *"A Modern Tomboy"*
as a traditional bound book at:
www.1stWorldLibrary.com/purchase.asp?ISBN=978-1-4218-8860-6

1st World Library is a literary, educational organization
dedicated to:

- Creating a free internet library of downloadable ebooks

- Hosting writing competitions and offering book publishing
scholarships.

Interested in more 1st World Library books? contact:
literacy@1stworldlibrary.com
Check us out at: www.1stworldlibrary.com

1ˢᵗ World Library Literary Society

Giving Back to the World

"If you want to work on the core problem, it's early school literacy."

- James Barksdale, former CEO of Netscape

"No skill is more crucial to the future of a child, or to a democratic and prosperous society, than literacy."

- Los Angeles Times

"Literacy... means far more than learning how to read and write... The aim is to transmit... knowledge and promote social participation."

- UNESCO

"Literacy is not a luxury, it is a right and a responsibility. If our world is to meet the challenges of the twenty-first century we must harness the energy and creativity of all our citizens."

- President Bill Clinton

"Parents should be encouraged to read to their children, and teachers should be equipped with all available techniques for teaching literacy, so the varying needs and capacities of individual kids can be taken into account."

- Hugh Mackay

CHAPTER I

OPENING THE SCHOOL

Mrs. Merriman and Lucy were standing at the white gates of Sunnyside, waiting for the arrival of the girls. Mrs. Merriman had soft brown hair, soft brown eyes to match, and a kindly, gentle face. Lucy was somewhat prim, very neat in her person, with thick fair hair which she wore in two long plaits far below her waist, a face full of intensity and determination, and a slightly set and formal way of speaking.

"Aren't you at all excited about their arrival?" said Mrs. Merriman, turning to her daughter as she spoke. "It will make a great change in the house, will it not?"

"How many of them are there, mother?" was Lucy's response.

"Oh, my dear child, how often I have explained all to you! There's Laura Everett, my dear friend Lady Everett's only daughter; then there is Annie Millar, whom I do not know anything about—but she is a friend of Laura's, and that alone is recommendation enough."

"Laura Everett, Annie Millar," quoted Lucy in a low tone. "Have you seen either of them, mother?"

"No, dear, of course not"

"Has father ever seen them?"

"No. But my dear friend Lady Everett—"

"Oh, mother darling, when have you seen your dear friend?"

"Not since we were girls. But it is so nice to think she should trust her daughter to me."

"Well, yes, mother, I suppose so. I suppose I must be quite satisfied. Well, that means two—Laura and Annie. How old are they, mother?"

"They are both fourteen."

"Then the others, mother?"

"Rosamund Cunliffe. I did meet her mother a year ago, who told me she was very pretty. I remember that. Then there is Phyllis Flower. Think of any one with such a dear name— Phyllis and Flower! The whole name is too sweet! I told your father that I knew I should fall in love with Phyllis."

"Mother dear, you really mustn't make favorites," said Lucy in a reproving tone. "If these girls must come to us and form the beginning of a school, why, we must behave accordingly. You are not half as steady as I am, mother, and I am fifteen, and you are—"

"Forty-five," said Mrs. Merriman; "but then I only feel twenty, and I am very happy about all this. The house is perfectly arranged, everything in apple-pie order, and they will have such a good time, dear girls! Well, now, let us count them over. Laura Everett, fourteen; Annie Millar, ditto; Rosamund Cunliffe, fifteen; and Phyllis Flower, thirteen. Then there is Jane Denton. Well, I know nothing whatever about her except that her mother says she is a good girl, and does her utmost to learn, and she is sure will be absolutely obedient. Then comes Agnes Sparkes. I quite expect she will be the witty one. Altogether that makes six girls, and you, my dear, are the seventh—the perfect number, you know."

"And the whole house turned topsy-turvy!" said Lucy. "Really and truly, mother, I wish we had thought it over before we did anything so queer."

"We could not help it, love. Your father's health is very bad, and he cannot continue his work as a professor. There is no other manner in which to earn money. Why not take the whole thing cheerfully, Lucy? Remember, you will have your education practically free."

"I don't suppose I'd mind the girls so very much," said Lucy, "if it were not for the horrid governesses. To think of having a creature like Mademoiselle Omont living in the house! And then, I am not specially in love with Miss Archer. But there, I suppose we must make the best of it."

"We must, and will, and can," said Mrs. Merriman in her cheery voice.

She had scarcely said the words before a wagonette was seen driving down the summer lane. Girls in different-colored dresses, with bright faces, eager eyes, suddenly appeared in view. The wagonette drew up at the gate, and Mrs. Merriman, to Lucy's disgust, went impulsively forward.

"Here you all are, dears!" she said. "Oh, I am so glad to welcome you! Now, you must tell me who's who. Won't you get down? It will be nice to stretch your legs in walking up the avenue. Your luggage, of course, is coming in the cart which was sent to meet the train.—Tell me, my love, are you Laura Everett?"

Mrs. Merriman darted forward and took the somewhat irresponsive hand of a tall, pale girl, who replied languidly that her name was Jane Denton.

"I beg your pardon, dear—I do truly. Then which is Laura? For I want to welcome the dear child of a very dear friend of my youth."

A girl with a merry face, bright blue eyes, and fair hair now extricated herself from the group of her companions. "I am Laura," she said, "and this is my friend Annie."

Mrs. Merriman rapturously kissed both girls.

"Welcome to Sunnyside!" she said. "You may be certain I will do my utmost to make you happy. This is my daughter Lucy."

"Can I show you the house, Miss Everett?" said Lucy, speaking stiffly; "and will you come, too, Miss Millar?"

The three girls went on in front.

"I must get to know the rest of you," said Mrs. Merriman, who was too much accustomed to Lucy to mind her ways. "Which is—now let me guess—which is Phyllis Flower? I am longing to know her. And which is Rosamund Cunliffe? —Jane Denton, I shall not forget you, dear. I am so glad to see you."

Here Mrs. Merriman gave Jane's hand an affectionate squeeze.

"And Agnes Sparkes—I have not noticed Agnes Sparkes. I am sure you—whoever you are, but I can't quite make out yet—will be the wit of the school. Ah! you are Agnes Sparkes?" and Mrs. Merriman pounced upon a small, very thin, dark girl, with no beauty whatever about her.

A peal of laughter greeted her ears. "Indeed, I am Phyllis Flower," said the young lady in question; and Mrs. Merriman started back with a look of disappointment. "You thought because I had rather a pretty name that I'd look it," continued the girl. "But I do not—I am neither witty nor beautiful, and I know I am not clever. I have got just nothing but my name. I'd rather like to live up to it; but somehow I don't think I can. Perhaps I may at Sunnyside. It seems such a novel idea to come to a sort of home school like this, and not to be treated a bit formally. Thank you so much, Mrs. Merriman!" and Phyllis held out a small, neatly gloved hand and clasped Mrs. Merriman's, looking at her all the time with delight beaming in her eyes.

The other girls followed suit. They managed to introduce themselves one by one, and presently Mrs. Merriman was seen trotting contentedly down the avenue, followed by her new pupils. She looked something like a well-groomed pony herself, and the girls were much amused at her way of greeting them, and so thoroughly pleased that peals of laughter reached the displeased ears of Lucy, who was waiting with Annie and Laura in the porch.

"Really," thought Lucy, "poor mother gets worse and worse. What sort of school will this be? Not the slightest vestige of order, and all these girls being spoken to at the gate. Mother has no dignity. It is really terrible. I shall be glad when Miss Archer and Mademoiselle Omont come. How are we to spend the present evening?"

The girls themselves seemed to arrange that matter. Having lost all shyness with regard to Mrs. Merriman, they were not likely to feel it towards Lucy. They accordingly requested to be taken into the house, and were much pleased with the arrangements made for their comfort. The old house of Sunnyside was one of the prettiest in the southwest of England. It had spacious grounds, beautiful gardens, and the rooms themselves, although somewhat low, were large and numerous. One or two girls had a room each, and the others were arranged two in a room, with a curtain between.

When Mrs. Merriman started the idea of a small school for the special education of special girls, she had spared no expense to have everything done in as thoroughly nice a manner as possible; and the girls themselves were delighted, and showed their appreciation by behaving in a hoydenish and school-girl fashion. They laughed and joked with each other, declaring that Mrs. Merriman was quite too funny for anything, but that she was also an old dear; that Lucy was rather a nuisance, and very prim, but that she shouldn't stand much in their way. And then they paced about in the garden arm-in-arm, and talked to one another, just, as Lucy said afterwards, as though they had lived there all their lives.

Poor Lucy in every respect was her mother's opposite. Neither did she specially take after her gentle, patient father, who was always satisfied to make the best of things, his motto being peace on any terms, and who was surprised now when Lucy ran up to him as he was pacing up and down in the walnut walk at some distance from the house.

"Ah, my little girl!" he said when he saw her approaching. "Why, what is the matter? How flushed your cheeks are!"

"And no wonder, father," answered Lucy. "If you could flush up at anything you'd feel hot and indignant now. Oh, father dear, I wish—I wish we weren't obliged to have those detestable girls!"

"What, Lucy! Have they come?"

"I should think they have. They'll waylay you in a minute or two."

"Oh, no, my dear. I don't specially want to see them now."

"Then let us go straight by this gate into the paddock. I don't suppose they will find the paddock before to-morrow. Father, I don't think mother is at all suited to keep a school."

"Lucy, I will not have your dear mother abused. Talk on any other subject, but I can't stand that."

"I suppose it is very wrong of me."

"It is more than wrong. You can scarcely realize what a good, brave, and noble woman she is. Who but she would have acted as she has done lately? She has taken the bull by the horns and saved us from absolute ruin. By her plucky ways and determination has she not just kept our heads above water? My dear Lucy, you little know what might have happened but for your mother's pluck and bravery."

"I know," said Lucy, softened on the spot. "But if she only wouldn't—wouldn't make so free with them when they come, and if there might be a little order, and if they could have been postponed till the resident governesses had arrived. But now they are there, all of them, as merry and jocular as you like, running about the place, racing here and there, and devouring all our best fruit, tramping in and out of the greenhouses and conservatory, and making such a noise just over your study. It would be much better to give up

Sunnyside—anything would be better than this."

"I don't think so, and you will find after a time that you will like your school friends. Your education will be finished without any extra cost whatever. We are being very well paid for these girls, we know they are all ladies, and your mother will be happy and in her element. How could you turn your dear mother into a precise, stately woman? It isn't in her, and you would not wish it to be."

"I don't know," said Lucy. "I think I would. But, father, you always make me ashamed of myself. You, who suffer so much, are so good, so patient."

"If I am good and patient it is because of my dear wife and my dear daughter," said the man sadly. "And now, Lucy darling, go back to them all and try to help your mother. The governesses will come to-morrow, and the day after lessons will begin. In a week's time you will see perfect order arising out of chaos, and you will be surprised at your present feelings."

Lucy raised her father's hand to her lips. She loved her mother, but she adored him, with his slight stoop, his scholarly face, his gentle smile, his kindly eyes. There were few men more beloved than Professor Merriman. He had given some really great books to the world, and was a scholar in the truest and best sense of the word. When he instructed Lucy, which he did now and then, she regarded those moments as the happiest and most sacred of her life.

"Well, whatever happens, I have got him," she thought as she turned to go back to the house. "And if it adds any years to his precious life, surely I can endure anything. But I do hope he won't get to like any of those girls. Perhaps he will. Perhaps he will even offer to teach some of them. I sincerely trust none of them are clever. Oh, who is this queer little creature coming to meet me?"

The queer little creature in question, dressed in brown holland, with a small brown hat and cotton gloves, was no other than Phyllis Flower. She ran up to Lucy, and stood in front of her, and said, "Is your father really the great Professor Ralph Merriman?"

"Yes," said Lucy, coloring and smiling, for it was delightful to her to hear the appreciative tone in Phyllis's voice.

"I thought so, but I was not quite sure. Agnes Sparkes and I were arguing about it. Agnes said it couldn't be, but I said it was. I am very glad. I hope we shall see him sometimes."

"He is not well," said Lucy. "He can't be disturbed."

"We would none of us dream of disturbing him; but we would love to look at him sometimes, and perhaps sometimes to hear him speak."

"I dare say you will see him. When he is well enough he will dine with us," said Lucy. "But you must not expect"—

"Oh, we expect nothing—nothing certainly from you," said Phyllis Flower, flushing angrily, for there was a tone in Lucy's voice which she could scarcely stand. Then she, continued, "Why are you determined not to be nice to us, Miss Merriman?"

"You had better call me Lucy," said the girl after a pause. "We are all girls together. You are at school and I am at school."

"How old are you, Lucy?"

"I am fifteen."

"And I am thirteen and a half. How old do you think I look?"

"Oh, any age. You are so thin."

"And wizened," laughed Phyllis. "Well, never mind. I dare say I shall grow tall enough by-and-by. Now, my dear," she continued after a pause, "you have nothing whatever to be jealous of in me. I am not clever, I am not good-looking; in short, I am nothing at all, just the most ordinary person. But I can tell you something about the characters of your other school-fellows if you like. Would you care? There is plenty of time. Shall we walk up and down for a little?"

Lucy could not resist the temptation. Phyllis, who was quite as frank and free as Mrs. Merriman herself, laid her hand on Lucy's arm. Lucy shuddered, but submitted.

"The person who has got the greatest character among us is Rosamund Cunliffe. She will rule us all."

"She won't rule me," interrupted Lucy angrily.

"You can't help it, my dear. She has always ruled every one with whom she comes in contact; and she does it quite nicely, too, for she isn't unamiable. She simply has a strong character."

"I hardly know what she is like," said Lucy.

"Oh, you must have observed her—that tall, dark, pretty-looking girl, with rosy cheeks and a pretty mouth."

"Yes, I think I know whom you mean."

"And she is clever, too. But I don't think it is her beauty or her talent that makes her curious charm. It is something beyond all this. I never saw her do a really unamiable thing, and yet I think she must love power very much. You will soon find out for yourself what she is like. As for Janey Denton, she is just a good sort, something like me. And Laura Everett is very proud of her family, and she is clever. And Annie Millar is Laura's shadow, and does nothing whatever except what Laura wishes. Then there is Agnes Sparkes. She is supposed to be my friend, and she is very pretty, fair, and lively and clever. But of all the girls who have come here to-day the two who will make their mark in the world are beyond doubt Rosamund Cunliffe and Laura Everett. Now, I think I will let you find out the rest for yourself."

CHAPTER II

ROSAMUND TAKES THE LEAD

Before that day had come to an end, Lucy had discovered how true were Phyllis Flower's words. For Rosamund Cunliffe, without making herself in the least disagreeable, without saying one single rude thing, yet managed to take the lead, and that so effectively that even Lucy herself found that she could not help following in her train.

For instance, after dinner, when the girls—all of them rather tired, and perhaps some of them a little cross, and no one exactly knowing what to do—clustered about the open drawing-room windows, it was Rosamund who proposed that the rugs should be rolled back and that they should have a dance.

Lucy opened her eyes. Nobody before had ever dared to make such a suggestion in the house of Sunnyside. Lucy, it is true, had dancing lessons from a master who came once a week to instruct her and other girls in the winter season, and she had occasionally gone to a children's party. But beyond that she had never danced, looking forward to it, however, as a possible recreation by-and-by.

Rosamund's clear voice was now heard.

L. T. Meade

"Let us push back the sofas. This is a splendid room. We can roll up the rugs in a twinkling. Where is Mrs. Merriman? She will play the dance music. Oh, there are seven of us—one too many. Perhaps you will play for us, Lucy?"

"But I don't know any dance music," said Lucy; "and then mother would not like the rugs being disturbed. The room is arranged just as father and mother wish it to be. I think perhaps"—

She colored painfully.

"We will do nothing without leave, of course," said Phyllis Flower. "I'll just run and find Mrs. Merriman and ask her."

Before Lucy could prevent her, Phyllis had darted out of the room, returning in a minute or two with the required permission.

"It's all right, girls," she said; "we can trip it on the light fantastic toe as long as ever we please, and the rugs may go to Hong-kong for all Mrs. Merriman cares."

Lucy colored with rage. Rosamund gave a quiet smile—a smile which seemed to denote power. Phyllis's dancing eyes lit for a moment on Lucy's face. Those eyes said in the most provoking manner, "I told you so." And then some one went to the piano, and a minute or two later all the girls, Lucy included, were dancing round and round the room in the merry waltz.

Even Lucy enjoyed it when once it had begun, and the little performer at the piano played well, and kept excellent time. And by-and-by Lucy forgot herself, and could not help laughing when Rosamund seized her round the waist and whirled her round and round, and taught her to reverse, and instructed her in one or two other matters unknown to Lucy up to the present.

The dance lasted for over an hour; and just in the midst of it, when Lucy was really laughing in quite a heart-whole manner, she raised her eyes and saw no less a person than Mr. Merriman himself standing in the doorway. He was smiling, and his eyes were fixed on Rosamund's face.

The moment Rosamund saw him she stopped at once, and said to Lucy, "Is that your father, the great professor?"

"Yes," said Lucy.

"Please introduce him to me."

Lucy longed to say, "It will tire him; I can't do it." She longed to give any sort of excuse, but none would come to her lips. She was forced to take Rosamund up to Mr. Merriman.

"This is Rosamund Cunliffe," she said, "and she wants to know you, father."

"I am very much pleased to see you, Miss Cunliffe," said Mr. Merriman; and then Rosamund stood in the doorway and talked.

Lucy went back and tried to dance with another girl, and the dance music still went on. But she could not help straining her ears and trying to catch the subject of Rosamund's conversation. Why, she was absolutely laughing, and the Professor, who was generally so grave and quiet, was laughing also. What did it all mean?

"Father, aren't you tired?—Miss Cunliffe, you are tiring

L. T. Meade

father," said Lucy at last, running up to the door and trying to speak calmly.

"No, my dear," said her father. "On the contrary, I am intensely interested.—You must tell me that story again, Miss Cunliffe. Would you like to come and see my library?"

The two went off together, and Lucy felt almost as though she must burst into tears. Phyllis's eyes again met her face, and she had to restrain her feelings. The "I told you so" look was too maddening almost for endurance.

Rosamund's love of power showed itself further in the arrangement of her bedroom. She took down the dividing curtain between herself and Jane Denton without asking any one's permission; and she slept in the bed intended for Jane, and rearranged the drawers, putting them into another part of the room; and complained about the wardrobe, saying that she would like it put opposite the door instead of in its present position. And whatever she wished was immediately done, and whatever she said was said so politely that no one took offense. And Lucy had to confess to herself that Phyllis was right, and that Rosamund would be a power—the leading power—in the school.

Early the next day the two teachers arrived. Mademoiselle Omont was very French in appearance, very dark, with sparkling black eyes and neatly arranged soft dark hair. She had a truly Parisian accent, and a pretty, graceful way about her. Miss Archer was a stolid-looking woman of about five-and-thirty years of age. She had a long talk, on her arrival, with Mrs. Merriman, and then she went to her room and stayed there for some little time, so that it was not until tea-time that the girls and the two resident governesses met.

Lucy looked with great approbation at Miss Archer when she

took her seat opposite the tea-tray.

"She will bring order into this chaos," thought the girl. "She will force all these girls to behave properly. She will insist on order. I see it in her face."

But as the thought passed through Lucy's mind, Rosamund jumped suddenly up from her own place, requested Phyllis Flower to change with her, and sat down close to Miss Archer. During tea she talked to the English governess in a low tone, asking her a great many questions, and evidently impressing her very much in her favor.

"Oh, dear!" thought Lucy, "if this sort of thing goes on I shall lose my senses. If there is to be any order, if the whole scheme which mother has thought out so carefully, and father has approved of, means to establish a girl like Rosamund Cunliffe here as our leader, so that we are forced to do every single thing she wishes, I shall beg and implore of father and mother to let me go and live with Aunt Susan in the old Rectory at Dartford."

Lucy's cheeks were flushed, and she could scarcely keep the tears back from her eyes. After tea, however, as she was walking about in front of the house, wondering if she should ever know a happy moment again, Miss Archer made her appearance. When she saw Lucy she called her at once to her side.

"What a nice girl Rosamund Cunliffe seems!" was her first remark.

"Oh! don't begin by praising her," said Lucy. "I don't think I can quite stand it."

"What is the matter, my dear? You are little Lucy Merriman,

are you not—the daughter of Mrs. Merriman and the Professor?"

"I am."

"And this house has always been your home?"

"I was born here," said Lucy almost tearfully.

"Then, of course, you feel rather strange at first with all these girls scattered about the place. But when lessons really begin, and you get into working order, you will be different. You will have to take your place with the others in class, and everything is to be conducted as though it were a real school."

"I will do anything you wish," said Lucy, and she turned a white face, almost of despair, towards Miss Archer. "I will do anything in all the world you wish if you will promise me one thing."

Miss Archer felt inclined to say, "What possible reason have you to expect that I should promise you anything?" but she knew human nature, and guessed that Lucy was troubled.

"Tell me what you wish," she said.

"I want you not to make a favorite of Rosamund Cunliffe. Already she has begun to upset everything—last night all the drawing-room arrangements, her own bedroom afterwards; then, to-day, the other girls have done nothing but obey her. If this goes on, how is order to be maintained?"

Miss Archer looked thoughtful.

"From the little I have seen of Rosamund, she seems to be a

very amiable and clever girl," she said. "She evidently has a great deal of strength of character, and cannot help coming to the front. We must be patient with her, Lucy."

Lucy felt a greater ache than ever at her heart. She was certain that Miss Archer was already captivated by Rosamund's charms. What was she to do? To whom was she to appeal? It would be quite useless to speak to her mother, for her mother had already fallen in love with Rosamund; and indeed she had with all the young girls who had arrived such a short time ago. Mrs. Merriman was one of the most affectionate people on earth. She had the power of taking an unlimited number of girls, and boys, too, into her capacious heart. She could be spent for them, and live for them, and never once give a thought to herself. Now, in addition to the pleasure of having so many young people in the house, she knew she was helping her husband and relieving his mind from weighty cares. The Professor could, therefore, go on with the writing of his great work on Greek anthology; even if the money for this unique treatise came in slowly, there would be enough to keep the little family from the products of the school. Yes, he should be uninterrupted, and should proceed at his leisure, and give up the articles which were simply wearing him into an early grave.

Lucy knew, therefore, that no sympathy could be expected from her mother. It is true that her father might possibly understand; but then, dared she worry him? He had been looking very pale of late. His health was seriously under-mined, and the doctors had spoken gravely of his case. He must be relieved. He must have less tension, otherwise the results would be attended with danger. And Lucy loved him, as she also loved her mother, with all her heart and soul.

When Miss Archer left her, having nothing particular to do herself and being most anxious to avoid the strange girls, she went up the avenue, and passing through a wicket-gate near the entrance, walked along by the side of a narrow stream where all sorts of wild flowers were always growing. Here might be seen the blue forget-me-not, the meadow-sweet, great branches of wild honeysuckle, dog-roses, and many other flowers too numerous to mention. As a rule, Lucy loved flowers, as most country girls do; but she had neither eyes nor ears for them to-day. She was thinking of her companions, and how she was to tolerate them. And as she walked she saw in a bend in the road, coming to meet her, a stout, elderly, very plainly dressed woman.

Lucy stood still for an instant, and then uttered a perfect shout of welcome, and ran into the arms of her aunt Susan.

Mrs. Susan Brett was the wife of a hard-working clergyman in a town about ten miles away. She had no children of her own, and devoted her whole time to helping her husband in his huge parish. She spent little or no money on dress, and was certainly a very plain woman. She had a large, pale face, somewhat flat, with wide nostrils, a long upper lip, small pale-blue eyes, and a somewhat bulgy forehead. Plain she undoubtedly was, but no one who knew her well ever gave her looks a thought, so genial was her smile, so hearty her hand-clasp, so sympathetic her words. She was beloved by her husband's parishioners, and in especial she was loved by Lucy Merriman, who had a sort of fascination in watching her and in wondering at her.

From time to time Lucy had visited the Bretts in their small Rectory in the town of Dartford. Nobody in all the world could be more welcome to the child in her present mood than her aunt Susan, and she ran forward with outstretched arms.

"Oh, Aunt Susy, I am glad to see you! But what has brought you to-day?"

"Why, this, my dear," said Mrs. Brett. "I just had three hours to spare while William was busy over his sermon for next Sunday. He is writing a new sermon—he hasn't done that for quite six months—and he said he wanted the house to himself, and no excuse for any one to come in. And he just asked me if I'd like to have a peep into the country; that always means a visit to Sunnyside. So I said I'd look up the trains, and of course there was one just convenient, so I clapped on my hat—you don't mind it being my oldest one—and here I am."

"Oh, I am so glad!" said Lucy. "I think I wanted you, Aunt Susan, more than any one else in all the world."

She tucked her hand through her aunt's arm as she spoke, and they turned and walked slowly along by the riverside.

Mrs. Brett, if she had a plain face, had by no means a correspondingly plain soul. On the contrary, it was attuned to the best, the richest, the highest in God's world. She could see the loveliness of trees, of river, of flowers. She could listen to the song of the wild birds, and thank her Maker that she was born into so good a world. Nothing rested her, as she expressed it, like a visit into the country. Nothing made the dreadful things she had often to encounter in town seem more endurable than the sweet-peas, the roses, the green trees, the green grass, the fragrance and perfume of the country; and when she saw her little niece—for she was very fond of Lucy—looking discontented and unhappy, Mrs. Brett at once perceived a reason for her unexpected visit to Sunnyside.

"We needn't go too fast, need we?" she said. "If we go down this path, and note the flowers—aren't the flowers lovely, Lucy?"

"Yes," replied Lucy.

"We shall be in time for tea, shall we not? But tell me, how is your father, dear? I see you are in trouble of some sort. Is he worse?"

"No, Aunt Susy; I think he is better. He has had better nights of late, and mother is not so anxious about him."

"Then what is the worry, my love, for worry of some sort there doubtless is?"

"It is the girls, Aunt Susy."

"What girls, my love?"

"Those girls that mother has invited to finish their education at Sunnyside. They came yesterday, and the teachers, Mademoiselle Omont and Miss Archer, arrived to-day. And the girls don't suit me—I suppose I am so accustomed to being an only child. I cannot tell you exactly why, but I haven't been a bit myself since they came."

"A little bit jealous, perhaps," said Aunt Susan, giving a quick glance at Lucy's pouting face, then turning away with a sigh.

"You will be surprised, Lucy," she continued after a pause, "when I tell you that I used to be fearfully jealous when I was young. It was my besetting sin."

"Oh, Aunt Susy, I simply don't believe it!"

"You don't? Then I will show you some day, when you and I are having a snug evening at the old Rectory at Dartford, a letter I once received from my dear father. He took great pains to point out to me my special fault, as he called it; and his words had a wonderful effect, and I went straight to the only source of deliverance, and by slow degrees I lost that terrible feeling which took all the sunshine out of my life."

"Tell me more, please, Aunt Susan," said Lucy.

"Well, you see, dear, I was not like yourself an only child. I was one of several, and I was quite the plain one of the family. I am very plain now, as you perceive; but I had two beautiful little sisters. They were younger than I, and Florence had quite a beautiful little face, and so had Janet. Wherever they went they were admired and talked about, and I was thought nothing of. Then I had three brothers, and they were good-looking, too, and strong, and had excellent abilities, and people thought a great deal about them; but no one thought anything about me. I was the eldest, but I was never counted one way or the other as of the slightest consequence. My people were quite rich, and Florence and Janet were beautifully dressed, and taken down to the drawing-room to see visitors; but I was never noticed at all. I could go if I liked, but it did not gratify anybody, so by degrees I stayed away. You do not know what bitter feelings I had in my heart, for they really were undeniably some of the most attractive children you could possibly find; and Florence was so witty, and Janet so delicate and refined and sweet in all her ways! I could not be angry with them, but I did think it fearfully unfair that so many blessings should be poured on their heads and so few given to me, for I was not even specially clever.

"Then I thought I would make a friend of my brother Roger. He was a very fine fellow, and for a time I did get into his confidence, and I was fairly happy. But he went to Rugby, and at Christmas he brought some of his school-fellows back with him, and they paid the most absurd attentions to

Florence and Janet, and they snubbed me; and I suppose Roger, poor dear! was weak enough to be influenced by them, for he took no notice of me either, so you can just imagine what a bad time I had.

"Well, my dear, one day there came a letter from an old cousin asking either of the two girls, Florence or Janet, or myself, to go to stay with her in the country. She had a very nice house, and a pony and trap, and she could take us about and give us a good time. My mother was exceedingly anxious that the twins—I forgot to tell you that they were twins—should go, and she said so to me. She said they wanted change of air, as they were looking quite cooped up in our poky town. But I said, 'I am the eldest, and I don't see why I shouldn't have the pleasure of going, as I also have been invited. I mean it is only fair to give me the first chance.'"

"Then she said, 'I think that is quite fair, and you shall have the first chance, Susan;' and so I went."

"Florence and Janet were not a bit angry, poor dears! They kissed me and helped me to pack my things, and Florence offered me one of her prettiest necklaces, and Janet some wonderful embroidered gloves which had been given to her by Roger at Christmas. But I was too jealous to accept any of their trinkets, and I went away with a sore feeling in my heart. Ah, Lucy! that was a long time ago."

Aunt Susan paused. A spasm of pain crossed her face. After a time she said slowly, "I enjoyed myself for a week or two. Then came news from home. The fever which had been lurking in the town for some time reached our house, and the two beautiful little twins were smitten with it. And before I could hear again they were both dead. Had I given up my own way, and let them go to see my old cousin, they might have been alive now."

"But you—you might have taken the fever. Oh! I think it is fearfully sad; but how could you know? And you could not be blamed—you could not really be blamed," said Lucy with great earnestness.

"Perhaps not," said Aunt Susan, recovering herself on the spot. "And I do not mean to be morbid about it; only, at the time, my conscience troubled me, and your poor aunty had a very bad time. It was soon afterwards that my dear father wrote to me, and I shall always keep his letter. Since then I have never been jealous of any one, and I would advise you to lay my story to heart, Lucy, and to do your utmost to keep down the seeds of jealousy, for they make a man or woman miserable, and they do no good in the world."

Lucy did not know why Aunt Susan's talk affected her so much. She still kept her hand on the old lady's arm, and they walked slowly up to the house. As they were approaching it she said suddenly, "Now that I have seen you, I mean to do my very best. I know it is remarkably brave of mother to have started the school and to have the girls here, and I know I ought to help her, and not to be cross because her ideas are not my ideas. And I will try, and I will remember your story and what you have said, for you always suit me, and you always understand me, Aunt Susan. But may I ask you one thing, one great favor?"

"What is that, my dear?" asked her aunt.

"If I find matters quite intolerable, may I come to you for a week to the Rectory at Dartford—just for one week? Will you invite me?"

"You have a hearty welcome, child. You know what it is

L. T. Meade

like: soup-kitchens, mothers' meeting, coal-tickets, reading aloud to the children, rushing about from this place to the other trying to help those who cannot help themselves. It will do you good, Lucy, and of course you shall come."

CHAPTER III

A GYPSY TEA

Lessons were not to begin until the following morning, and the six boarders were feeling in consequence a trifle disconsolate. They did not know what to do with themselves. They had explored the place the day before. They had visited the kitchen-garden and the flower-garden, and the paddocks and the shrubberies and the lawns, and they had wandered down towards the river. There seemed to be nothing special to do. The tennis-lawn was not properly mowed for tennis, and anyhow the net was not out, and there seemed to be no croquet-ground anywhere. In consequence, there was nothing whatever to do but to pace up and down under the shadow of the trees a little way from the house.

Rosamund Cunliffe walked with Phyllis Flower, Jane Denton with Agnes Sparkes, and Laura Everett with her special friend and factotum, Annie Millar. They were all good-natured, kind-hearted girls, ready to make the best of things; but as they walked now, pacing up and down, Rosamund suddenly stopped, faced round, and addressed the rest of her companions.

"Well, girls," she said, "I must say that I think we are placed in a rather disagreeable position at Sunnyside."

"What do you mean?" asked Laura, opening her wide blue eyes to their fullest extent.

"Why, can't you judge for yourself? That little Lucy Merriman is determined to be disagreeable to us. We cannot get her to make herself the least pleasant; whatever we do she interprets in the wrong manner, and how we are to keep the peace I don't know. I am sure I don't want to dislike her or be disagreeable to her; but she is at home, and we are strangers. She is exceedingly ill-bred, there is no doubt of that. Why should we put up with it? Ought we not at once to declare our independence, and to let her know that as we pay—or, rather, our parents pay for us—a very good sum for our education, she is bound at least not to make herself obnoxious?"

"Oh, I don't think she is obnoxious," said Agnes Sparkes. "She is just a little bit jealous. I used to be jealous of a girl once. It is a horrid sensation."

"Oh, my dear!" said Rosamund slowly, stamping her foot in her endeavor to speak with emphasis, "it is absolutely ridiculous for any one to give way to those morbid feelings in these days. If her mother wished us to come here to be educated, I suppose she had her good reasons for it, and that Lucy should be such a goose is really past enduring."

"I quite agree with what you say," replied Laura in her quiet voice, "and my only remedy is this: don't take the least notice of her."

"But that is not so easy when she pokes her disagreeable little face in at every turn."

"And her still more disagreeable little words," said Phyllis Flower.

"Now, Phyllis, don't you make mischief," said Annie Millar. "You know perfectly well that you are cleverer than the whole lot of us put together, whether you like to acknowledge it or not."

"I am not a bit clever, and I always say so," was Phyllis's response. "I have got far less than most people: no looks, no stature, no abilities. No one need ever come to me for anything, for I have nothing to give, having got nothing for myself."

"You have one gift, dear," said Rosamund, looking at her kindly; "you are an excellent listener, and you can make as pertinent a remark as any one in the school. I maintain that I consider you clever, and you will prove my words before many terms are over."

"But the point now," said Laura, "is Lucy. We begin lessons to-morrow. I should say that Miss Archer is an exceedingly nice woman—in fact, she is vastly superior to most—and the French governess is very good, too. They are both busy arranging our work for us; and of course we shall have masters innumerable, and several mistresses also, and we shall go to Dartford twice a week for lessons, so we shall be just as busy as bees. I think the only plan is to let Lucy alone."

It was while this conversation was going on, and the girls were standing together in a group, that Mrs. Brett, accompanied by no less a person than Lucy herself, appeared in view. Lucy shrank from the six girls who stood together under one of the big elm-trees, and she was about to loosen her hold of Mrs. Brett's arm, but that good lady drew her forward.

"Now come, Lucy; don't be silly. Now is your chance. I want

to be introduced to those nice girls. Exceedingly nice they look, and pleasant companions they will be for you. Come and do your duty, my love."

"Oh, if only mother had such dignified manners!" thought the girl. She found herself yielding to Mrs. Brett's commands, and in a minute was standing amongst the other girls, introducing one after another to the wife of the rector of Dartford.

"My dears, I am heartily glad to see you," said Aunt Susan in her cheerful voice. "I am Aunt Susan, or Aunty Susy, to all the world, and any one who comes to Dartford finds his or her way to my cosy little bower sooner or later. Lucy is a special friend of mine.—Aren't you, Lucy?"

"You are my aunt, remember," said Lucy in a choking voice.

"She is her aunt, remember," said Phyllis Flower in a sort of mocking tone.

The other girls tittered. Mrs. Brett's calm voice continued: "I am a very plain old woman; I have no youth to boast of, and no looks to boast of; but I think I have got a somewhat capacious heart, and it is amply willing to take you all in if you wish to come. Now, let me see. This is Wednesday. I think you will come to Dartford on Saturday for lessons. Will you all come and have tea with me? You shall meet my husband, who is a very jolly sort of man, and we can show you some of our curiosities, which we have collected from time to time in our scanty travels. We are precious poor, so you mustn't expect anything but a very plain tea—bread and butter and jam; but you will have enough, and that is something, and you will see the inside of a plain working-man's house."

"Oh, Aunt Susy! Not a working-man!" said Lucy.

"Yes, a working-man, my dear," persisted Aunt Susy. "He is a minister of the Gospel, and he works hard for his Lord; and he is very proud of his Master, and very proud of the service among his Master's work-men.—So, girls, you can come if you like, or stay away if you like. We can all be very jolly together. Do you accept my invitation?"

"Indeed, we shall be delighted," said Agnes Sparkes eagerly. "What do you say, Jane?" she continued, turning to Jane Denton.

Jane Denton signified her approval with sparkling eyes, and the other girls followed suit.

"Well, that is settled," said Mrs. Brett. "You may call me Aunt Susy, those of you who like."

Lucy looked at her aunt almost as though she hated her at that moment. Mrs. Brett did not pretend to see the glance.

"Now," she said, "what are you going to do this afternoon? Why should not we all go and have tea down by the river? Why shouldn't we? Your mother wouldn't object, would she?"

"Oh, no; mother never objects to anything," said Lucy, with a little sigh.

"But you do, don't you, Lucy?" said Rosamund in a low voice.

"I dislike innovations," said Lucy.

Their eyes met. Rosamund's flashed angrily. Lucy felt that

all the jealousy which she had promised Aunt Susan to bury for ever in a low grave was rising up stronger than before. Aunt Susan was in reality watching her niece, and was quite determined to have her way.

"Won't some one go into the house," she said, addressing the girls in a mass, "and ask Mrs. Merriman if you may yourselves carry down the cups and saucers and teapot, and jam and bread and butter, and whatever is required for a gipsy tea? I have just one hour before I must trot back to catch my train, and during that hour I can help you to get it. There is a lovely bank just above the river, where we can make our gipsy fire and enjoy ourselves."

Where was the *ennui* now? Agnes Sparkes rushed off to fulfil Mrs. Brett's bidding. Lucy, ashamed, she knew not why, followed her more slowly. In a few minutes, owing to Mrs. Brett's breezy talk, there were seven girls, all apparently happy, very busily preparing tea. The fire soon crackled and blazed; the kettle quickly did its part by singing merrily and boiling sturdily. Tea was made in the old brown teapot which was always kept for such occasions. How good it tasted in the open air! how different from any made indoors! No longer was Sunnyside a dull place, for Mrs. Brett kept all the girls laughing with the funny stories she told and the extraordinary sort of free-and-easy manner in which she did everything. And yet she was so good-natured, so full of fun and *bonhomie*!

With regard to Rosamund, Mrs. Brett saw at once that she would be Lucy's worst enemy, and she determined in her own mind to take the girl in tow.

"I will just knock some of her pride out of her, to begin with," thought the good lady.

Accordingly, when tea was over, and every scrap of bread and butter had been consumed, she selected Rosamund as the person to wash up the tea-things.

"Why me?" said Rosamund, opening her pretty brown eyes in some astonishment.

"Because you are the tallest, and you look the strongest," said Aunt Susan. "Now, be quick about it.—Lucy, did you bring out the towel?"

"I did," said Lucy; "and the little wooden bowl, and here is hot water. And do you want me to help, Aunt Susy?"

"Help, child? Of course you shall help. Rosamund shall wash and you shall dry. Now then, be as quick as ever you can."

The two girls were thus brought face to face with each other. Mrs. Brett looked at her watch, said that she had quite another ten minutes to spare, and suggested a walk down a favorite path, where they could gather some delicate maidenhair which she happened to know grew there.

How they walked and talked! Even Rosamund, left behind washing the tea-things while Lucy dried them, felt her ill-humor vanish.

"Isn't she charming?" she said.

"Yes," said Lucy; but then she added, "I don't want you to like her. That would be the last straw."

"And why shouldn't I like her?" asked Rosamund.

"Because she belongs to me."

Rosamund was quite silent for a minute. "While Mrs. Brett was here," she said slowly, "I was quite happy. Now I do not feel happy, and it is owing to you, Lucy. Can we not meet and talk this over, and come to a sort of compact, a sort of armistice? Do you mind if we do?"

Just then Mrs. Brett was seen returning. Lucy stood up hastily. "I will talk to you. It would be best," she said then.

"To-night," said Rosamund—"to-night, after prayers, let us meet outside under the elm-trees. We can talk there and put things a bit straight. I don't think we can go on as we have begun. It would make us both unhappy."

"My dear girls," called out Mrs. Brett—"ah! I see the tea-things are all washed up and put away in the basket. Well, they will be quite safe; there are no gipsies in these parts. Now, who will come with me as far as the station? Don't all speak at once. I shall be very glad of the company of those who like to come; but those who don't may stay behind, and they won't offend me in the very least."

But all the girls wanted to accompany Mrs. Brett; and, surrounded by a crowd of eager young people, the good lady walked to the railway station.

CHAPTER IV

CASTING OF THE DIE

Rosamund and Jane Denton shared the same bedroom. They had been friends from childhood, for they had lived in the same street and gone to the same kindergarten together, and their mothers had been old school-fellows before marriage, so their friendship had grown up, as it were, with their very lives.

But Jane was a girl of no very special characteristics; she leant on Rosamund, admiring her far more vivacious ways and appearance, glad to be in her society, and somewhat indifferent to every one else in the wide world.

She sat now on a low and comfortable seat near the open window. Prayers were over, but the time that Rosamund had fixed for meeting Lucy Merriman had not quite arrived. She yawned and stretched herself luxuriously.

"I shall go to bed. Our work begins to-morrow. What are you sitting up for, Rosamund?"

"I am going out again in a few minutes," said Rosamund.

"Are you indeed?" cried Jane. "Then may I come with you? I

shan't be a bit sleepy if I am walking out in the moonlight. But I thought—However, I suppose rules don't begin to-day."

"What do you mean by that?"

"I heard Miss Archer say that we were not to go out after half-past nine unless by special permission."

"Oh, well, as you remarked, rules don't begin until to-morrow, so I can go out at any hour I like to-night."

"I wonder why?" said Jane, and she looked up with a languid curiosity, which was all she could ever rise to, in her light-blue eyes.

Rosamund knelt by the window-sill; she put her arms on it and gazed out into the summer night. She heard people talking below her in the shrubbery. A few words fell distinctly on her ears, "I hate her, and I shall never be her friend!" and then the voices died away in the distance.

Jane had risen at that moment to fetch a novel which she was reading, so she did not hear what Rosamund had heard.

Rosamund's young face was now very white. There was a steady, pursed-up expression about her mouth. She suddenly slammed down the window with some force.

"What is it, Rose? What is the matter? Why shouldn't we have the window open on a hot night like, this?"

"Because I like it to be shut. You must put up with me as I am," said Rosamund. "I will open it if you wish in a few minutes. I have changed my mind, I am not going out. I shall go to bed. I have a severe headache."

"But wouldn't a walk in the moonlight with me, on our very last evening of freedom, take your headache away?" said Jane in a coaxing voice.

"No; I would rather not go out. You can do as you please. Only, creep in quietly when I am asleep. Don't wake me; that's all I ask."

"Oh, I'll just get into bed, dear, if you have a headache. But how suddenly it has come on!"

"This room is so stifling," she said. "After all, this is a small sort of school, and the rooms are low and by no means airy."

Jane could not help laughing.

"I never heard you talk in such a silly way before. Why, it was you who shut the window just now. How can you expect, on a hot summer's evening, the room to be cool with the window shut?"

"Well, fling it open—fling it open!" said Rosamund. "I don't mind."

Jane quickly did so. There was a crunching noise of steps—solitary steps—on the gravel below. Jane put out her head.

"Why, there is Lucy Merriman!" she said.

Lucy heard the voice, and looked up.

"Is Rosamund coming down? I am waiting for her," she said.

Jane turned at once to Rosamund.

"Lucy is waiting for you. Was it with Lucy you meant to

L. T. Meade

walk? She wants to know if you are going down."

"Tell her I am not going down," replied Rosamund.

"She can't go down to-night," said Jane. "She has a headache."

"I wish you wouldn't give excuses of that sort," said Rosamund in an angry voice when her friend put in her head once more. "What does it matter to Lucy Merriman whether I have a headache or not?"

Jane stared at her friend in some astonishment.

"I do not understand you, nor why you wanted to walk with her. I thought you did not like her."

"I tell you what," said Rosamund fiercely, "I don't like her, and I'm not going to talk about her. I am going to ignore her. I am going to make this house too hot for her. She shall go and live with her aunt Susan, or she shall know her place. I, Rosamund Cunliffe, know my own power, and I mean to exercise it. It is the casting of the die, Jane; it is the flinging down of the gauntlet. And now, for goodness' sake, let us get into bed."

Both retired to rest, and in a few minutes Jane was fast asleep; but Rosamund lay awake for a long time, with angry feelings animating her breast.

In the morning the full routine of school-life began, and even Lucy was drawn into a semblance of interest, so full were the hours, so animated the way of the teachers, so eager and pleasant and stimulating the different professors. Then the English mistress, Miss Archer, knew so much, and was so tactful and charming; and Mademoiselle Omont knew her own tongue so beautifully, and was also such a perfect German scholar! In short, the seven girls had their work cut out for them, and there was not a minute's pause to allow ambition and envy and jealousy to creep in.

Lucy had one opportunity of asking Rosamund why she did not keep her appointment of the night before.

"You surprised me," she said. "I thought you were honorable and would keep your word. I had some difficulty in getting Miss Archer out of the way, for she was talking to me so nicely and so wisely, I can tell you, I was quite enjoying it. But I managed to get right away from her, and to walk under your window, and you never came."

"I suppose I was at liberty to change my mind," said Rosamund, her dark eyes flashing with anger.

"Oh! of course you were. But it would have been more polite to let me know. Not that it matters. I was not particularly keen to talk to you. I am so glad that Miss Archer is my friend. She gave me to understand last night how much she liked me, and how much she meant to help me with my studies. I believe from what she says that she considers I shall be quite the cleverest girl in the school. She believes in hereditary talent, and my dear father is a sort of genius, so, of course, as his only child, I ought to follow in his footsteps."

"Of course you ought," said Rosamund in a calm voice. "Then be the cleverest girl in the school."

"I mean to have a great try," said Lucy, with a laugh; and Rosamund gave her an unpleasant glance.

CHAPTER V

AN INVITATION

If any girl failed to enjoy herself on the following Saturday at Dartford, she had certainly only herself to blame. As a matter of fact, the whole seven, without exception, had a right good time. Even Lucy forgot her jealousies, and even Rosamund forgot her anger. They were so much interested in Mrs. Brett and her husband, in the things they did, and the things they could tell, and the things they could show, and the whole manner of their lives, that they forgot themselves.

Now, to forget yourself is the very road to bliss. Many people take a long time finding out that most simple secret. When they do find it out and act on it they invariably live a life of great happiness and equanimity, and are a great blessing to other people. Lucy and Rosamund were far— very far—from such a desirable goal, but for a few hours they did act upon this simple and noble idea of life, and in consequence were happy.

But Saturday at the Bretts', with all its bliss, came to an end, and the girls returned to beautiful Sunnyside and to the life of the new and rather strangely managed school.

Sunday was a long and dreary day, at least in Rosamund's

eyes, and but for an incident which occurred immediately after morning service, she scarcely knew how she could have got through it.

Mr. Merriman had a pew at one end of the church, which had belonged to his people for generations, and which was not altered when the rest of the church was restored. It was large enough now to hold his wife and himself and the seven girls; but the two teachers were accommodated in another part of the church. Rosamund found herself during the service seated next to Mr. Merriman. It was the first time she had really closely observed him, and she now noticed several peculiarities which interested her a good deal. He had a dignified and very noble presence. He was tall, with broad shoulders, had an aquiline nose, very piercing dark eyes, black hair, which he wore somewhat long, and an olive-tinted face.

Lucy did not in the least resemble her father, but took more after her mother, who was round and fat, and proportionately commonplace. Rosamund at first felt no degree of elation when her place was pointed out to her next to the Professor. But suddenly encountering Lucy's angry eyes, she began to take a naughty comfort to herself in her unexpected proximity. She drew a little closer to him on purpose to annoy Lucy; and then, when she found that he was short-sighted and could not find his places, she found them for him, thus adding to poor Lucy's torment; for this had once been Lucy's own seat, and she herself had seen to her father's comforts. From attending on him, Rosamund began to watch him, and then she found a good deal of food for meditation. In short, it is to be feared that she did not follow the service as she ought to have done. For the matter of that, neither did Lucy.

The Rectory near Sunnyside was occupied by a clergyman who had several young daughters. These girls were very prepossessing in appearance. Their father was a widower, their mother having died some years ago. There were six girls, and as they trooped up the aisle, two by two, they attracted Rosamund's attention. They were dressed very simply in different shades of green. The two eldest had the darkest tone of color, both in their hats and their quiet little costumes. The two next had one shade lighter and the two youngest one shade lighter again. They looked something like leaves as they went up the church, and they all had one special characteristic—a great wealth of golden-brown hair, which hung far down their backs. The two eldest girls must have varied in age between fourteen and twelve, the two next between ten and eight, and the little ones between seven and five. They had quiet, neatly cut features, and serene eyes. They walked up the church very sedately, and took their places in the Rectory pew. Rosamund longed to ask a thousand questions about them. They were so much more interesting than the girls who were staying at Sunnyside; they were so fresh, and their dress so out of the common.

A somewhat prim and very neatly dressed governess followed the six girls up the aisle and took her place at the end of the pew. But Rosamund could still see from where she sat the heads with the six green hats and the wealth of fair hair hanging below. She was full of interest, and altogether her thoughts were occupied first by the Professor and then with her neighbors.

By-and-by the rustle of a very rich silk caused her to turn her attention again to the outside world, and she observed a lady of about forty-five years of age, richly dressed in deep mourning, with a good deal of crape and a widow's bonnet, walking up the church. This lady entered a pew which she occupied all alone.

Then the choir, the rector, and the curate appeared, and the service began. It began, went on, and finished. Just as it came to a conclusion, Mrs. Merriman, bending towards Rosamund, said, "We will wait, if you please, until the rest of the congregation have dispersed. I am anxious to see Mr. Singleton, to ask him a question."

Rosamund wondered who Mr. Singleton was. But she was only too anxious to see her neighbors leaving the church, and was pleased at the idea of waiting.

The congregation filed down the centre aisle one by one, in orderly fashion, and the six little girls in their green costumes and their fair hair disappeared from view. The elderly governess primly followed, and then the lady in black silk also left her pew. But as she did so she paused and said something to the verger, who was in the aisle. Rosamund, whose eyes were fixed on her, noticed that the verger pointed to the pew in which she herself was sitting, and a minute later the lady came to the door of the pew and said something in a very low voice to Mrs. Merriman.

To Rosamund's amazement, Mrs. Merriman stretched out her hand across the pew and took one of hers.

"My dear, Lady Jane Ashleigh, an old friend of your mother's, wishes to see you. Will you go very quietly out, talk to her for a minute or two outside the church, and then wait for us in the porch?"

Rosamund obeyed, filled with the keenest interest. Lady Jane walked on in front, and Rosamund followed. They both entered the porch, whereupon the widow turned, grasped one of Rosamund's hands, and said, "If it were not church-time I should long to kiss you. I was a very, very great friend of your mother's. She wrote to me two days ago to say that you were coming to live here. I intended to call yesterday, but was prevented. I came to church to-day hoping to make your acquaintance. When will you come and see me? Can you come this afternoon?"

"Oh, indeed I can!" said Rosamund. "I remember mother quite well telling me about you. Your name used to be Lady Jane Stanisford, was it not?"

"Quite right, my dear. Oh, what a look you have of your mother! You must come and spend the rest of the day with me. You can come now; you can come in my carriage."

"Oh! I ought not to, for the others will be waiting for me."

"I will wait with you here. But no; I must hurry home at once. Then come this afternoon, and bring any one of your school friends that you like. I shall be glad to see you and to talk over old times. Dear Mrs. Merriman, she is a great friend of mine. Give her my love, and a message that you are to come and have tea with me, and supper, too. I will send you back to Sunnyside in my carriage late this evening. Good-bye for the present, dear."

It was a very beaming face that greeted Lucy and the rest of the party when, accompanied by Mr. Singleton (the father of the fair-haired girls, and the rector of the parish), they all appeared in the church porch. Lucy went straight up to Rosamund.

"What in the world are you smiling at?" she said. "You look as though you were thinking of something extremely funny; and it makes your face look so strange, not at all like the face of a person who has just been in church."

"Will you introduce me, Miss Lucy, to this young lady?" said Mr. Singleton's pleasant voice.

Lucy was obliged to comply. She muttered the introduction in a somewhat surly tone; but Mr. Singleton was by no means proof against Rosamund's bright and clever face, her smile, which was now quite charming, and her animated manner.

"You must come and spend a day with my little girls—that is, when you can obtain leave," he said.—"Ah, Mrs. Merriman! it will be very unlike you to be over strict with your young people. They must all come to the Rectory. When is your next half-holiday?"

"You must ask Miss Archer," said Mrs. Merriman.

Miss Archer replied that Wednesdays and Saturdays would be half-holidays, and Mr. Singleton clinched the invitation by asking the party to the Rectory for the following Wednesday.

On their way home Rosamund left Lucy's side, with whom she had been walking, and ran up to Mrs. Merriman.

"Lady Jane Ashleigh is a friend of mother's, and she has asked me to go to her after lunch to spend the rest of the day with her. May I go?"

"Not on Sundays, dear. We never allow our young people to pay visits on Sundays," said the professor, just turning his head and glancing kindly at Rosamund.

The smile vanished from her countenance. She colored high with annoyance.

"But I promised her I would go, and she is an old friend of mother's, and please may I go on this occasion?"

"I make a rule which cannot be broken, that no girls accept invitations for Sunday. That is the end of the matter."

He turned to speak to his wife, without giving Rosamund any further thought. He was feeling ill that day—worse than usual—and he did not notice the consternation, rage, and also determination which filled Rosamund's face. Lucy had not heard her words, but she exclaimed eagerly when the girl returned to her place among her school-fellows, "Well, what is it? What did Lady Jane say to you?"

"Oh, nothing—nothing particular."

"But you did seem so eager and pleased. You don't look at all pleased now."

"She said nothing in particular, really. How nice that field looks, with all that grass growing up so green after the haymaking."

"Oh, don't talk platitudes," said Lucy. She watched Rosamund narrowly.

By-and-by they reached the house. Rosamund went straight up to her own room. There such a wave of passion, anger, and revolt swept over her that she scarcely knew herself.

"I will go. I won't obey. Mother wrote to her about me. She is mother's friend. I will slip off and spend the day with her, and take the consequences, whatever they may be. I cannot stand those girls, and she is delightful! I win go to her, come what may."

Jane Denton did not understand Rosamund as she brushed her long hair and tidied herself for the early dinner.

CHAPTER VI

VISIT TO LADY JANE

Rosamund made herself altogether charming during the ensuing meal. She was so clever that even Lucy's watchful eyes could detect nothing unusual about her. The professor was charmed with her intelligent remarks, her interest in the architecture of the very old church where they had just enjoyed the service, and her eagerness to acquire a more profound knowledge of church architecture in general. This was one of his own special hobbies, and he promised to lend Rosamund books on the subject, and even invited her to go into his library in the course of the afternoon to look at some illustrations which he thought would interest her.

"But I like to spend Sunday quietly and alone," said Rosamund, raising innocent eyes to the professor's face. "Will it matter if I come to see your illustrations and your books to-morrow?"

He gave her a paternal glance of almost affection.

"You shall certainly spend your Sunday as you like best, my dear," he said. "For my part, I love to see spirited and happy girls like yourself devoting themselves to periods of thought and meditation. In no other possible way can they attain to true knowledge of what Sunday means."

Jane Denton looked at her friend in some astonishment, but Rosamund calmly returned her gaze.

When the meal came to an end the girls scattered here and there, and Jane ran up to Rosamund to know what she meant to do.

"To stay quietly by myself," was Rosamund's answer, "so for goodness' sake don't interfere with me, Janey. I am going to my room, to begin with. I want to have a good long think, and—But don't question me, and keep the others away— won't you?—there's a dear."

Jane promised readily enough, and Rosamund went to her room. There from her window she watched the whole party disappearing in different directions: some to the neighboring woods, three girls together to the bank of the river, others with books into hammocks or cosy seats in the pretty garden. The two teachers had gone for a walk some miles into the country. The professor was in his study, where Mrs. Merriman kept him company.

"Now is my time," thought Rosamund.

She changed her dress for one of the prettiest she possessed— a pale-blue muslin, beautifully made. She put on a large, black, shady hat, and catching up her gloves and parasol, started on foot to Lady Jane's place. She had not an idea where to go, but trusted to find the way by making inquiries. Once she was safe out of the neighborhood of those odious girls, as she was pleased to call them, she thought all would be easy enough. She soon reached the high-road, which was far more dusty than she had anticipated, and did not suit her pretty patent-leather shoes.

Presently she met a girl on her way to Sunday-school in the village, and asked her the direct road to Lady Jane Ashleigh's.

"Oh, my!" was the girl's response; "won't you find Miss Irene in a tantrum this afternoon! Do you mean to say you are going there? And on Sunday, too!"

"Yes," said Rosamund, forgiving the girl's apparent impertinence on account of the interest which her remarks aroused. "But who is Miss Irene?"

"Lady Jane's daughter, bless you! Why, I live there as kitchen-maid, and I tell you the tantrums of that young lady is enough to upset the nerves of the stoutest person. I have come out now, and glad I am to be away. You are a strange young lady, I take it, from your appearance. You had best not go there if you want rest."

"But I am going there," was Rosamund's reply, "so please tell me how; and what is the name of Lady Jane's place, for she did not tell me?"

"Why, anybody here must know The Follies, and the place is true to its name as place can be. Oh, Lady Jane is well enough, but it is Miss Irene. Well, I wish you luck. You walk straight down this road for a mile or so, and turn in at the first gates you come to, and there you will be; and I 'opes you'll enjoy yourself."

The girl dropped a somewhat impertinent curtsy and marched on her way.

Rosamund also went on, feeling more interested and pleased than ever.

L. T. Meade

"Irene—what a pretty name!" she said to herself. "And from all accounts she seems to be what old people would call a difficult young person, and to young people she is doubtless delightful. Anyhow, I expect I shall have some fun; and as my absence is certain to be found out, and I am certain to get into a row when I go back to the horrid Merrimans', I may as well enjoy myself while I can."

So she hurried her footsteps, and presently found that the kitchen-maid at The Follies had given her correct instructions. There, directly before her, were massive gates leading into the winding avenue, sheltered by tall trees, beech and elm. The place looked cool and soothing. Oh, what a contrast it made to the hot and dusty road over which Rosamund had traveled! When she found herself inside she stepped on the grass in order to get some of the dust off her pretty patent shoes. She shook out her pale-blue muslin dress, arranged her hat becomingly, and went up the drive, looking as dainty and as unlike an-ordinary English school-girl as girl could look. She knew, the value of appearances, and was determined to make the best of them. Of course, her mother had told her much of Lady Jane. Lady Jane was her mother's greatest friend when they were both girls together; and when she had married a certain Mr. Ashleigh, a man of great wealth, although their acquaintance had very much dropped into the background, yet still the stories about the beautiful and willful Lady Jane had delighted Rosamund when she was a little girl herself. Now, it seemed that Lady Jane was blessed with a daughter, and as naughty as she must have been in her own early days. This made matters exceedingly interesting to Rosamund.

She reached the front door and rang the ponderous iron bell which hung from a chain by the side of a Gothic column, and a man-servant in livery, with powdered hair, appeared in reply to her summons.

"Is Lady Jane Ashleigh within?"

"Yes, madam," he replied respectfully, and he motioned Rosamund into a large, cool hall, beautifully furnished with all sorts of antique specimens of oak and Sheraton furniture. From here he took her into a little room rendered beautifully cool by green silk blinds, which were partly let down at the windows, one of which was altogether open and looked out on a flower-garden partly sheltered by trees. Here Rosamund saw, just for a brief moment, a girl in red, swinging backward and forward idly in a swing suspended from two stalwart boughs. The girl had somewhat wild eyes, a very bright face, and a mischievous expression round her lips. When she saw Rosamund she leaped from the swing, and disappeared from view, and the next moment Lady Jane sailed into the room. The contrast between the girl in red and the lady in deep mourning who now appeared puzzled the girl a good deal; also the extreme calm and graciousness of Lady Jane's bearing, the absence of all that wildness in the eyes which Rosamund's own mother had explained so fully. In short, the graciousness of a perfectly balanced nature seemed to surround this charming woman. She thanked Rosamund for coming, and sitting down near her, proceeded to question her with regard to her mother.

"It is years since we met," she said, "but I have never forgotten her. She was my favorite school-fellow. Our paths in life led very much apart afterward, for I married my dearly beloved husband and lived in the country, whereas she traveled a good deal over the world. But still we did contrive to correspond from time to time, although we have not met, I verily believe, since your birth, Rosamund. How old are you, my dear?"

"I was fifteen my last birthday," replied Rosamund.

"In some ways you look older than that."

"I am glad," said Rosamund, her eyes brightening. "I want to be grown-up," she continued. "I want to have done with school."

"Why did your mother think of sending you to Mrs. Merriman's?"

"Oh, there were a lot of reasons. Jane Denton, who is my greatest friend—although I don't know why I am so fond of her—was coming here, and her mother knew Mrs. Merriman, and mother hates ordinary schools, and she thought this would just do. And then all of a sudden she remembered that you lived near, although she did not say anything to me about that, or you may be sure I should have been quite interested. I am so glad to see you, Lady Jane! And, please, when am I to be introduced to Irene?"

Rosamund was sorry the moment she had said these words, for over Lady Jane's face there passed an expression of absolute pain. After a moment's pause, she said, "Who has told you about my little daughter?"

"Does it pain you for me to speak about her?"

"Answer my question, dear. Who has told you?"

"I think it might have been your kitchen-maid. I will explain to you the very truth, Lady Jane. You know you asked me to come here to-day, and you said you would send me back to-night, and I was so pleased; but when I spoke about it to Mr. Merriman, he said at once that he did not allow girls to visit friends on Sunday, and that that was one of his strictest rules."

"And yet you came?" said Lady Jane, her eyes darkening.

"Yes, I came," replied Rosamund, "for I simply couldn't stand it. Why should I be coerced and told that things were wrong by a man like Mr. Merriman?"

"A great scholar and a noble gentleman," said Lady Jane quietly.

Rosamund felt herself coloring, and a sense of annoyance swept over her.

"Well, anyhow, I came," she said; "and I suppose you are not going to send me back now that I have braved the displeasure of every one to come to you?"

"I will drive you back myself after we have had tea together; and you must come and spend a week day with me. It was wrong to come, dear, and it was a pity. When you get to know Mr. Merriman well you will understand that when he says a thing he means it. I will try and intercede for you on this occasion. I myself do not think it at all wrong that you should come and minister to the wants of a lonely woman on Sunday. I noticed your bright face in church; and although you are not very like your mother, you have got something of her expression, and many of the tones of her voice, and it gives me pleasure to converse with you."

"But why should you be lonely when you have got"—

Just at that moment there was a noise outside, followed by a fierce scuffle and the banging about of furniture, and the room door was opened, and the girl whom Rosamund had seen swinging at the other end of the sunlit lawn appeared on the scene. She was one of the most beautiful girls Rosamund, who thought herself very good-looking, had ever beheld in

L. T. Meade

her life, but her eyes were wild and almost unsteady. Her laugh was harsh and her voice unpleasant.

"Irene," said Lady Jane, turning pale, "what is the matter with you? Won't you behave?"

The girl gave a laugh, flung herself into a chair, then drew herself a little closer, and stared full at Rosamund.

"Never mind mother," she said. "Who are you?"

"My name is Rosamund Cunliffe," was Rosamund's reply.

She spoke steadily. There was a certain calm about her voice which seemed to exercise a beneficent influence over the queer girl.

"And my name is Irene Ashleigh. Won't you come out, and I'll swing you? You'd like to have a good swing this hot day, wouldn't you?"

"If you will promise, Irene, to be very careful," began Lady Jane; but Irene's only reply to this was to jump up as suddenly as she had seated herself, take Rosamund's hand, and pull her through the open French window.

"Never mind mother," she said again. "She is nothing but an old croak. There's a bit of spirit about you. Oh! they all tell stories about me; but I'm not half bad, only I think I'm a changeling. Did you ever think you were a changeling?"

"Of course not. I don't know what you mean."

"I'll explain to you. I quite like your look. May I put my arm round your waist?"

"If it pleases you," said Rosamund.

"How stiffly you speak! But I like you all the same. You are what might be called a good old sort, and there's nothing prim about you. Do you know why I came into the room just now?"

"I'm sure I cannot tell."

"Well, I'll let you know. I was listening at one of the windows, and I heard you tell mother—dear old puritanical mother—that you had crept away without leave from the learned professor, and had got into difficulties. Oh, didn't I just love you for it! There's a Miss Frost here who tries to teach me; but, bless you! she can't knock much learning into me. She is as terrified of me as she can be, is old Frosty. She and I had a squabble in the passage; she said I was not to come in because I had my red dress on. You know, it's only a year since father died, and mother is in deep mourning still; but I will wear red—it is my sort of mourning. I suppose we can all do as we please. Well, when I discovered that you were one of the naughty sort, I thought I'd have a nearer view of you, and I like you very much. You are pretty, you know, quite pretty. Not so pretty as I am! Now, look me full in the face. Did you ever see any one prettier?"

"Irene, you do talk in a wild way!"

"It is rather cheeky of you to call me Irene; but I don't much mind. I like you to be cheeky. Well, here's the swing. How high up do you want me to push you?"

"Not any way at all just at present. Let us walk about and talk before you swing me. I must know something about you. How old are you?"

"I'm sure I don't know—I've forgotten. Oh, by the way, you didn't understand me when I said I was a changeling."

"I didn't, and I don't. But why do you talk in that silly way?"

"Well, I seriously think I am, for if you had seen father when he was alive you'd have said if there was a dear—I was very fond of dad—if there was a dear, sober, conscientious old man—he was a good bit older than mother—you'd have pronounced that he was he."

"That is very funny English, Irene."

"Oh, never mind! I like to talk in a funny way. Anyhow, you'd have said that he was he. And then there is mother. You see how good she looks. She is very handsome, I know, and every one adores her, and so does her loving daughter Irene; but, all the same, I was made in a sort of fashion that I really cannot keep indoors. No rain that ever was heard of could keep me in, and no frost, either. And I have lain sometimes on the snow for an hour at a time and enjoyed it. And there's scarcely a night that I spend in bed. I get out, whatever poor old Frosty may do to keep me within bounds. I can climb up anything, and I can climb down anything, and I like to have a boat on the lake; and when they are very bad to me I spend the night there in the very centre of the lake, and they can't get at me, shout as they may. No, I never take cold."

"The only thing I am keen about is to be allowed to wear colors that I like. I love gay colors—red one day, yellow the next, the brightest blue the next I hate art shades. I am not a bit aesthetic. Once they took me to London, but I ran away home. Oh, what a time I had! I am a wild sort of thing. Now, do you suppose that any mother, of her own free-will, would have a daughter like me? Of course I am a changeling. I suppose I belong to the fairies, and my greatest wish on earth is to see them some day. Sometimes I think they will meet me in the meadows or in the forest, which is two miles away, or even in the lake, for I suppose fairies can swim. But they have never come yet. If they came I'd ask them to let me go back to them, for I do so hate indoor life and civilization and refinement. And now you see the sort I am, and if you are the sort I somehow think you are, why shouldn't we be friends? Perhaps you are a changeling, too. You know that dress doesn't suit you one bit; it is too grand and fine-ladyish; and you ought to let your hair stream down your back instead of having it tied behind with that ribbon. And you ought to have a hole in your hat instead of that grand black feather. And—oh, good gracious!—what funny boots! I never saw anything like them—all shiny, and with such pointed toes. How can you walk in them? I as often as not go barefoot all day long; but then I am a wild thing, a changeling, and I suppose, after all, you are not."

Rosamund felt herself quite interested while Irene was delivering herself of this wild harangue. She looked back at this moment, and saw Lady Jane standing in the French window. Irene's arm was still firmly clasped round Rosamund's waist. Rosamund could just catch a glimpse of the expression of Lady Jane's face, and it seemed to signify relief and approval. Rosamund said to herself, "We all have our missions in life; perhaps mine is to reclaim this wild, extraordinary creature. I shouldn't a bit mind trying. Of course, I don't approve of her; but she is lovely. She has a perfect little face, and she is just like any savage, quite untrained—a sort of free lance, in fact. Irene," she said aloud, "I am not going to let you swing me just now; but you may sit near me, and I will tell you something which may alter your views about your being a changeling."

"What do you mean by that?" said Irene, and she looked

L. T. Meade

doubtful. "I cannot sit long," she continued. "Be as quick as ever you can."

"Yes, I will, and afterward"—

"Afterward I will go into the house and get Frosty to give us tea, and we will take it in the boat together. We will get into the very middle of the stream, where no human being can call us back, and we will have a right good time."

"Will you ask your mother's leave first?"

"Indeed I won't. I never ask her leave. I never ask any one's leave. I never trouble mother much, because she cries so badly when I vex her; but I don't mind how hard Frosty cries. Frosty is terribly afraid of me, but she has stayed with me longer than any other governess. They mostly go at the end of a week or a fortnight; but Frosty has been with me for close on four months. She is very worried. She was quite fat when she came, and now she is a sort of walking skeleton, and it is all owing to me, because I do work her so hard and terrify her so; and she can't teach me anything, however hard she tries. I tell you I'm a changeling, and changelings can't be taught. She told me the other night that she believed me. She looked as white as a sheet when she said the words, and I did laugh so, and clapped my hands. I woke mother, and mother came into the room; and Frosty told mother what I had said, and poor mother cried. I said, 'Never mind, mother. I am fond of you, but I like frightening Frosty.'

"Then Frosty went away to her own room, and I thought, of course, she would give notice the next day, but she didn't. She is very poor, and has to earn her own bread somehow. I expect that is why she stays."

"Well," said Rosamund stoutly, "I will say this, Irene, that you are—whether changeling or not—an exceedingly naughty girl. There, now!"

Irene opened those deep sapphire-blue eyes, which were one of her greatest charms, to their fullest extent; her little mouth pouted, and some pearly teeth showed beneath. She clinched her small hands, and then said stoutly, "Hurrah! I admire your courage. They never dare tell me I am naughty. I rule the house; they are all quite terrified of me."

"Well, I am not a scrap afraid of you," said Rosamund.

"Aren't you? What a relief! Well, come on; I can't sit still any longer. I have got to order our tea to be sent to the boat, and we will get into mid-stream and keep all the world at bay. Can't you tell me there what you wanted to say?"

"No; I will tell you now, and I am not at all sure that I am going in the boat with you, for Lady Jane said I had done wrong to come here; and if I did wrong to come, I suppose I must try and do right, for I can't talk of your faults while I have such a lot of my own."

"Oh, hurrah! You are nicer than ever. I am glad you are full of faults too. Do say why you think I am not a changeling."

"Because my mother told me that long ago your mother was rather naughty, although she is so good now. So I think, perhaps, when you are her age you will be good too."

"Oh, horror! Heaven preserve us!" cried Irene. "That is the final straw. Ever to sink into the apathy of my beloved mother would be beyond endurance. But there, I am off to Frosty, and you will have to come into the boat with me."

Irene flew fleet as the wind from Rosamund's side.

Notwithstanding her exceedingly ugly red dress, its shortness, its uncouth make, she ran as gracefully as a young fawn. Soon she had disappeared round the corner, and as soon as she had done so Lady Jane was seen tripping across the grass. She motioned Rosamund to her side.

"She took to you," she said. "She seems to like you. Are you going to be good to her?" said the lady, her lips trembling as she spoke.

"If I can. Oh, I know she is very naughty; but she is so beautiful!" said Rosamund, with sudden enthusiasm, her own pretty dark eyes filling with tears.

"You are a sweet girl!" said Lady Jane. "Perhaps God has sent you here to effect the means of reform. Only sometimes I fear—But here she comes. She must not see me talking to you. If she thought that we were in league all would be lost."

Before Rosamund could reply, or even ask Lady Jane if she might go into the boat with Irene, that young lady had darted to her side.

"Now, what were you saying to the Mumsy-pums? I don't allow any one to talk in a confidential way to my Mumsy-pums except myself. Now, I was just watching you, and you kept nodding your head all the time. What were you saying? I know you were talking about me. What was the dear Pums saying with regard to her changeling? Was she running me down—eh?"

"No, nothing of the sort," said Rosamund stoutly.

"Then I know," said Irene, knitting her black eyebrows till they almost met in her anxiety to express herself clearly; "she was telling you to have a good influence over me. She always begins like that with the new governesses. She has an interview with them the morning after they arrive. They are generally by that time reduced to a state of pulp, and she has them, as she thinks, alone. But I generally contrive to listen. I am a great eavesdropper. Oh, I am not a bit ashamed of it— not a bit—so you needn't begin to preach. She tells them to try and reform me. She says money is no object if only I can be reformed. As though a changeling could be reformed! She has been asking you to reform me, hasn't she? I know her little ways, dear, good old Mumsy-pums. But she can't reform a changeling. Now the boat is ready, and Betty is toiling for dear life with our tea-tray. I darted into the kitchen, where she was having a Sunday doze. I sprang upon her back, and she gave such a shriek as though something awful had happened; and I said, 'Tea in a twinkling, or I'll dress up and frighten you when you are in bed to-night.' Oh, didn't she hop round as though she were walking on red-hot irons! And there she is now, panting down the path with our tea. Come along, Rosamund."

"But I don't think I must. I ought not to come," said Rosamund.

She was tempted, fascinated. To feel conscious that she was not one scrap afraid of this queer girl, to feel conscious also that the girl herself, notwithstanding her extreme naughtiness, could in the end be managed by her, brought such a rush of interest into her life that she forgot everything else for the moment; and, besides, Irene was exceedingly strong, and although she was much slimmer and not so tall as Rosamund, she dragged her down the path with a power that it was almost impossible to resist.

"That will do, Betty. I won't frighten you to-night by dressing up and making my eyes fiery," said Irene as the cook appeared with the tea.

"Oh, bless me, miss!" replied the cook, "for heaven's sake keep out of my bedroom. If you will only give me back my key and let me lock my door I wouldn't have such dreadful nightmares. I wish you would, Miss Irene."

"I give you back your key?" said Irene. "I'd have no fun if I hadn't power over you. There, that will do. You may sleep sound to-night. I always keep my word."

The cook departed, red and panting. She was as much afraid of Irene as any of the other servants. But the place was a good one, the wages exceedingly liberal, and Lady Jane the kindest and most patient of mistresses. In short, many of the servants stayed for her sake, notwithstanding the life of terror which naughty Irene gave them.

The little boat, painted sky-blue and tipped with white, was now pulled out of the boat-house. Irene put in the basket of provisions, and a moment later she and Rosamund were skimming across the smooth bosom of the lake. It was quite a big lake, being a quarter of a mile across and half a mile long, and in the centre was a rapid current which was considered, and really was in times of storm, somewhat dangerous. For this current Irene made, and when they got there she suddenly rested on her oars, and looking at Rosamund, said, "Are you afraid, or are you not? If the current gets a little stronger we will be drifted to the edge of the lake, and at the edge of the lake there is a waterfall, and over it we will go, and, splash! splash! splash! I took a girl there once; she was my governess, but I was quite tired of her, and knew the fright she would get in when I took her out in the boat. I never take those who are dead sick with fright; but I took her, and she was nearly drowned—not quite, for I can swim in almost any water, and I held her up and brought her safe to land. But she left that evening. She was a poor thing, absolutely determined to stop. I hated her the moment

I saw her face, it was so white and pasty; and she wasn't at all interesting. She couldn't tell stories; she didn't believe in changelings. She had never read the *Arabian Nights*. She knew hardly any history; but she was great at dates. Oh, she was a horror! She was rather fond of grammar, too, and odds and ends of things that aren't a bit interesting. And needlework! Oh, the way she worried me to death with her needlework! She did criss-cross and cross-criss, and every other stitch that was ever invented. So I said to myself, 'Miss Carter must go,' and I took her out on a rather stormy day, and we got into mid-current. Mother and the servants came shouting to us to get out of it; but of course we couldn't, and poor Miss Carter, how she did shriek! And I said, 'We are certain to go over the fall; but we won't get drowned, for I won't let you, if you will promise faithfully to give notice the very instant you get back to the house.' Oh, poor thing, didn't she promise! Her very teeth were chattering. She was in a most awful state. Now, we can go over the waterfall to-day if you don't mind. You wouldn't be frightened, would you?"

"Frightened? Not I! But I don't intend to go over the waterfall, all the same."

"Now, what on earth do you mean by that remark?" asked Irene.

"I am quite as strong as you, and if it comes to a fight I can take the oars. The current is not yet very strong; but I wish to get out of it, for the see-sawing up and down makes me a little bit sea-sick. I am not your governess. I am just a girl who has come to live at the Merrimans', and I can make myself very pleasant to you if you make yourself pleasant to me, or I can take not the slightest notice of you. There are heaps and heaps of other girls about. There are all the Singletons."

"Oh, for primness!" began Irene. "Oh, those Green Leaves! they are positively detestable. But you shall have your way, Rosamund. You really are not afraid, so just you take one oar and I will take the other, and we will get into smooth water and enjoy ourselves for once. It is a comfort to talk to some one who hasn't a scrap of fear in her."

"Nobody ought to be afraid of you," said Rosamund, taking up an oar as she spoke; and with a few vigorous strokes the girls got out of the current into the still, blue waters of the lake.

Poor Lady Jane, who was watching them from her boudoir window, breathed a sigh of relief.

"I knew that girl was sent to be a blessing to me," she said to herself; "and my dear old friend's child, too. Oh, why was I given such a creature as Irene to bring up and look after? I can no more manage her than an old hen could manage a fierce young ostrich."

Meanwhile Rosamund and Irene began to enjoy themselves. The tea, as it was called, consisted of a bottle of cold tea; but the rest of the provisions were first-rate, the most delicious cakes of all sorts and descriptions, with a few other dainties in the shape of sandwiches. The girls ate and talked, and Irene, perhaps for the first time in her life, became almost rational in her behavior.

"And now," said Irene, "I want you to tell me again what you said about mother being naughty, because it will give me a most tremendous hold over her. I wish you would tell me some of the sort of things she used to do; because if I can say, 'I got it from you, mother, and you are the one to blame,' it would be an immense pull. I wish you would tell me. Do, won't you?"

"She never did the sort of things you have done," said Rosamund.

"How in the world do you know that?"

"Well, for instance, she was never cruel."

"I cruel? Well, I like that! I often and often put slugs and snails and worms, and that sort of thing, out of the path for fear any one should tread on them. I cruel?"

"You are in one way," said Rosamund. "I am not a scrap afraid of you, and I say you are cruel when you terrify the servants and your poor mother, who has no one but you, and"—

"We will get back into the current if you say another word," said Irene.

"No, we won't," replied Rosamund, "for I will keep this oar, and you cannot wrench it from me."

She grasped it more firmly as she spoke. Irene looked at her for a moment, and her small, wild, charming face seemed to lighten as though with sudden passion. Then she broke into a merry laugh.

"I declare it is refreshing to hear you," she said. "Only don't scold me too much at first. Let us be jolly for a little bit. When will you come to see me again?"

"That depends on your mother and, I suppose, on the people I am living with—the Merrimans."

"I don't know them."

"Don't know them? Why, they live quite close."

"I don't know any of the girls round here. There is a Merriman called Lucy, a horrid prig, isn't there?"

"I must confess that I don't care for her," said Rosamund.

"Ah! then we have something in common. I shall cultivate her just for the express purpose of finding out her faults, and then we will have more in common. Only, promise me one thing, Rose."

"What is that?" said Rosamond, suddenly struck by the gentle tone which the queer child's voice could assume.

"You won't take up with the Leaves. Do let the Leaves alone. Mother is always harping on them, and bringing them up to me. But the fact is, they are afraid to come here. They have been invited scores of times; but they always make excuses at the last moment. I know the reason, for that terrible Miss Carter, who was nearly drowned, went straight from us to them, and has remained with them ever since. Of course, she told them about the boat, and the current in the middle of the lake, and the waterfall. I have been rather curious to see them, and to give them a good round fright, every one of them, till they blanch to the color of ghosts, and then their green dresses wouldn't suit them any longer. But they wouldn't come. I have got no friends. That is why I am so anxious to have you as a friend. You don't think me so dreadful, do you?"

"I think you could be splendid; but at the present moment I consider that you are exceedingly naughty," said Rosamund. "But then, I am not a bit too good myself, so I suppose that is why I tolerate you. Now, will you please row back to the shore, for I am afraid I must be returning to the Merrimans'?"

CHAPTER VII

TEA ON THE LAKE

It was with some difficulty that Rosamund persuaded Irene to obey her orders; but firmness won the day. That young lady was accustomed to ruling with a rod of iron, but she had at last found a girl who was not the least afraid of her, who really did not mind what she did, and who insisted on taking one oar while she took the other. This was a new experience, and she could do nothing, try as she would, to terrify Rosamund, who laughed when she assured her that she was a changeling, and might perhaps take any form at any time, and might return to her real home with the fairies at any moment; who laughed still more merrily when she vowed she would upset the boat.

"I can swim like a duck," said Rosamund, "and I am a great deal bigger than you are; and, clever as you think yourself, you would be no match for me in the water."

In the end the merry laugh, the good nature, the charm and beauty of the face, touched something which had never yet been awakened in Irene's wild little heart. She turned to her oar, and they rowed quite silently, and soon both girls landed on the shore. There they found Lady Jane awaiting them.

L. T. Meade

"As you did not get leave, dear, to come here to-day, I think I had better take you back myself to the Merrimans', for I should like to see Mr. Merriman and have a chat with him; so will you come straight with me to the carriage?"

"May I come too?" asked Irene suddenly.

"No, dear, I think not. I could not take you in that red frock. If you were to put on a white dress, perhaps; but I think not to-day, Irene."

Lady Jane looked anxiously at her little daughter. Irene gave a wild laugh, which really sounded to poor Rosamund as scarcely human, and the next moment, with a whoop, she disappeared into the thick shrubbery of young trees near by. Her voice could then be heard calling, "Frosty! Frosty! come at once;" and then a thin and very emaciated woman was seen coming out of a summer-house just beyond.

Meanwhile Lady Jane put her hand on Rosamund's arm.

"You have done wonders," she said. "You amaze me. I scarcely know how to thank you. Come with me at once. I must see more of you; but you will have to go home now."

Rosamund took the lady's hand, and they walked up to the house, where an open landau was waiting for them. They drove quickly through the summer air. Rosamund remained silent, afraid to speak, and yet longing to say something. It was not until they had gone nearly a mile that Lady Jane broke the silence.

"I have always felt that if her heart could be touched she would be all right," was her first remark. "I think, somehow, you have touched it. She has been a great and dreadful trial to me—her extraordinary spirits, the way she fears nothing, the impossibility of giving her the slightest discipline, the—the"—

Here the poor lady burst into tears.

"Oh, don't, Lady Jane!" said Rosamund. "I am not a very good girl myself, and perhaps that is why I partly understand her. At the present moment I hate my position. I like Mr. and Mrs. Merriman very well, and some of the girls; but I can't stand that priggish Lucy. Perhaps that is why I comprehend Irene—anyhow, if I may sometimes come to see her."

"Sometimes, dear! Sometimes! But I am going to see Mr. Merriman on that very point this evening. I want you to be constantly with her."

"How can I be if I have to do all my lessons?"

"I will write to your mother. Something will have to be done. I can't lose this one chance. It was Heaven directed me; and, oh, your face in church—so like your mother's, and withal so spirited and so sweet! And then I felt that if only my little darling were in any way like you! I have had sorrow in my life; but no sorrow has been so great and terrible as that which I have endured with regard to that poor child."

"She has a lovely face," said Rosamund; "but the fact is, she is untamed. She wants some one to tame her; and no one can break her in. She must be led, not driven."

"I know it; but then I cannot lead her, and she has got the whole house so thoroughly in her power that she gloats over the position. But I must not say any more."

"I am afraid Mr. and Mrs. Merriman will be very angry with me," said Rosamund; "but, to tell the truth," she added, "I should not mind a bit if I had not met Irene. But somehow, now, I would rather be good than naughty, because I want really to help her."

They had now turned in at the avenue and were driving up to the house. They could see several girls coming to meet them. Jane Denton was the first to notice Rosamund. She went up to her at once.

"Oh, Rose," she said, "they are making such a fuss!" and then she colored and glanced at Lady Jane.

"Don't say a word against Rosamund. Whether she has been disobedient or not, she has done a splendid afternoon's work," said Lady Jane. Then she added, "Introduce me to your young friend, my dear."

Rosamund did so. Jane was much pleased. She had heard a good deal about Lady Jane in the course of the afternoon, and when Lucy and Mrs. Merriman and one or two other girls were inveighing against Rosamund's extreme naughtiness in going to see the great lady without permission, Jane was envying her in her heart.

Now Rosamund jumped lightly from the carriage, put her hand inside Jane's arm, and conducted Lady Jane into the house. She walked straight toward the study, that sacred room which was seldom invaded, and opening the door, announced Lady Jane Ashleigh, then at once closed it behind the good lady, and went with her friend Jane Denton into the grounds.

"You have got into a scrape," said Jane. "I never knew anything like it. What a pity you went!"

"Oh! don't bother me, Jane. I really don't care a bit if they do punish me. What punishment can they inflict?"

"Lucy said that you ought to be expelled," said Jane. "You never knew anything like her rage. But I rather think she did harm than otherwise, for the Professor said to her, 'Oh, gently, Lucy—gently. It is her first offense.' So I don't expect they will do that."

"It would be rather delightful if they did," said Rosamund, "for then I could go to Lady Jane and have a right good time. There, come along. I have a lot to tell you, but nothing at all to tell the others. Here they are coming to meet us, with that precious Lucy at their head. Wouldn't I like to take her out on the lake?" thought Rosamund, but she did not utter her thought aloud.

The fact was, seeing these good, well-behaved girls brought back a great deal of her naughty spirit, whereas terribly naughty Irene made her feel more or less good.

"What a strange creature I am!" she thought, with a sigh. "And how can I hope to influence any one?"

Meanwhile Lucy came straight up until she stood a few feet away from Rosamund.

"I wonder," she said, speaking in even a more formal way than usual, "how you can look me in the face, Rosamund. Have you ever been at school before?"

"I don't call this school," said Rosamund; "it is a private house. It is true we are subject to rules." Then she added, making a great effort to control herself and to speak quietly, "I will tell your father and mother what I feel with regard to this day's expedition; but I will not tell you, for you are only a school-girl like myself, and I expect, when all is said and done, not a bit better."

"Not a bit better?" repeated Lucy, her voice almost choking. "Why, I never disobeyed my parents in the whole course of my life."

"I am not aware that I have disobeyed mine," said Rosamund. "But," she continued, turning to the other girls, "I will talk of this to my master and mistress, Professor and Mrs. Merriman, and not to you, Lucy."

Then she linked her hand through Jane Denton's arm, called to Laura Everett to follow her, while Annie Millar, Laura's special friend, immediately turned to join the little group, and the four children soon found themselves in the shade of one of the thickest plantations in Sunnyside.

"Oh dear! oh dear!" said Laura, speaking excitedly, "there has been a fuss made. I always did admire you, Rosamund; but I must own I was disappointed at your creeping away in the manner you did, without telling anybody. And as to dear Professor Merriman, his face was quite full of pain. I could scarcely bear to look at him."

"I am sorry I went," said Rosamund. "At least, in one sense I am sorry, but it was a mistake to prevent me. The fact is," she continued, "I am not made like ordinary girls; I know I am not, and I could not stand the narrow point of view which it seemed to me the Professor had assumed."

"But at school, remember, if there were no discipline there would be no chance of education," was Laura's next remark.

"I am sure Laura is right," said Annie Millar.

"Well, I hold with Rosamund to a certain extent," exclaimed

Jane Denton.

Rosamund turned round to her own friend and smiled.

"Now, I will tell you something," she said. "I hold a distinct brief against myself. I did wrong, and yet in some ways I suppose I did right to go. Girls, have you ever heard any particulars with regard to Lady Jane Ashleigh?"

Laura's face turned very red.

"Of course, every one in the place respects her," she said.

"Yes, I know, and I am not a bit surprised. I told her quite frankly that I had come without leave, and she said she was sorry for that; and although she did wish to see me so much, she would insist on not allowing me to stay to supper, and brought me home, as you see, comparatively early. So you will understand that she at least is not to blame. Nevertheless, have you heard anything more of that household?"

"Only that there is a girl—a very queer girl—there," said Annie Millar in an almost spiteful voice.

"Some people say she is mad," said Laura Everett.

"Well, now, I am going to tell you something," said Rosamund. "I have seen the girl. Her name is Irene. She has quite one of the most beautiful little faces I have ever looked at. And she is the wildest, queerest creature; but not a scrap mad in the ordinary sense of the word. She and I spent a good deal of the afternoon together, and I mean to see more of her, and to make her my friend."

"But you will have so many friends!" interrupted Jane.

"Yes, every one wants to be your friend, Rosamund," said Laura in a gentle tone.

"And I am quite glad to be everybody's friend, if only Lucy Merriman may be left out of the category," was Rosamund's answer. "But, all the same, I mean to make Irene Ashleigh my special friend above all others, and you must none of you be jealous, because—because—well, I can't explain."

"There are the Singletons," said Laura quickly. "Mr. Singleton came over this afternoon with two of the girls, the two eldest ones; their names are Maud and Alice, and they told us a lot about Irene. They seem to have a perfect horror of her. They are awfully nice girls, and we are to go there on Wednesday afternoon, and I for one am looking forward to it. But, Rosamond, it is extraordinary that you should take up with her. They told us an awful story about how Irene treated their dear governess, Miss Carter. They wouldn't tell us quite all, but they said that, for their parts, nothing would induce them to go to The Follies, although they had been asked ever so often. And as to poor Miss Carter, her nerves have not yet got over the awful shocks that Irene subjected her to. Once she was almost drowned."

"Oh! I know all about that," said Rosamund, with a laugh. "Well, don't keep me now. I see Lady Jane driving away, and I am going straight to have an interview with the Professor."

The girls watched her, in a little group, as she marched out of the wood, across the front lawn, and passed into the house by a side-door which led straight to the Professor's study.

He was alone, expecting no one. He was somewhat tired, and life seemed to him a little more bewildering than usual. He had never greatly approved of his wife's scheme of having girls to live with them, but had yielded to it at last under the pressure of necessity. He had no objection to the scheme on any score except that he was afraid it might absorb all his time and thoughts; for he was so constituted that he could never see a human creature, particularly a human creature in trouble, without taking that person's part and endeavoring if possible to set wrong right. And now, just what he feared had happened. He was weak and ill, and his nerves shaken, and Lady Jane had been to him, and Rosamund Cunliffe, the girl whom he most admired of all those who had come to live at Sunnyside, had directly disobeyed him, and Lady Jane had made a somewhat painful appeal to his sympathy. What was to be done?

Mrs. Merriman had hurried into the room the moment Lady Jane had left.

"Well," she said—"well, and what did Lady Jane say? And what are we going to do with that naughty girl? We ought to be firm with her. We really ought, Ralph."

The Professor looked gently at her, but did not speak.

"For Lucy's sake we ought to be firm," continued Mrs. Merriman. "Of course, I don't want to be hard on any girl; but a direct act of disobedience—"

"It is her first offence; and, after all, the girl is impulsive and has never been subject to control, and there are extenuating circumstances," said the Professor. "My dear," he continued, laying his hand on his wife's very plump shoulder, "you must speak to Lucy from yourself, not from me, dear; for I am too tired. But you must speak to her from yourself, and tell her that she is not to dictate any terms to us with regard to the pupils who come to be educated at Sunnyside. She herself is but one of the pupils. And now, dear, leave me, please."

L. T. Meade

Mrs. Merriman did so, and a moment later Rosamund entered the room. She advanced proudly, her head well thrown back, a spot of additional color on each cheek, her brown eyes brighter than usual.

"Professor," she said before he could speak a word, for he was amazed at her entering into his presence, "I know I have been a very naughty girl. I did disobey you. I did go all by myself to The Follies. I was annoyed at your strict views, and I had not been accustomed to self-control. I beg of you to forgive me, and to forgive me although I am not particularly repentant."

"What do you mean by that, Rosamund?" asked the Professor, his eyes darkening and a look of pain crossing his face.

"Because I think I have helped Lady Jane, and I want, please, Professor, your forgiveness and then your help."

As she spoke she suddenly dropped on her knees by his side and laid one hand on his knee.

"I want your help," she said, looking up into his face, "for dear Lady Jane was mother's friend, and she has got such a strange, wild, beautiful little daughter, whom nobody under-stands, and who is, I confess, exceedingly naughty. But I—yes, I, Professor—want to tame her."

"I have heard of her," said Professor Merriman. "There is no one living in the place who has not heard of Irene Ashleigh. The fact is, her name is a terror to the neighborhood. I have heard dreadful stories of that child, and the thought of her has weighed on my mind."

"As it is weighing on mine now," said Rosamund in a low

voice, her eyes suddenly filling with tears.

"My dear, you have been sent to me to be trained as I would train my own child—to be trained in this little simple school, to be educated in mind and body, not to be thrown into contact with a girl who is in no way fit to know you. At present, Rosamund, you are under masters and governors, and have, according to scriptural precepts, to obey them. By-and-by your time of emancipation will come, and you will owe allegiance only to God and those whom you love, my dear; but until that time comes it seems to me scarcely fit or advisable that you should have anything to do with Irene. I told Lady Jane so this evening."

"You told Lady Jane that?" said Rosamund, rising to her feet, her face very pale, her eyes dark as night.

"Yes, I did, for I considered it my duty."

"Then you would like me to leave you, Professor? You would like me to write to my mother and explain all the circumstances to her, and beg and implore of her to take me away?"

"You must please yourself, Rosamund," said the Professor; and now he rose and in his turn laid his hand on her shoulder. "You have a generous heart, I can see. But you have never been subjected to the rigorous laws of self-control. You showed a sad want of self-control when you disobeyed me to-day, and again I perceive it breaking out. If you cannot obey me, Rosamund, you must go. Yes, I shall be sorry to have to say it, but you must go."

"And does that mean," said Rosamund, "that I am not to see Irene, that I am not to try to help her, that I am not to be a friend to Lady Jane, that my mother's wishes in this matter are to be disregarded?"

"It means," said the Professor very gravely, "that, for the present at least, you are to have nothing whatever to do with Irene Ashleigh—nothing whatever to do with her. You understand that, Rosamund. And I give you a week, my dear, to decide. Think over the advantages of this home. Think what it means to your friends, and will eventually mean to yourself, and try to discover that I am wise in my generation, although you doubtless consider me foolish. If at the end of the week you have found out that you cannot really obey me—or, rather, that you will not—I shall have, reluctantly, to write to your mother and ask her to remove you, for the other girls cannot be contaminated with that most fatal of all sins, the sin of direct disobedience."

Rosamund bowed her head. The tears she could not repress brimmed to her eyes. Suddenly she flung off the Professor's detaining hand.

"Oh, you are hard!" she said. "Is no one to help a girl who will soon become irreclaimable? Why, already I have an influence over her."

But the Professor did not answer.

"Give yourself a week," he said after a long pause; "then come to me again with your resolution."

She was about to leave the room when he again laid his hand on her arm.

"Give me your word of honor, Rosamund Cunliffe, that you do not go again to The Follies until the week is up."

She looked at him, struggled to speak, but remained silent.

"Your word of honor," he repeated, "you do not go to The Follies until the week is up."

"My word of honor!" she said then in a faltering tone. "I will not go on one condition, that you allow me to write to Lady Jane."

"You may do that if you promise to tell her the exact truth, that you are on parole for a week. At the end of that time you may come to a decision. God grant it may be a right one! I trust you, but leave me now, please, dear."

Rosamund left the room.

CHAPTER VIII

THE RECTORY

On the following Wednesday all the girls belonging to Mrs. Merriman's school, accompanied by Miss Archer, went to have tea with the Singletons. Even Rosamund was interested in this visit. She did not say much about it. She had been rather silent and, as Jane Denton said, "off color" for the last few days. She had forgotten to be wild or cantankerous. She had even ceased to notice Lucy; and as to her lessons, she had gone through the tasks assigned to her with sufficient promptitude and sufficient correctness to win fairly good remarks from the two governesses and from the different teachers who came to visit the little school. Of Irene Ashleigh she absolutely refused to speak. With regard to her adventure on Sunday she also kept a profound silence. No one, not even Jane Denton, could induce her to alter her mind with regard to this particular. Jane was anxious about her friend. Laura Everett said that she did not think Rosamund Cunliffe nearly as interesting as when she first met her. Phyllis Flower looked wise and mysterious, as she always did, and everything settled down to a monotonous and yet harmonious contentment at Sunnyside.

Nevertheless, Wednesday was thought a good deal about, and the girls of the entire school—for every single one was invited—headed by Lucy and accompanied by Miss Archer, started to walk to the Rectory.

Now, Rosamund's interest in this expedition was on no account to examine the "Leaves," as naughty Irene called the rector's daughters; but she wanted to watch Miss Carter, and if possible to get a word with her, and to induce her to tell her something more with regard to the wild and mischievous girl whom, nevertheless, she could not get for a moment out of her head.

When the young people arrived at the Rectory they found the rector's daughters waiting for them, not dressed in their quaint green dresses as on Sunday, but in simple white, with green ribbons, however, round their white straw hats. They looked particularly pretty and interesting, and Rosamund could not help feeling that under different circumstances she might have been glad to make friends with them. Maud, the eldest girl, had very straight, well-formed features. She was intensely fair, with large, clear blue eyes; and her hair, golden, with warm shades in it, hung below her waist. Her little mouth was small and rosy and very firm. She had a pretty cleft in her chin, a good carriage; and, in short, she was just the sort of girl to captivate other girls. Beyond doubt she had for some time acted as mother to her sisters; for Alice, the next in age, was about two years younger. Then came Bertha and Mary, pretty little girls of nine and ten years of age, and then Ivy and Jasmine.

They made an interesting group as they clustered round the girls from Sunnyside and bade them welcome, Maud taking the lead, and finally attaching herself to Rosamund; for she guessed, in some sort of instinctive way, that Rosamund had more character than the other school-girls, and would be more likely to interest her.

"Come and walk with me, won't you?" she said. "I want to introduce you to dear Miss Carter. She is longing to see you. She knows—we all know—about your wonderful escapade on Sunday."

Rosamund felt herself turning pale just for a moment: then the color flooded her cheeks.

"I would rather not speak about Sunday, if you don't mind," she said.

"Certainly I don't mind," replied Maud in a very quiet and lady-like way. "That is, if you would really rather not," she continued after a pause. "We know a great deal of Irene Ashleigh from Miss Carter, and we are all interested in her."

"I should have thought you would have hated her," said Rosamund suddenly.

"No—not exactly. She has a sort of fascination for us. Whenever we want dear Carter to make us thoroughly happy, or to give us a great treat, we get her to tell us about this wild, this formidable little Irene. She could not do it at first, poor thing! for, you know—but I can't speak of that to-day. Oh! here she is, coming down the path. Ah, Miss Carter," called Maud, "this is Rosamund"—

"Rosamund Cunliffe," said Rosamund.

"Rosamund Cunliffe, the girl who was so plucky and went on the lake with Irene Ashleigh on Sunday afternoon."

"You were very fortunate," said Miss Carter, speaking in a prim voice. "It was, I regret to say, otherwise with me. I could not command her, and she took me"—Miss Carter's lips trembled.

"Don't speak of it now, dear Cartery. It always upsets you, doesn't it? Let us talk of something else. You are very happy with us, aren't you, Cartery love?"

"Cartery love" expressed that she was, and Maud slipped her hand affectionately through her governess's arm.

Rosamund gave the latter lady a keen glance. She saw that she was naturally extremely kind, but also shy and wanting in courage.

"She could never master Irene," thought the girl. "Irene is going to be given to me. She shall be mine. I mean to help her. I mean, whatever happens, to save her. But I don't mind talking a wee little bit about her to 'Cartery love,' as that funny Maud calls her."

The rest of the girls came up in a group, and the next hour or two were spent wandering through the pleasant gardens, while laughter, jokes, and good-humored chatter of all sorts filled the air.

Then came tea. Now, the rector's teas were celebrated. They were, in fact, that old-fashioned institution, now, alas! so rapidly disappearing from our English life, known as "high tea." Eggs, boiled ham, chickens, stewed fruits, fresh ripe fruit of every sort and variety, graced the board. No dinner followed this meal; but sandwiches and lemonade generally concluded the happy day.

The girls knew that they were not expected back until bedtime, and gave themselves absolutely up to the pleasures of the time. The Rectory was a charming old house, being quite a hundred and fifty or two hundred years old; and the study, or schoolroom, as the girls called it, where they invariably partook of tea, was a low-roofed apartment running right across the eastern side of the house. It was, therefore, at this hour a delightfully cool room, and was rendered more so by the bowery shade of green trees.

Rosamund found herself sitting near Maud at the meal, and she suddenly turned to her and said, "I quite understand now why you wear green, and why some people call you the Leaves."

"One person, you mean," said Maud, coloring slightly.

Lucy gave Rosamund an angry glance, and even managed to kick her under the table. This kick was highly resented by that young person, who, as she said to herself, stiffened her neck on the spot and determined to show what mettle she was made of.

"I'm not going to be mastered by that horrid Lucy, come what may," she thought.

Although it was impossible to be absolutely rude to Maud, who was one of those charming girls, unaffected, affectionate, and natural, who must delight every one, yet Rosamund's real object was to have a talk with "Cartery love." Now, Cartery's hands were full at that moment, for she was absorbed pouring out coffee at the other end of the table, never thinking once of herself, attending to the wants of every one else. She was one of those retiring people who may come and go in a crowd without any one specially noticing them; but if a kind office is wanted to be done in the most unobtrusive and gentle way, then "Cartery love" was sure to be at the fore. On this occasion she did glance once or twice at Rosamund, and something which was not often seen in her eyes filled them for a moment—a look of mingled admiration and fear. Rosamund determined to bide her time.

"I have not come here to make friends with the stupid Leaves," she said to herself. "I have come here to talk to Miss Carter, and talk to her I will. The week is coming to a close, and I have to give my decision. How that decision will turn out depends as much on 'Cartery love' as on anybody else."

Tea, good as it was, came to an end at last, and the children went out into the grounds, some to play tennis, some croquet, and some to wander away, two and two, each talking, as girls will, of their hopes and fears and ambitions.

Rosamund, to whom Maud devoted herself, turned suddenly to that young person.

"I will confide in you," she said. "You are longing to play tennis, are you not?"

"Oh no, thank you, not at all," said Maud, who was one of the champion players of the neighborhood, and could never bear to be out of any game that was in progress.

"But I know you are. I can read through people pretty well," said Rosamund, speaking in a low tone. "Now, I want to have a little talk with Miss Carter. Won't you go and play, and forget all about me, and let me have a chat with Miss Carter?"

"With our darling Cartery? Why, certainly, you shall if you like. I see you want to get her to tell you about Irene. I doubt if she will. Do, please, be merciful. She is very nervous. When she came to us she was almost ill, and we had to take great, great care of her. Would you like, first of all, to know how she came to us?"

"I should very much."

L. T. Meade

Rosamund forgot at this juncture all about Maud's passionate love for tennis.

"Well, it was in this way. We had no governess; we used to go to a sort of school—not the Merrimans', for they had not started one at the time—and I used to teach the little children, and things were rather at sixes and sevens. Not that father ever minded, for he is the sort of man who just lets you do what you like, and I think that is why we have grown up nicer than most girls."

"Indeed, I didn't know it would have that effect," said Rosamund, trying to suppress the sarcastic note in her voice.

"Don't speak in that tone, please. I think we really are quite nice girls—I mean we never quarrel, and we are always chummy and affectionate, and we try to do our best. We are not a bit self-righteous or conceited, or anything of that sort; for, you see, when our dear mother was alive she taught us so beautifully. Her rule was such a very simple one. She never punished us; all she ever said was, 'Do it because it is right. You cannot quite understand why it is right while you are very young; but, nevertheless, do it because it is right and because you love me.' And when God took her, and we thought our hearts would break, we all sat in a conclave together, and we determined to follow our mother's rule, and to do the right because it was right and because we loved her. I cannot tell you what a terrible time we had; but we stuck to that resolve. Nevertheless, our education was a poor affair, although father never noticed it.

"One day I was out driving with father, and we saw a poor lady sitting by the roadside. She looked so forlorn, and her eyes were red with crying. We did not know her; but she knew us, for she stood up at once, and said to father, 'You are Mr. Singleton?'

"Then, of course, father remembered her, only I did not. She was one of the many governesses who had come to try to tame Irene Ashleigh. So father and I both got down from the gig, and she told us that she had left The Follies and was going back to London to try to get another situation. She said that she had sent on her trunks by a porter to the station, and she meant to walk, for Lady Jane was very, very angry with her. She could not go on. She broke down, poor dear! and very nearly fainted. She said she did feel very faint and bad, so we just got her into the gig—as, of course, any people who had any feelings would do—and we brought her straight back to the Rectory, and she has stayed with us ever since.

"For the first month she was not our governess at all; she was our sort of child, to be petted and loved and fussed over. We put her in the sunniest room, and when we found that her nerves were so terribly shaken that she could scarcely sleep alone, one of my sisters had a little bed made up in the room and slept with her at night. We fed her up, didn't we just? and petted her; and when we found she liked it we took to calling her 'Cartery love,' and she did not mind it a bit. Then she got better, and said she must seek another situation, and father said she should stay and teach us and look after things in the house a bit. So she stayed. She knows such a lot, and does teach us so beautifully, and she isn't half nor quarter as shy as she was; we all love her, and she loves us. I think if Irene were not so near she would be perfectly happy."

"Thank you for telling me so much," said Rosamund when Maud ceased speaking.

"I had to tell you, for I want you, if you talk to her, to be very careful, for she is still exceedingly nervous. And no wonder. What she lived through at The Follies was enough to destroy the nerves of any woman, even the stoutest-hearted in the world."

"Well, I should like to speak to her, and I will certainly not harm her," said Rosamund.

Maud left her for a little while, and in a few minutes Miss Carter was seen coming down the path with Maud hanging on her arm.

"Now, Cartery dear," she said, "you talk to Rosamund Cunliffe, who is a friend of mine, and I will go and have a good, romping game of tennis. Oh, I see they are just breaking up the present set, so I am just in time."

Off ran Maud. Miss Carter's light-blue eyes followed her with an expression of the deepest affection.

"You seem very fond of her," said Rosamund suddenly.

"I don't know what I should have done without her. She saved my life and my reason."

"I don't want to talk about what has evidently given you very great distress," said Rosamund after a time; "but I should like to tell you that I know."

"You know?" said Miss Carter, beginning to tremble, and turning very pale.

"Yes, for Irene told me."

"My dear, dear Miss Cunliffe, how had you the courage to go with her in that terrible boat? She actually took you into the current—that appalling current where one is so powerless—and you escaped!"

"Oh, yes," said Rosamund lightly. "It was a mere nothing. You see, I am stronger than she is. All she wants is management."

"I could never manage her," said Miss Carter. "I could tell you of other things she did."

"No, I don't want to hear unless you are going to tell me something nice about her. Every one seems to speak against that poor girl; but I am determined to be her friend."

"Are you really?" said Miss Carter, suddenly changing her tone and looking fixedly at Rosamund. "Then you must be about the noblest girl in the world."

These words were very gratifying to Rosamund, who did think herself rather good in taking up Irene's cause; although, of course, she was fascinated by the exceedingly naughty young person.

"Yes, indeed, you are splendid," said Miss Carter; "and I know there must be good in the child. Such courage, such animal spirits, such daring cannot be meant for nothing. The fact is, her mother cannot manage her. Her mother is too gentle, too like me."

"Dear Lady Jane! Miss Carter, when my mother was young she was her great friend, and she said that Lady Jane was rather naughty."

"Ah!" said Miss Carter, with a sigh, "she has left all that behind her a long time ago. The only time I found her hard and unsympathetic was when I told her that I could not stay any longer at The Follies. She begged and implored of me to stay; but, of course, you know the story. I was under a promise to go, and I could not let out that Irene had wrung it from me at the risk of my life. So I went, and she took no notice of me, although it seemed to me that a sort of despair filled her face. Anyhow, off I went, and I am a happy woman here. I don't know what is to be done with Irene."

How long were you with her?

"A month altogether; but that month seems like years. I was very glad to get the post, for I must tell you, Miss Cunliffe, that I am poor and dependent altogether on what I earn for my daily bread. I have an old mother at home; I help her to keep alive with some of my earnings; and Lady Jane offered a very big salary—over a hundred a year—and there was only one child to teach, and I thought it would be so delightful. She mentioned the charms of the country-house, and that she did not require a great deal of education; and she even spoke of the lake and the boat. Oh, I was so glad to come! for I am not certificated, you know, and cannot get the posts that other women can. Well, anyhow, I arrived, and for a month it was really a reign of terror."

Miss Carter began to tremble.

"You must not do that, really," said Rosamund. "You are not suited to it. But do tell me what you think a very strong-minded person would have made of Irene."

"Well, you see, the first and principal thing was not to fear her, and it was impossible not to fear her, for she was up to so many tricks; she was worse than the most mischievous school-boy who ever walked. She would suddenly come into the drawing-room in her gymnasium clothes, and turn somersaults up and down the room in the presence of Lady Jane's distinguished guests. Oh! I cannot tell you half she did—I dare not tell you. There was no trick she was not up to; but you will know for yourself if you really mean to have more to do with her."

"I certainly mean to have a great deal more to do with her, although at the present moment I am forbidden by Professor Merriman even to speak to her."

"I know the Merrimans have a very bad opinion of her," said Miss Carter.

"Yes, that is just it; but she is the daughter of my mother's dearest friend, and I am not going to give her up."

"Yet you are at school at Mr. Merriman's!"

"That is true."

Miss Carter looked in a puzzled way at Rosamund.

"I cannot reveal any more of my plans," said Rosamund, speaking in a rather lofty tone; "but now I want to know a few things about her. Is she stingy or generous?"

"Oh! absolutely and perfectly generous, and in her own way forgiving too; and I do not think she could tell a lie, for she has no fear in her, and I suppose it is fear that makes us tell lies. She has never feared any mortal. She has no respect for authority, not even her mother; and although she rushes at her sometimes and smothers her with kisses, she seems to have no real affection for her. If I could be sure that she was absolutely affectionate I think something could be done for her. Now, that is all I can tell you. You can scarcely believe how this subject distresses me and causes that terrible trembling to come on. I don't think, Miss Cunliffe, young as you are, and brave as you doubtless are, you ought to undertake the reform of that wild girl at your age. Allow me to say that you are sent to school by your parents for a definite purpose, and not to undertake the reform of Irene Ashleigh."

A frown came over Rosamund's face, and Miss Carter, glancing at her, saw that her words had caused displeasure.

"Forgive me," she said gently; "I don't really mean to be

L. T. Meade

unkind. Indeed, I admire you, and admire your bravery beyond words. To be as brave as you are would be a noble gift, and if it were only my own heritage, how happy I should be!"

"I tell you what it is, Miss Carter," said Rosamund suddenly; "if ever I want your help, and if I can assure you that you can give it without personal danger to yourself, will you give it to me?"

"If I think it right I will truly do so."

"Then the day may come," said Rosamund; "there is no saying."

Just then Ivy's pretty voice was heard calling Miss Carter.

"She is my second youngest pupil, and such a darling child!" said Miss Carter, her eyes brightening. "Yes, dear," she continued as Ivy danced up to her; "what is it?"

"We want a game of Puss-in-the-corner, and the silliest and youngest among us are going to play."

Jumping up as she spoke, Miss Carter said she belonged to that group, and Rosamund turned somewhat disdainfully away.

CHAPTER IX

AN UNEXPECTED ROOM-MATE

It was on that very same day that Jane Denton, Rosamund's special friend, complained of sudden chill and headache. She was a little sick, too, and could not touch her supper. Mrs. Merriman always kept a clinical thermometer handy, and on discovering that the young girl's temperature was considerably over one hundred degrees, she took fright and had her removed to a room in a distant part of the house.

"If she is not better in the morning we will send for the doctor," was her verdict. "Now, girls, one thing: I do not wish the Professor to be annoyed. I undertook this school in order to save him anxiety, and if he knows of every trifling indisposition he may be terribly vexed and put out. I therefore take charge of Jane to-night, sleeping in her room and looking after her, and administering to her simple remedies. If in the morning she is no better I will send for the doctor, and then we will know how to act. Meanwhile you, Rosamund, have your room to yourself."

Rosamund was distressed for her friend, and boldly announced at once that she would act as nurse.

"I ought to," she said. "She is my friend, and I have always been fond of her. Besides, it seems exceedingly hard that you, Mrs. Merriman, who work so much for us all day long, should have to work at night as well. Do let me undertake this."

Mrs. Merriman could scarcely keep the tears back from her eyes when Rosamund spoke. She could not help liking the girl, notwithstanding her eccentricities and her very bold act of disobedience on the previous Sunday. But she was firm in her resolve.

"No, dear," she said; "I am obliged to you for making the offer."

"Hypocrite!" said Lucy angrily to herself. "She knows it cannot be accepted."

Mrs. Merriman was not looking at Lucy; on the contrary, she was looking full into Rosamund's face.

"I am obliged to you for making the offer," she continued; "but it is impossible for me to accept it, for the simple reason that there is just the possibility that Jane may be going to have some infectious disease, in which case I could not hear of any other girl in my establishment running any risk. Therefore you see for yourself that I cannot accept your offer. I should be unfaithful to your mother if I did."

"Oh, come, Rosamund!" said Laura Everett; "do let us go out and have a chat together. Of course, Mrs. Merriman is right. We will help you all we can, Mrs. Merriman, by being extra good girls. Isn't that the best way?"

Mrs. Merriman admitted that it was, and the two girls, their arms entwined, went out into the soft summer night. Laura Everett, with her merry face, blue eyes, and fair hair, was a great contrast to Rosamund Cunliffe. She was exceedingly clever and fond of books. Most of her tastes lay, however, in a scientific direction. She was devoted to chemistry and mathematics, and could already work well in these two branches of science. She was intensely matter-of-fact, and in reality had nothing whatever in common with Rosamund.

Lucy Merriman had a great admiration for Laura Everett: in the first place, because her mother, Lady Everett, was Mrs. Merriman's old friend; and in the next place, because she possessed, as Lucy expressed it, the invaluable gift of common-sense. She had rather taken Laura under her own wing, had intended to make her her special friend, had meant to trot her round and to show her to other friends; in short, as much as possible to divide her from Rosamund, whom she considered a most dangerous and pernicious influence.

But Laura had character of her own, and admired Rosamund; and now that she saw the girl looking rather pale, with an almost pathetic expression in her brown eyes, her heart smote her with a sense of pity, and she went up to her eagerly.

"I want you to tell me just what you think about the Singletons," she said. "Let us walk about under the trees. Isn't it nice and home-like here? Don't you think so, Rosamund?"

"Perhaps," said Rosamund in a dubious voice. Then she added impulsively, "You see, Laura, it is somewhat difficult for me to talk to you, for Lucy is your friend and she is not mine."

"I know you do not like her—I mean I know she is in every way your opposite; but if you only would take no notice of her little peculiarities, and accept her as she really is, you would soon find good points in her. She is devoted to her parents, and is very true. I know, of course, she is a little matter-of-fact."

"Yes, that is it," said Rosamund. "For goodness' sake, Laura, don't waste time talking about her. We can say as much as ever we like about the Singletons. I must say I am rather charmed with them."

"And so am I," said Laura, "particularly with Maud. She is so bright and unselfish."

"The person I like best of the entire group is Miss Carter," said Rosamund stoutly.

"What!" exclaimed Laura, with a laugh. "That poor, thin, frightened-looking governess—'Cartery love,' as they call her?"

"Yes, 'Cartery love,' or anything else you like to name her. I took a fancy to her, and thought her awfully nice. I may see more of her; there's no saying."

"You are so odd, Rosamund—so different from the other girls!"

"Mother told me that before, but somehow I never believed it. Of course, I have never been at school before."

"You can scarcely call this homely, pleasant house, school."

"I should enjoy it but for Lucy. But there, we are treading on dangerous ground."

"So we are," said Laura. Then she added stoutly, "I like it in spite of Lucy; or, rather, I like Lucy as much as anything else belonging to the school. I hope," she continued as they paced slowly under the fir-trees, "that you are not really anxious about Jane. I know that you and she are friends."

"We have been friends almost since we were babies," said Rosamund. "Not that we are a bit alike in character."

"Indeed you are not. Jane hasn't a quarter of your spirit."

"Perhaps it is because we are such opposites that we are such great friends," continued Rosamund.

"Perhaps; but do say you are not anxious about her."

"Not a scrap. I know Janey's ways. She is a little bit of a glutton is my Jane, and she overate herself at tea at the Singletons'. Now, you must not breathe it to mortal; but when I saw her taking that third plate of strawberries and cream, and that fifth hot buttered cake, I guessed there'd be something up to-night. She gets attacks of indigestion very severely; but if she has a chance of making a good meal—I mean a meal that she likes, for, of course, although the food here is good and plentiful, it is very simple—she never can resist it. There's my Janey to the life, so you needn't suppose that I am a little bit anxious about her."

"Well, that's all right," said Laura. "Somehow I thought by your manner you were."

"That is because I offered to stay in her room to-night. It did seem such a pity that dear Mrs. Merriman should be tired out."

"You have a very kind heart, Rosamund. Come, you know it."

"Have I? I don't think I do know it. But do you know what it

L. T. Meade

is, Laura? I am tired and would like to go to bed. Do you mind if I leave you?"

Laura, who saw Lucy in the distance, and was not so taken up with Rosamund as she had imagined she would be, consented without a moment's hesitation to part from her friend, and Rosamund presently went up to her own room. She had said good-night to the rest of the party, and wondered what she should feel like when she entered her room with no Jane to keep her company. Not that she was anything like as attached to Jane as Jane was to her; for she was Jane's idol, her ideal of all that was noble and princess-like and beautiful. Jane, to Rosamund, was an ordinary good-tempered girl, with whom she could put up, and on whom she could impose to a certain extent.

Nothing could exceed Rosamund's amazement, and a scream almost rose to her lips, when she entered and saw, curled up snugly in Jane's bed, no less a person than Irene Ashleigh. Irene's exceedingly bright face peeped up above the clothes. She gave a low, impish laugh, and then said slowly:

"Don't scream. Keep your nerve. I climbed up by the wistaria. I have been in bed for the last hour, expecting you. I happened to be hiding just below the window, clinging on for bare life to the wistaria and the thick ivy, and I heard the conversation between you and Mrs. Merriman, so I knew that you would have your room to yourself, and decided that I would share it with you. Now lock the door, for I have a great deal to say."

"But we are not allowed to lock our doors," said Rosamund.

"You will lock it to-night, because I order you to," said Irene.

"I shall do nothing of the sort. It is my room, and I will do exactly as I like."

Irene sat up in bed. Nothing could be more picturesque than her general appearance. She was in the red frock that she usually wore; her wild hair curled in elf-locks all over her head; her eyes, bright as stars, shone in the middle of her little elfin face; her charming lips pouted just for a moment. Then she said in a clear tone, "What if I get up and strike you right across the face? Will you lock the door in preference to that?"

"I will not lock the door."

Like a flash, Irene was out of bed and had struck Rosamund a resounding blow on her cheek. Rosamund felt the blow tingling, but she stood firm.

"Will you lock the door now?"

"No."

"What if I give you a blow on the other cheek?"

"Here it is for your majesty," said Rosamund, turning her other cheek to the foe.

Irene burst into a laugh.

"What a creature you are! But you know we are in danger. I have such a lot to say to you, and any one may nab us. Won't you lock the door just to please me? I won't slap you any more. I am sorry I hurt your dear cheek. I came because I could not help myself, and because I could not live without you any longer. Sunday, Monday, Tuesday, Wednesday, and no sign of you, and I just hungered for you. I am pining for you through all the days and all the nights, through every hour, in the midst of every meal; not speaking about you, for that is not my way, but just hungering and hungering, and yet you say you will not lock the door."

"No, Irene; and you ought not to be here. What is to be done?"

Poor Rosamund had never felt more bewildered in her life. She had given her word of honor; and her word of honor was, to her, worthy of respect. She had never yet broken it. Should she break it now? Irene looked at her for a few minutes in wonder. The two girls were standing in the centre of the room, for, of course, Irene was fully dressed. Compared to Rosamund, she was a small girl, for Rosamund was tall and exceedingly well developed for her age. Irene was a couple of years younger, but she was as lithe as steel. Her little fingers could crush and destroy if they pleased. Her thin arms were muscular to a remarkable degree for so young a girl. She had not a scrap of superfluous flesh on her body. At this moment she looked more spirit than girl; and if Rosamund could have got herself to believe that there were such creatures as changelings, she might almost have given credence to Irene's own story of herself.

As it was, however, she knew quite well that there must be a fight between them, and that if ever she was to influence Irene for good she must conquer her now.

"Look here," she said, going straight up to the younger girl; "you did wrong to come in here."

"I did wrong?" said Irene, with a little impish laugh. "But then I always do wrong. That doesn't matter."

"It may not matter to you. I am not concerning myself about your morals at this moment, but I am thinking about my own. When you did wrong now you injured me, and I am not going to put up with it."

"You are not going to put up with it? And how are you going to prevent it, darling?"

Before Rosamund could utter a word, Irene had sprung upon her, seized her round the waist, and compelled Rosamund to seat herself upon the side of the bed, which she herself had been occupying a few minutes ago.

"Now, darling," she said, "you are not going to get away from me, and I believe in your heart you don't want to."

Poor Rosamund! a great wave of longing to help this queer child swept over her heart; but there was her word of honor. She was a passionate, head-strong, naughty girl; but she could not give that up. Besides, she could not do anything with Irene in the future if she did not conquer her now.

"You are not going to—to say you don't like me?" said Irene, an expression of absolute terror filling her eyes and making them look wilder than ever. "Nobody ever dared to say that to me, and you are not going to be the first."

"As a matter of fact," said Rosamund, "I like you very much."

"There, then, I am satisfied," exclaimed Irene, and she flung her thin arms round Rosamund's neck, squeezed herself up close to her, and kissed her again and again.

"Ah!" she said, "I knew that all my life I was waiting for somebody; and that somebody was you, just you, so big, so brave, so—so different from all the others. I should not be the horrid thing I am if the others had not been afraid of me.

I got worse and worse, and at last I could not control myself any longer. I did things that perhaps I ought not to have done; but if you give me up I don't know what will happen—I don't know where things will end. Are you going to give me up?"

"I will tell you now exactly what has happened, Irene, and will leave it to you to judge how you ought to act for my sake at the present moment. You say you love me—"

"I suppose that is what I feel," said Irene. "It is a queer sort of sensation, and I have never had it before. It seems to make my heart lighter, and when I think of you I seem to get a sense of rest and pleasure. When you are away from me I feel savage with every one else; but when you are near I think the best of others. And I think it is just possible that if I saw much of you I'd be a sort of a good girl—not a very good one, but a sort of a good girl, particularly if you'd manage mother and manage the servants, and tell them not to be such geese as to be afraid of me. For, of course, you know, I can't help being a changeling."

"Now, Irene, you must listen to me. I ought to be in bed and asleep. People will hear us talking, and I won't allow the door to be locked, whether you like it or not, because it is against the rules."

"Gracious!" said Irene, "couldn't we both get out of the window, and climb down by the wistaria and the ivy, and reach the ground, and go and hide in the plantation? We could spend the night there, locked in each other's arms, so happy—oh, so happy! By the way, I saw a little summer-house—we could spend the night in the summer-house, couldn't we? Couldn't we?"

It was a temptation. Rosamund was fond of adventures. The

night was a very hot one; the room was close. Outside, there were stars innumerable. Mrs. Merriman, the only person who ever invaded the girls' bedrooms after the hours of repose, would certainly not intrude upon Rosamund. It would be nice to spend one night with her friend. Could she call Irene her friend? Anyhow, it would be nice to spend one night in the open air, and she could influence Irene and help her, and—But then there was the word of honor.

"I can't," she said. "I would have liked it, of course. But I will tell you what happened. When I got back home the other night I saw Professor Merriman, and he was very angry with me, and he said that I ought not to have disobeyed him. I told him all about you, and"—

"Of course he hates me, horrid old frump!" said Irene. "But you are not going to mind him. Why, mother has been writing to him, and writing to your mother, too; and the one thing about you that I don't quite like is that mother had evidently been thinking that you have been sent as a sort of Providence here to reform me. You must see by my making that remark that I tolerate you very much indeed, or I should not endure it. There, it's a fact that I do care for you. I don't mind mother, and I don't mind your mother; but I am willing to be a little bit good if you are with me. But I am not going away from you now. You can choose whether you have me in your room all night or whether you and I spend a happy time in that dear little bower in the plantation."

"I cannot choose either," said Rosamund stoutly, "for I will tell you what did happen. I promised Professor Merriman that I would have nothing to do with you for a whole week. At the end of that time I was to give him my decision. Now, this is Wednesday, so the week won't be up until Sunday. So you must go, Irene. You must go at once. I will meet you at the end of the week, or, if you prefer it, I will go down to

Professor Merriman now and tell him that you came in, and that I asked you to go."

"Oh, what a mean spitfire of a thing you'd be if you did that!" said Irene, her eyes flashing with anger. "You can't mean it—you simply can't."

Just then there was the noise of approaching footsteps on the landing outside, and the handle of the door was turned. In a flash, so quickly that even Rosamund could not believe her own eyes, Irene was hiding under the bed, and Lucy Merriman entered.

Lucy looked prim and neat, as usual, in her white dressing-gown and her hair in a long plait down her back.

"I have come for—but surely you were talking to some one?" she said, addressing Rosamund.

"I sometimes repeat poems to myself," said Rosamund, who was standing with her back to Lucy, quivering all over with indignation.

"But I heard two voices; and it is against the rules for any noise to be made in the bedrooms after ten o'clock. I have come for—"

"Do you mind telling me what you have come for, so that you may get it and go?" was Rosamund's response.

"You are exceedingly impertinent," said Lucy. "Why do you always address me as you do? You try your utmost to make me unhappy in my own home."

"And you, instead of treating me as an honored guest, try your utmost to make me miserable," was Rosamund's quick reply. "Never mind," she continued, hot passion getting the better of her; "I shall not be with you much longer."

"That is quite nice—that is what I hoped," said Lucy almost gleefully. "Well, Jane Denton is very bad, and they are thinking of sending for the doctor. Of course, you don't care whether your friend lives or dies. Anyhow, I have been sent to fetch a bottle of aromatic vinegar which Jane, poor girl! said she had left on her washhand-stand. Ah! here it is."

Lucy took it up. She looked round the room. Poor Rosamund's terror can be better imagined than described, for the wicked Irene had lifted the valance of the bed, and her bright eyes and a tiny portion of her face could be distinctly seen by any one who happened to glance in that direction. Had Lucy seen her she must have screamed, for nothing more elfish than that face could be imagined. As it was, all might have been well had not Irene, just as Lucy was reaching the door, given a low, wild whoop, and then disappeared again under the valance of the bed.

"Now, I know you have some one there."

"If you are not afraid of rats you had better look," was Rosamund's quick response. But she turned very pale, and Lucy, who was something of a coward herself, said after a minute's pause:

"Rats! You know there are no rats in the house. What fresh insult will you bestow upon us?"

A moment later she had vanished from the room. Rosamund put both her hands to her hot ears. Irene sprang from her hiding-place.

"Didn't I do it well? Oh, what a hateful, hateful girl she is!

Now, Rosamund—Rose—whatever you call yourself—you had better just get right out of this window with me as fast as ever you can, or you'll have Lucy bringing her precious governesses, and her mother, and that sick girl, Jane Denton—how dare she call herself Jane, my dear mother's name?—as well as the Professor himself, on the scene to hunt for the rats. Come, Rose, out with you! We will lock the door first, and then all will be safe."

It seemed to Rosamund at the moment that even her word of honor had vanished out of sight, for her hatred of Lucy had really reached boiling-point. She did turn the key in the lock, knowing well that no one would break open the door until the morning; and a minute later she and Irene had escaped by the window, and gone down hand over hand by the wistaria and ivy until they reached the ground. Three minutes later they were ensconced in the old summer-house, where they sat very close to each other, Irene not talking much, and Rosamund wondering what was to become of her.

"It seems to me," said Rosamund to herself, as she looked down on the little creature who nestled up almost like a wild bird in her arms, "that I have burnt my boats, and that I cannot go back. But there is one thing certain: I will tell the Professor the truth in the morning."

All that Irene did, however, during the long hours of that summer's night was to lie fast asleep with Rosamund's arm round her. But just before she fell into slumber, Rosamund said:

"Aren't you cold, Irene? Surely you are not accustomed, even in the middle of summer, to wear so little clothing at night."

"Bless you!" said Irene, "half the nights of my life I sleep in the boat. I go out just as night falls, and none of them can ever catch me; and there I sleep, curled up in the bottom of the boat. Oh! it is splendid to wake in the early morning and to hear the birds singing, and to feel the fresh, fresh air on my face. I was never meant for civilization. When you come to live with me we will do the same, both of us. We'll be an uncivilized pair of terrors—that is what we will be. If you come to me, Rosamund, will you promise to be quite naughty? You won't turn awfully goody-goody, just to make me goody-goody?"

"I can promise nothing at present," said Rosamund. "You did exceedingly wrong to come, and I did worse to yield to you, and to get out of the window, and to spend the night with you, as I have done. I don't know what will happen in the morning—I really don't—and my friend so very ill, too."

"Oh, bother your friend!" said Irene; and then she dropped off asleep, and Rosamund sat and thought things out.

At first the night-air was delightful; but as the hours went by poor Rosamund, who had not brought any extra wrap with her in her hasty flight, felt chilled and tired. She woke Irene when the sun was high in the heavens.

"Come," she said, "I have broken my word of honor, and for you; but I am going now to take you back as far as The Follies. What will happen afterwards I do not know, and you mustn't ask me. If you don't come quietly at once I will never have anything more to do with you as long as I live. Get up! come along!"

"Why, you are quite cross; but you look very handsome, and I admire your ways," said Irene. "Dear, dear! Wasn't it lovely sleeping in your arms? We will sleep together in a cosy bed at The Follies, won't we, darling?"

L. T. Meade

"I can't make any promises. I don't know what is going to happen. Come quickly. I want to be in the house and up in my own room before any one discovers that I spent the night out."

There seemed reason in this to Irene, and she suffered her friend to walk with her along the road. It was a glorious summer morning; but at so early an hour—not yet five o'clock—the air was cool. Exercise, however, soon revived Rosamund, and she lost that feeling of chill and fatigue which had made the latter part of the night so unpleasant to her. As to Irene, she was as fresh as a young bird, and the pranks she played, and the somersaults she turned, and the extraordinary manner in which she went on would have terrified many girls, although Rosamund scarcely noticed them. She had already discovered that Irene's bark was worse than her bite, and the best plan was to let her alone and not to take too much notice of her vagaries.

The two girls parted at the gates of The Follies, Irene assuring Rosamund that she was going to lay all sorts of traps for the servants during the next couple of hours.

"I shall have great fun," she said. "They have been more than usually troublesome lately, and I want every one to go, so that we can have a fresh batch in their places when you come, darling; for you will come—I know you will—early next week. And, Rose, I will even be a little bit good for you."

There was a suspicion of tears in the wild, star-like eyes, and then the queer little creature flashed out of sight.

Rosamund stood still for a minute with her hand to her forehead. She then slowly retraced her steps. She was so lost in thought that she did not notice the milkman as he rattled along with his cart; nor did she notice the doctor, who passed in his gig, driving rapidly back to Dartford. He, however, stared very hard at the good-looking girl, evidently a lady, who was out all alone at that early hour.

By-and-by Rosamund got back to Sunnyside. She climbed up the ivy and wistaria and re-entered her own room. She carefully shut the window, unlocked her door, undressed, and got into bed. Her first impulse had been to tell the whole story of her night's adventure to Professor Merriman; for she felt that, stern as he could be, there was also something gentle about him, and he would certainly understand her. But on second thought the desire to confide in him passed out of sight, more particularly as there was a noise and confusion— a sort of stifled confusion—in the house: people hurrying backwards and forwards, and voices sunk to whispers, which came sometimes to Rosamund's ears, and sometimes receded in the distance.

By-and-by she looked at her watch and saw that it was half-past seven, the usual hour for the girls to get up. But no one had brought hot water, and no one had called her. She felt really dead-tired at last. What did anything matter? She had got herself into such a serious scrape that she did not think she could possibly stay more than a day or two longer at the Merrimans' school. Of course she would be dismissed, expelled, disgraced. But she did not care. She was sorry for Jane—quiet, gentle Jane—who had always been her devoted friend; but she did not mind anybody else. Laura Everett she rather liked; but the other girls were indifferent to her, with the exception of Lucy, whom she cordially hated. Before she knew where she was, Rosamund was sound asleep.

L. T. Meade

CHAPTER X

JANE IN DANGER

Rosamund was awakened from her slumbers by Laura Everett, who shook her lightly by the shoulder.

"Why, Rose," she said, "I wish you'd wake up. We are all in such a state of confusion and anxiety. Have you the least idea what the hour is?"

"No. Where am I?" said Rosamund, sitting up in bed and pushing back her hair.

"Well, it is close on nine o'clock. We had breakfast anyhow this morning, for nothing is in order. I cannot even explain how bad things are."

"Try and tell me, Laura; don't keep me in suspense."

"It's Jane, of course."

"My friend Jane?"

"You heard last night that she was very ill. Lucy told you. Lucy has been talking about you. She said you were very queer when she came in here last night, and didn't show a scrap of feeling. But I am sure you are sorry for her. She is in great danger, Rosamund."

"Jane in danger!"

Rosamund had always been fond of Jane, but she had never thought her of the slightest importance. She had always thought of her as just a good sort to have as a friend; but all the admiration must be on the friend's side, who must do all that Rosamund wished—for she, Rosamund, would not put herself out for her friend. But now things were changed. Jane Denton was the heroine of the hour. No one else in the whole of that house was thought of in comparison with Jane. For the symptoms of the night before had developed in a most aggravating way. She had grown worse and worse; in short, she was so alarmingly ill that when Lucy came into the room Mrs. Merriman had decided to send for the doctor from Dartford. He was obliged to drive over, there being no train so late at night. When he saw her he pronounced her illness to be diphtheria. How she had got it nobody knew; but diphtheria Jane had, and of the most malignant type.

"What is it?" said Rosamund, now turning to Laura, who sat down on the edge of her bed. "You think I have no heart, but you are mistaken."

Her bright eyes filled with tears, and Laura was softened at once.

"I knew you had a heart, dear," she said. "But the fact is, you never understood Lucy. I like Lucy, and you don't—there lies the difference between us. Lucy misunderstood you. She said that, instead of going to bed, you were making a most awful noise, reciting poetry to yourself in two distinct voices, and that an extraordinary noise came from under the bed, and you declared it was rats. But she thinks you are a sort of ventriloquist, and can throw your voice anywhere you like. She was absolutely frightened, and rushed out of the room."

"Well, the doctor arrived about two o'clock in the morning, and he stayed until early morning; and now the whole school knows, and what is to be done is more than I can tell. The doctor wants us all to leave the house."

"I shan't go," said Rosamund stoutly.

"What do you mean, Rose? You mustn't think of yourself at a moment like this."

"I shall stay and nurse Jane. She is my friend. Don't keep me, please, Laura. What a horrible creature I have been! Oh, dear! oh, dear! Do you know where the Professor is, Laura?"

"I believe he is out, but I don't know. Mrs. Merriman is looking after Jane at present. But, Rose, you won't be allowed to see her. The doctor has forbidden any single individual except Mrs. Merriman to go into her room, or to have anything whatever to do with her. You mustn't disobey orders. A trained nurse is coming, and will be here in a very short time. Perhaps there will be two nurses. They are going to try that new treatment—antitoxin. Poor Jane's room is not so very far from where I sleep, and I heard her groaning in the night. To think of our all being so happy yesterday, and now this coming!"

"I know," said Rosamund in a low tone. She had never expressed herself so before. There was a lump in her throat.

Laura went away and soon entered the schoolroom, where Lucy and the other girls, all looking pale and anxious, were standing about. Laura went straight up to Lucy.

"Well," said Lucy, "is that thoughtless, heartless creature awake yet? Is she thinking of any one but herself?"

"Oh, yes, I woke her. She isn't heartless. I wish just at present, when we are in such anxiety, you would try to be kinder, Lucy, and"—

Laura's voice suddenly broke.

Rosamund presently came downstairs. She wanted to find the Professor. She wanted she knew not what. As a matter of fact, he was not to be found, for he had gone by the very earliest train to Dartford to see Mr. and Mrs. Brett.

The upshot of this visit was that soon Mrs. Brett's large, pale face, with its light-blue eyes and gentle smile, was seen passing the window. The Professor was with her. All the girls rushed out with a sudden sense of relief to greet her.

"Oh, Aunt Susan, we are so glad you have come!" said Lucy, her own little face quivering with sudden emotion.

"My dear, dear children," said Mrs. Brett, "I have come to take you away with me—that is, all of you who can come. My husband and I are a childless couple, and we have plenty of room in our house. You must just pack your things and come along. That is what I have come for. There is a nurse coming to look after the poor girl who is so dreadfully ill.— Lucy, dear, your father is particularly anxious that you should come—yes, and all the rest of you, for that matter. I can squeeze you all in; but I cannot manage the governesses, that is the only thing. All the rest—every single one of you— must come. Rosamund, you, of course; and, Laura, you also. Annie Millar—yes, certainly—and Phyllis Flower, and Agnes Sparkes—every single one of you shall come back with me. It will be Poverty Castle, my loves, and we'll have to stint and scrape and contrive; but at any rate we'll be merry when we can be merry, and we'll forget our troubles in doing good to others."

Nothing could exceed the heartiness of Mrs. Brett's manner. Her very smile brought sunshine with it, and her firm voice confidence. It seemed in a minute to those agitated and unhappy girls that a ray of sunlight had fallen upon them, and that the world was not quite so miserable after all.

They were still standing talking eagerly in the hall when a fly drew up at the door and Dr. Marshall stepped out. He had, in fact, followed Mrs. Brett and the Professor up from the station. He saw Rosamund, and recognized her as the girl he had seen some hours before walking alone along the high-road. He went up to her and put his hand on her shoulder.

"Are you one of the young ladies who live here?"

"Yes," she replied, glancing at him in surprise, for so lost had she been in her own thoughts that she had positively hardly observed him when he swiftly passed her in the early morning.

"Then I congratulate you upon your powers of early rising."

Rosamund colored. Lucy's eyes were fixed on her face.

"My dear Miss Lucy," said the doctor, "your friend, Miss"—

"My name is Rosamund Cunliffe," said Rosamund.

"Your friend Miss Cunliffe has put all the rest of you young ladies to shame. She was walking abroad this morning between four and five o'clock at some distance from here."

Lucy's eyes flashed fire. Rosamund found herself turning pale. The Professor looked at her. Suddenly Rosamund went up to the Professor and took his hand.

"I want to speak to you, and alone," she said.

"In a moment, my dear," he answered.

He then turned to the doctor.

"Mrs. Brett, my kind sister-in-law, has promised to take all my young people to her house in Dartford," he said. "She proposes that they should return with her immediately. Then the house will be quite quiet for the invalid, and there will be no danger of the disease spreading."

"If it does spread I shall be on the spot to grapple with it," said Dr. Marshall.—"What an excellent plan, Mrs. Brett, and how exactly like you!—Now then, young ladies, the sooner you pack up the better. You needn't take a great many things; they can be sent to you afterwards. The great thing is to get away. It may be in the air; it may be—we cannot tell what; but the sooner all of you young people are out of Sunnyside the safer it will be."

"It would not be fair," said the Professor, "to ask the Singletons to take any of them in. We did think of that at first. We know how particularly kind Mr. Singleton is. But there are his own children to be thought of; and as he is the rector of the parish he has also to consider his parishioners."

"I am the woman who has to act in this emergency," said Mrs. Brett; "and now the sooner we drop the subject of whys and wherefores the better.—Run upstairs, my dears, and get ready.—I will not even see my dear sister, Mrs. Merriman, for fear of infection; but you will know where to find me if you want my help."

"I don't think we shall need it," said the doctor. "Two excellent nurses are coming by the next train, and I shall leave full directions, and my assistant will come out to see the patient this evening.—Now, if you will kindly allow me to pass, young ladies, I will go and see the invalid, and I will not see any of you again afterwards. It is safer not."

There was a look on his face which startled and brought back some of the nervousness of most of the girls. But Mrs. Brett, or Aunt Susan, as Lucy called her, was all smiles and benediction.

"My dears," she said in her motherly way, "there is room enough and to spare in my house for every one of you— room enough and to spare. You shall have the heartiest welcome."

Here Mrs. Brett went up to Rosamund, and, rather to the surprise of the others, elected her for a resounding kiss on the cheek.

"My dear, a girl who can go out and take a walk at so early an hour in the morning is quite after my own heart."

"But, Aunt Susan," interrupted Lucy, "do you really approve of a girl who burns the candle at both ends? It so happens that I was obliged to invade Rosamund's room last night, and I heard her reciting poetry in two voices, and then I heard her throw her voice into a distant part of the room, so that you might almost imagine that she was a ventriloquist. It was nearly eleven o'clock, and the doctor said he saw her walking along the high-road between four and five this morning. Don't you think it is too much for her strength?"

"Never mind, dear," said Mrs. Brett, who was as kind in heart as her face appeared. "I admire energy; but the energy of the young is sometimes misdirected. When dear Rosamund comes to stay with me I will show her one or two things.—You won't mind getting a wrinkle or two from an old woman, will you, Rose?"

"No," said Rosamund, who was absolutely torn in the midst of many conflicting emotions: her anxiety for her friend, her knowledge of what had happened the night before, her ever-increasing dislike to Lucy—and, in fact, the whole false position in which she found herself—all distressed her beyond measure.

Again she touched the Professor on the arm.

"I want to say something," she remarked, and she turned and faced the other girls.—"Before I decide to go with Mrs. Brett I must speak to Professor Merriman."

"But there is no time, my dear," said Mrs. Brett. "Our train leaves in three-quarters of an hour. Each girl will please pack a small bag, if she possesses such a useful commodity, and we must walk as fast as ever we can to the station, for my poor dear husband has no end of things for me to attend to to-day, and the moment we get to Dartford we shall have to bustle about, I can tell you. There'll be no time for whims and fancies, or even for lessons; for there is to be an enormous tea-fight, as I call it, for the young folk of the parish in the schoolhouse this afternoon, and games afterwards, and recitations; and if you, Rosamund, can recite as well as Lucy has described, why, you will be invaluable."

"But I can't recite. Lucy is mistaken," said Rosamund.— "Professor, may I speak to you?—Mrs. Brett, if you are in a hurry, I will follow you by a later train, if it is decided that I am to go to you."

Here the determined girl took the Professor by the arm, and leading him into the study, shut the door behind them, and turned and faced him.

"I have been exceedingly naughty. I have broken my word of honor."

Now, the Professor, who was always extremely dreamy, had nearly forgotten Rosamund's transgression of the previous Sunday. He did not speak at all for a minute, but looked at her in puzzled astonishment.

"You have broken your word of honor?" he said. "We are in great trouble. I hope you are not now beginning to be taken up with whims and fancies. If so, please transfer them to a more convenient season. I am harassed about my books, my—my dear wife, and that poor girl. By the way, she is your friend, too. I can quite understand that you are grieved on her account."

"I am terribly grieved. I do not wish to leave. I should like to stay and help to look after her."

"But that cannot be permitted. That would be an act of the greatest selfishness. What we require you to do is to leave the house before you are infected—you even more than the others, for you have been in the same room with her."

"I do not think I am infected. I cannot imagine how Jane caught diphtheria. I did see her bending down over a drain the other day. She had dropped her pencil and was trying to find it. I told her not to do it, and even dragged her away. I am sure I am all right, and I should not allow her to breathe on me, and I think I could help."

"It is generous of you, my dear, but it cannot possibly be permitted," said the Professor. "I will relate that little circumstance to my wife. Not that it matters, after all, how we get our diseases; the thing is to cure them when we have acquired them. However, I will mention the circumstance to my dear wife."

"Please do. Now, I have something to confess. You heard what Lucy said: that I was reciting poetry, that I was using two voices, that I was a sort of ventriloquist. You heard what Dr. Marshall said: that he saw me on the high-road at a very early hour this morning. Now, I was not reciting last night; I was talking to another girl, and no less a girl than that one I had promised you to have no communication with for a whole week—Irene Ashleigh. Please hear me out before you speak. I did not ask her to come to me. She came on her own account. I did mean to keep my word of honor; but Irene, poor little girl! had taken a liking to me. I had managed, I don't know how, to touch something sympathetic in her heart, and she was hungering for me, and you had forbidden me to go to her. So last night, after I came to bed, she was in my room. She had got in by the window. Oh, don't look at me with those startled eyes! I do not wish her to be blamed, and I was not to blame when I found her there, for I did mean to keep my word of honor. She begged of me to lock the door, but I refused; and I think I was almost inducing her to leave the house, and to go home, when Lucy burst into the room. Lucy came to fetch something for Mrs. Merriman— something that Jane wanted—and Irene was under the bed like a flash. It was she who made that noise that Lucy attributed to me. Then afterwards I felt reckless, and I did lock the door, and I did go out by the open window, and I spent the night in the summer-house with little Irene, and this morning I walked back with her to The Follies. Now you know what I am. You see I am not worth saving; and I want to tell you that if you will not have me here, then I will go to

Lady Jane, and tell her the entire story, and ask her if I may stay with her—at least until the time of infection is over. That is what I wish to do; but I will not go in the dark. I have told you how naughty I have been, and you can punish me by expelling me from the school. But, please, quite understand that your daughter has provoked me a great deal, and that I did make an effort—at least at first—to keep my word of honor."

Rosamund's voice dropped. In truth, the emotions of the previous day, the night before, and this morning had been too many for her. She trembled, and finally, to the great astonishment of the Professor, burst into tears. Now, no one ever had higher principles than Professor Merriman, but no man ever had a greater horror of tears. He could not bear what Rosamund had told him; he could not understand how, under any provocation, a girl could act as Rosamund had done; and yet, at the same time, her tears so maddened him that he would have done anything to get rid of her.

"You bewilder me," he said. "Of course, you did wrong. Do you wish to go with Mrs. Brett? I will see you presently and speak to you."

"If you will not have me here, I will not go with Mrs. Brett. I will go to Lady Jane; for there is one person who wants me, although you will not believe it!"

"Then please yourself; but I grieve to tell you that after your recent conduct I cannot receive you again at the school."

Rosamund left the room with a proud step, but there was something in her heart which danced.

CHAPTER XI

BOOBY-TRAPS

Lady Jane Ashleigh was sitting at her early breakfast. She always breakfasted alone in a beautiful little room which her late husband had specially furnished for her. It was a room full of memories, for she had passionately loved her husband, and had never ceased to mourn his death. If she had been a more cheerful and less self-concentrated woman she might long ago have won the love of her queer and erratic little daughter. As it was, during her husband's lifetime she thought of no one but him, and since his death her best thoughts were devoted to his memory: to keep flowers always on his grave; to see that his portrait was dusted day after day, and that flowers were put under it; to kneel there and utter prayers that he and she might be reunited in a better world, absorbed her strongest thoughts.

Of late, however, Irene's queer conduct had terrified her very much. Too late she discovered that she had no hold over the child, and the child was now a source of misery to her. She could not manage Irene. The servants were afraid of her. No governess would stay long. In short, she was drifting from bad to worse; and yet it was impossible for Lady Jane not to love the queer, erratic little creature. Often at night, when Irene was sound asleep, the mother would steal into the room and look at the pretty face, quite soft then, with all the wildness gone out of it. She used to look down at the long, curling black lashes, on the pale, smooth, rounded cheeks, at the wealth of dark curling hair, and wonder and wonder why the child ever and always turned from her, why she never reposed confidence in her, why she left her to live apart. If by any chance Lady Jane made a noise while she was in Irene's room and awakened that small sprite, then the scene would change. Irene would spring up in bed, dare her mother to invade her slumbers, and frighten her with immediately vanishing into the night-air and spending the rest of her time in the boat.

A short time ago, Irene had insisted on locking her door, and on one occasion had managed through utter carelessness to set fire to a curtain. Her own bravery had quenched the flames before any mischief was done; but the household had been alarmed, the room forcibly burst open, and the child, whose arm was badly burned, was carried fainting from the room. After that Lady Jane removed all keys and bolts from the door, and no entreaties on Irene's part could induce her to have them put back.

On this lovely summer's morning Lady Jane was eating her delicate breakfast in her usual delicate way. Her thoughts were divided between her husband, whom she would never see again in this world, and the child whom she could not manage. She was also thinking of Rosamund, the daughter of her dear friend.

A servant came in with the letter-bag. Lady Jane never had any special correspondence, and she was in no hurry to open it; but having quite consumed her breakfast, she thought she might as well do so. She therefore languidly took a key from her chatelaine, inserted it into the lock, and took out the contents. She found amongst many other letters one from her old friend, Rosamund's mother.

Mrs. Cunliffe wrote to say that she was glad Lady Jane liked Rosamund, and gave her hearty consent to Rosamund's spending a good deal of her time at Lady Jane's house.

"I may as well tell you," continued the mother, "that Rosamund herself is somewhat difficult to manage. I have always found her so; but hitherto nothing has gone very wrong between us, because I have led her by the golden rule of love. I have never driven her in any respect. I heard a great deal of the Merrimans, the dear Professor, whose books are so well known, and the charming little school they proposed to open; and when I found that the school was in your neighborhood, my dear old friend, I decided to send Rosamund there. I am writing now to Professor and Mrs. Merriman to say that I wish Rosamund to spend as much time as ever she can spare at your house and in the company of your sweet little girl. By the way, you have told me nothing about her. She must be about twelve years old now. Rosamund, dear child, is fifteen. I can fancy what a comfort the little Irene must be to her mother, so gentle and sweet, just like what that mother was when I was a somewhat wild and erratic girl myself."

"Alas and alack!" thought poor Lady Jane, "how very little my dear friend knows of the sort of creature whom Providence has bestowed upon me as a child!"

Just at that moment the room door was burst open, and Miss Frost, in tears, her nose very red, her agitation extreme, followed by Irene, entered the room.

"She has poisoned me! She has absolutely poisoned me!" said the unfortunate governess, sinking on the first chair she could find. "She brought me my pills as usual this morning—you know I am ordered pills for indigestion—and after I had swallowed them she announced that she had changed them for wood-lice, which curl up as you touch them."

"It was such fun!" laughed Irene. "Oh, Frosty, Frosty, it was delicious!"

"But what a wicked thing for you to do, Irene!" said her mother.

"They will multiply inside me," said poor Miss Frost. "Oh, what is to be done? Can a doctor be summoned at once?"

"I am sure there can be no danger," said poor Lady Jane; "but it was a wicked trick to play, Irene. But I believe wood-lice are harmless, and I suppose they are dead. Still, Irene, your conduct is disgraceful. You are really past bearing."

"All right, mumsy!" said Irene in a most cheerful tone. "I don't mind how much you scold me, for I had such a happy time while I was watching Frosty swallowing those digestive pills! She thought me so attentive, because as a rule I don't take any interest in her pills. I found a lot of the dear little wood-lice in the garden this morning, and it suddenly darted through my mind that they could be swallowed just like pills. So I put them into a box and rattled them well, and brought them to Frosty, and opened the box and said to her, 'Here, Frosty, here are your digestive pills;' and she had swallowed two before she found out what she had done. The rest began to uncurl in the box, and she discovered what had happened. Oh, it was lovely to see her face!—You do feel bad, don't you? You'd like to go at once, wouldn't you, darling? I am so awfully anxious for you to go!"

"But if—if," said poor Miss Frost—"if you really think that

the pills—I really can't call them by the other name—will do no harm, it seems almost a"—

"I tell you what I will do," said Lady Jane. "I will send you straight into Dartford to see Dr. Marshall. He will tell you what is best to be done. But I feel sure you are quite safe.— Irene, you are so naughty that I cannot speak to you."

Miss Frost, who did not dare to give up her lucrative situation, left the room. Lady Jane went to the bell and rang it. A servant was desired to have the carriage ordered immediately, and the unhappy and perplexed governess was soon out of the house on her way to Dartford to see Dr. Marshall or one of his assistants.

Meanwhile Irene, in the red dress she had worn all night, very much crumpled, very much disheveled and soiled, sat down and fixed her bright eyes on her parent.

"So she is not to go!"

"Was that why you did it, Irene?"

"Of course," said Irene in a laconic voice, "I'll have to think of something else. She is an extraordinary woman is Frosty. I got rid of Carter. You know how I got rid of her."

"You mustn't speak of it—it is too painful."

"Well, I'll have to get rid of Frosty."

"Now listen to me, Irene. Your governess is not to go."

"Mumsy dear, why that tone? You know you are a little bit afraid of your Irene, aren't you?"

Irene danced up to her parent and looked at her with eyes bright as stars. Suddenly she flung herself on her knees by her mother's side.

"You didn't by any chance come to see me in my little bed last night?" she asked. "You didn't come perhaps in the early morning? You didn't quote those well-known lines:

What does little birdie say
In its nest at peep of day?

Mumsy dear, did you?"

"No, Irene; I was occupied with other things—with sad, very sad memories. This is the anniversary of your dear, your precious father's death."

Irene had the grace to be silent for a moment. After a pause she said, "I did remember that yesterday morning; and knowing that you'd be frightfully dumpy—oh, mummy! you know you never are cheerful—I thought I'd have a spree on my own account. So I tell you what I did, mothery."

Lady Jane looked with absolute fear into Irene's face. After a time her eyes slowly welled up with tears.

"I can't imagine what I have done," she said. "I often wonder beyond words why I am given such a very naughty child—a child who understands me so very little, who cannot sympathize with my sorrows and cannot understand my griefs, and who contrives to make others miserable. It is your cruelty that is so terrible, Irene."

"My cruelty!" said Irene, opening her bright eyes wide. Something seemed to hurt her. It was the first time Lady Jane had ever seen a spark of real feeling in this extraordinary child. "Well, now, listen," she said. "I spent the night with Rosamund—dear Rosamund Cunliffe."

"You ran away from home and spent the night at the Merrimans'?"

"Oh, you needn't be afraid. I didn't even occupy one of their rooms long, and certainly didn't break bread with them. I wouldn't break bread in the house with that Lucy for all you could give me. Nevertheless, I spent the night with Rosamund. Oh, she is a splendid creature! She is jolly enough, and she is brave enough. Why, she let me strike her on the cheek as hard as ever I could, and didn't utter a word. I wanted her to lock the door, and she had some queer notions about it that I couldn't fathom; and when I struck her on her cheek, she only just offered me the other, and said, 'You may do what you like, but I will not lock the door.'

"Now, mother, if you'd stand up to me like that I'd just respect you. Anyhow, I respect Rosamund, and I dare say I'd have had to spend the night in her room, or perhaps even have had to come home, but something most welcome happened. Thank goodness, Rosamund isn't a prig! She's awfully passionate, and has plenty of strong feelings. She's not a bit a goody-goody; I'd just hate her like anything if she were. But that Lucy—you know that prim thing, the daughter of the Professor and Mrs. Merriman? Well, she came into the room, and I was under the bed in a twinkling. She argued with Rosamund and found fault with her, and got dear old Rose into a towering passion. Well, after that I could do what I liked with her. She did lock the door, although she vowed she wouldn't at first; and we got out through the window, and spent the night in the summer-house in the plantation. I put my head on her lap, and she put her arms round me and tried to keep me warm; and then I went off to sleep so happily, for somehow or other—I didn't think I could ever love anybody, but somehow or other there is a sort of feeling in me that perhaps is love for her. I think I could even be good for her.

"In the morning she walked with me as far as The Follies, and I have been for the last few hours very busy. There'll be a good deal of excitement amongst the servants to-day. I did hope that the wood-lice would settle Frosty; but now you have interfered. Why can't you let her go? She's no manner of use to me. Can't you give her whatever salary she has now, and send her back to London, or wherever she lives?"

"And let you grow up wild, Irene, with no one to teach you—for you will not learn from me?"

"Well, mother, I shall never learn anything from Frosty. Oh, what a morning it is! Is that the footman I hear outside? I expect he has discovered."

Just then James, who had been in the family for the last five or six years, came staggering into the room. He had been caught by a booby-trap which Irene had placed just over his pantry door, and a shower of spiders and caterpillars and other offensive insects had fallen all over him. His face was deadly pale, and he declared that he had been severely stung.

"There were wasps there," he said, "and I have been stung in the cheek and on the hand; and, madam, I don't really know what to do."

"It was a booby-trap. You look beautiful, James!" said Irene.

James flashed her an angry glance. Poor Lady Jane started to the rescue. What was she to do with this intolerable child?

"There are a lot more traps laid for the other servants," said Irene under her breath. "I didn't want poor old James to be stung by the wasps. They stung me when I was catching them, but I didn't cry out. I never cry out when I have pain. I wonder which insect stings worst? I ought to have a few handy for the worst of the servants. The only one I don't want to part with is cook, for cook is so much afraid of me that she will give me any unwholesome food I like to ask her for. When dear Rose comes we will have a feast. Oh, won't we have fun! I wonder—I do wonder—when she will come?"

Lady Jane left the room, and returned with a blue-bag, which she applied to James's swollen hand and cheek. The frightened servant said he did not think he could keep his situation much longer; but Lady Jane begged of him to be patient. Irene had disappeared.

"It is the kind of shock, your ladyship," he said to his mistress. "It's that I can't bear. There was I a-walking in as innocent as you please into my pantry, carrying the hot dishes from your ladyship's breakfast. I just touched a string, and found a shower of the most venomous insects crawling all over me. I dropped the dish on the spot, and if it hadn't been a silver one it would have been in shivers. And how was she to know that it wouldn't be your ladyship's best Sevres or Crown Derby? How am I to endure it, my lady?"

"She is a very naughty girl, and I will certainly punish her," said Lady Jane, with a sigh. "But now, James, go about your business. The remedies I have used will soon take the pain out of your stings, and you will be all right again."

"There's poor Miss Frost," continued the man; "she has swallowed living beasts. It's all over the house, the story of Miss Irene giving her them horrors instead of her pills. It's the most dreadful thing I ever heard tell of."

"I don't believe she is really seriously hurt at all. But I will see what can be done," said Lady Jane.

She sat for a time lost in thought. Irene must be sent away—school must be resorted to. She must not any longer be allowed to render The Follies a home of terror to every individual who lived there. But what school would take such a naughty girl? For an instant Lady Jane thought of the Merrimans. But no, that was worse than useless. Was there any school in any part of the world that would receive such a hopeless character as poor Irene seemed to be turning into? Lady Jane could not tell.

CHAPTER XII

ROSAMUND TO THE RESCUE

Lady Jane was in the midst of her meditations, and a more confused, distracted poor woman it would be difficult to find in the length and breadth of the land, when suddenly she heard a step in the hall, a frank young voice—not Irene's, but bright and young and full of courage—and the next instant Rosamund Cunliffe entered the room.

"May I speak to you, Lady Jane?"

James was mournfully removing the remainder of the breakfast. His face was not improved by the blue-bag, and his expression was that of a hunted animal. The butler, in high dudgeon, had retired to his own apartment, where he had locked and barred the door in order to prevent any pranks of that imp, as he privately styled Irene. The other servants were tremblingly attending to their duties; but all smelled mischief in the air.

Two such awful things did not often occur on the same day as the possible poisoning of Miss Frost and the terrible usage to which innocent James had been subjected.

"We're none of us safe!" quoth the cook. "It's best to

L. T. Meade

give notice."

"But then wages is so high," said the kitchen-maid. "There ain't a place like it in the country round—plenty of us, and half our time our own. What my mother says to me is, 'You must put up with something, Sukey; and if you hadn't Miss Irene you'd have low wages and 'ard work.' So I said I'd grin and bear it."

"Well, that's my notion, too," said the cook. "I say over and over, 'I'll grin and bear it;' and when the child comes to me and asks me so pretty for the most unwholesome food—though nothing, for that matter, seems to disagree with her—why, I haven't the 'eart to refuse."

"You haven't the courage, you mean," said James, who entered the kitchen at that moment. "If you had my poor face you'd have something to say."

"Oh, your poor face!" said the cook in an indignant tone. "It'll be well afore you're twice married. You take note of that."

James left the kitchen in a huff to return to his duties in the breakfast-room. It was there that Rosamund found him when she burst in upon Lady Jane.

"I have come to see you. Can I have a talk with you where we can be alone?" said the girl.

Perhaps in all the world no sight could have been so welcome at that moment to poor Lady Jane as Rosamund's bright face. The courage in it, the knowledge that Irene respected and, yes, loved this girl, cheered her inexpressibly. She was not jealous. The fact was, had she been jealous, had she felt any very deep mother-love for her orphan child, things might have been quite different. But her whole heart was absorbed in memories, and Irene, in consequence, had never given her a true daughter's affection. But she was terribly perturbed about the naughty child; and Rosamund looked to her, with her straight carriage, her fine open face, like a very tower of strength.

"I am in great trouble, my dear. I am very glad to see you. But how is it that you have got away from school so early?"

"I will tell you all about it. There has been great trouble at Sunnyside. Poor Jane Denton, my special friend and room-mate, is dangerously ill with diphtheria."

"Diphtheria!" said Lady Jane, starting back as she spoke. "But is not that very infectious?"

"I don't think it really is. I mean, of course, that if any one bent over a person who is ill, that person would be very likely to get it. Anyhow, all the girls have been sent away. Mrs. Brett, Mrs. Merriman's sister, has taken them to Dartford to stay with her for the present; and two trained nurses are coming to look after Jane; and—oh, Lady Jane! perhaps you won't speak to me again, but I am expelled from the school."

"Expelled from the Merrimans'?" said Lady Jane in a low tone of intense distress and feeling.

"It is true. They have expelled me—or at least the Professor has. I am never going back. Now, I want to know whether I am to go to mother at Brighton, where she is at present, or whether I shall stay with you for a little, and—and help Irene."

Lady Jane's eyes filled with tears.

L. T. Meade

"You must tell me all about it. Why are you expelled?"

"It is all on account of Irene. I must tell you that I took a great fancy to her."

"You did? How sweet of you!" said Lady Jane.

"I know she is very wild and naughty; but there is something lovable about her, and I think I could manage her. I think she cares for me, so I wanted to be with her; and I asked the Professor, but the Professor did not wish it. You see, Lady Jane, I am sorry to hurt you, but Irene has got quite a bad name in the place. Most of the people are dreadfully afraid of her. They don't like her. They say she is always up to mischief."

"Indeed she is. Miss Frost has just gone to see the doctor because the naughty child made her swallow some repulsive insects instead of her pills. But—oh, dear!"

"Don't go on, Lady Jane. I think I can guess how exceedingly naughty Irene is. But, you see, I have taken a great fancy to her in spite of her naughtiness. Anyhow, on Sunday last I managed to conquer her, which was something."

"Indeed you did. It was most wonderful! Poor Miss Frost and I were amazed. We could scarcely contain our astonishment as we watched you."

"Well, now, I must tell you the whole story. The Professor said I was to have nothing to do with Irene, for if I did he would not allow me to stay with them; and he begged of me to consider how important it was for me to stay at the school selected for me by my parents. So I gave him my word of honor that I wouldn't see Irene or have anything to do with her for a week. I meant to keep it, of course."

"Your word of honor!" interrupted Lady Jane. "That was very strong, was it not? Your letter astonished me, for you did not explain anything."

"I could not—it was impossible. At least, I felt so at the time, although now I don't much care what happens. Anyhow, I fully intended to keep my word, although at the end of the week I meant to tell Professor and Mrs. Merriman quite plainly that unless I could see you, who had been mother's dearest friend, and Irene sometimes, I would ask mother to remove me from the school. You see, mother is quite reasonable, and when I explain things to her she does what she can. I sometimes think that is because she was exceedingly naughty herself when she was a little girl. Anyhow, that was how matters stood. But last night, when I went to my room to go to bed—poor Jane had been removed to a room in another part of the house, as she was so ill—whom should I find in the room but Irene herself, and"—

"She has told me that part. Now I understand," said Lady Jane.

"I am glad you understand. But I had rather a fight with her. In the end I lost my temper, but that was owing to Lucy Merriman. Well, this morning, when it was discovered that Jane—my dear Jane—had such terribly bad diphtheria, the whole school was scattered on the spot. Kind Mrs. Brett has taken all the girls, with the exception of myself, to Dartford. I insisted on taking the Professor aside and telling him just what had happened, and how I had broken my word of honor. I said I wouldn't go to Dartford with Mrs. Brett, and he told me if I went to you I was never to return to the school. So here I am. What do you mean to do with me?"

Lady Jane sat still, looking very pale and troubled. Rosamund, seeing that no answer could be expected immediately, sank on the nearest chair. She was now deadly tired; her night of absolute want of rest, added to the excitement which she had lived through, was beginning to tell on her; and, strong as she was, she turned white as death. It was that look on her face which first roused Lady Jane's attention.

"How cruel I am," she said, "and you your mother's child!"

She got up and rang the bell. The much-afflicted James answered the summons.

"Get some breakfast immediately for Miss Cunliffe. Tell cook to send in anything nice and appetizing that she possesses. Not a word to Miss Irene on the subject whatsoever."

He withdrew, and in a short time a really appetizing breakfast was placed before the nearly famished girl. Breakfast at Sunnyside that morning had been a farce, and when Rosamund came down the meal was over. She had, therefore, not tasted food that day until now. The hot coffee, the nice fish-cakes, the delicious bread-and-butter, all had their due effect. She owned that she was hungry, and when she had finished, fresh courage and energy came into her voice and manner.

"Now, what do you want me to do?" she said. "Please tell me. I have given up school. I have given up to a certain extent my reputation, for this will always be brought up against me; and I have come to you to become Irene's friend, and to stay with you for the present if you want me. But until I saw your face it did not occur to me that you might perhaps be afraid—afraid that I might have the seeds of the same complaint within me as poor Jane Denton. Is that so?"

"She is my only child," said Lady Jane, "and, to tell you the honest truth, I am afraid."

Rosamund got up restlessly and walked to the window. She had not looked for this complication.

"I'd have done better to have gone with Mrs. Brett after all," was her first thought. Then she turned to Lady Jane and said in a determined voice, "I don't think you ought to fear me, for I'm quite sure there is no danger. Even if there were, Irene would not have contracted the disease through me, for she lay for some time last night in Jane's bed."

"Heaven help me!" said Lady Jane.

She wrung her hands, and then got up and also stood by the window.

"It strikes me," she said after a pause, "that God is punishing me more cruelly than He punishes most people, and I cannot understand it. In any case, whether this means life or death, that child's present behavior and present prospects are intolerable. You shall come, Rosamund. I will take the risk. Come to me, and welcome, only let me have the satisfaction of knowing that your mother approves."

"Then will you wire to her?" said Rosamund.

"That would be an excellent plan," replied Lady Jane. "I will take your telegram to the village, for you don't want the servants to see what you are saying. Write it out at once, and I will take it."

"I have not brought any of my things with me, except just what I am wearing, so you will have to provide me until mother sends me a boxful from London. I am sure I am safe, and if—if Irene were to get ill, I think I should be able to nurse her better than any one else."

Lady Jane suddenly went up to the girl and kissed her.

"You are extraordinary!" she said. "You are brave above the common. I believe God has sent you. Does Irene know you are here?"

"No; I have not told her."

"Then she needn't know for the present. But where is she?"

"I wish you would write that telegram, Lady Jane. You ought to have mother's consent. I shall not be happy until it has come."

"At present Irene is supposed to be in the schoolroom. Where she really is I do not know, poor Miss Frost being absent. Anyhow, I will take this telegram myself, and ask you to remain quietly in a bedroom in this house until the reply comes from your mother. Just give me this promise—that you will not see Irene until I have heard from your mother."

To this proposition Rosamund was forced to submit. Indeed, she was not sorry at the prospect of a little rest, for she was beginning to feel very acutely her adventures of the previous night. Lady Jane wrote the telegram, ordered a carriage to be sent round, and drove into the village, a small place, which contained, however, a telegraph office, about a mile and a half away. Before she went she conducted her young guest to a beautiful bedroom on the first floor, which she said she would give her not only for a bedroom but also as part sitting-room. It was furnished in a style that Rosamund, well off as her parents were, had never seen before. The room was full of quaint and beautiful things, and there was a bookcase of delightful books—Kingsley's, Miss Yonge's, and many other favorite authors.

"Lie down, dear," said Lady Jane. "You look very tired. Forget Irene for the time. I shall be back before long, and will send your lunch up to you. We will just have your mother's permission, and then we shall feel in a straightforward position. She may, of course, wish you to return at once to her."

"I do not think mother will do that. She is not a frightened sort of person. Anyhow, you know what I feel about your daughter."

"I do, and God bless you, my love!"

Lady Jane departed, and Rosamund found herself alone in her great room. She looked around her, uttered a weary sigh, and sank into a chair near the window.

Presently she heard a scuffling noise and cries outside, in the passage. She heard the voice of a maid-servant saying, "Oh, Miss Irene! Miss Irene! don't do it; you oughtn't—you oughtn't!" then a scream, and then a girl's hurrying footsteps dying away in the distance.

"I wish I could fly out and give Irene a good box on the ears," thought Rosamund. "I'll soon break her off those horrid tricks. Of course I am going to stay here, and of course I am going to reform her, and of course—oh, how strange everything is! I think I'll lock the door. I don't choose her to come in now until I get mother's consent. Afterwards all is plain sailing."

Rosamund got up softly and locked the door, not a minute too soon, for she had scarcely done so before the handle was turned and the voice of Irene was heard outside crying through the keyhole, "What changeling is in this room? Which of you housemaids has dared to lock herself in? Come out! I've got a big spider ready, and"—

But Irene's voice died away for some extraordinary reason, and Rosamund for the time was left in peace. She drew the chair near the window, took up Kingsley's *Hypatia* from the shelf, and tried to interest herself in a story which always had the deepest fascination for her. But by-and-by sleep over-powered her young eyes, and she only awakened from it by hearing a very gentle tap at her door. She went to it and called out, "Who is there?"

The gentle voice of Lady Jane answered in response:

"I have brought you some lunch, dear."

Rosamund immediately unlocked the door, and received a daintily prepared little tray, which she took in, Lady Jane following her into the room.

"As soon as the telegram arrives I will let you know. I am very anxious that your time of servitude should be over. That child seems worse than ever. I never knew anything like her manners to-day. Three of the servants have given notice, and even cook was in violent hysterics in the kitchen, for she found that Irene had put a live toad into the bread-pan. She said she can stand most things, but that toads are beyond bearing. The thing foamed at her in a most terrible manner, and the consequence is, all the bread had to be thrown away, as no one can possibly attempt to eat it. Really, Rosamund, you will have your hands full."

"I shall not mind that," said Rosamund. "But has Miss Frost come back?"

"Yes, poor thing! she is lying down. She says she feels that those dreadful creatures are crawling about inside her. The doctor assures her that there is nothing to fear, and that they are quite dead; but she will not believe him. It will be all right when she knows that you are here. You can do lessons with her, my dear, if your mother consents to your staying, for she is very highly educated, though she really has no control over Irene. I trust you may be able to do something with her."

"I will subdue her," said Rosamund. "There is no fear whatever on that point. Only, don't tell her so, please, for that would put her against me; and I think at present she has a sort of fancy for me. Do you know, I am quite hungry, and longing to attack those delicious cutlets."

"Then you shall, dear, and in peace. You had better lock your door again, for the girl is as suspicious as she is mischievous, and scents out any fresh person in the house. She says that she has a strong sense of smell, and knows each person by a sort of delicate perfume which emanates from them. Really, Rosamund, there are times when I almost doubt if she is quite human."

"Oh! she imagines all that," said Rosamund in a low tone. "I wouldn't fret if I were you, Lady Jane. Be sure you let me know when mother's telegram arrives."

"Yes, dear; I will bring it up here and read it to you. It will probably not be long now before we get it."

Lady Jane left the room, and Rosamund rebolted the door. Then she sat down to enjoy her lunch. She had just eaten a mouthful of the cutlet when she was aroused by a whoop— that familiar whoop which Irene had given vent to under poor Jane Denton's bed the previous night. Rosamund turned round, and there was Irene's face pressed against the window-pane. She had run up a ladder which she had forced one of the gardeners to bring to the window, and was looking in. Her face was all wreathed in smiles. She beckoned to Rosamund, who refused, however, to pay the slightest attention to her. Fortunately the window was shut, and Rosamund did not suppose that the naughty girl would go to the extreme of breaking the glass.

She now deliberately turned her back upon Irene, and continued to eat her cutlets without taking the least notice of her. In vain did Irene whoop and call out, and sing and shout, all for Rosamund's benefit. At last she said in a threatening tone, loud enough to pierce through the shut window, "I will run down the ladder and fetch a hammer, and come up again and break the window, and get in that way if you don't let me in. You don't suppose I am going to be conquered in my own house?"

But Rosamund was even with her. In one minute she had gone to the window, had flung it wide open, and taken both Irene's hands.

"Irene," she said, "you told me you loved me."

There was something in the tones, something in the absence of fear, which caused Irene to pause; the color faded from her little face, leaving it very white and almost imploring.

"I do—I do!" she said after a minute's pause.

"Now, do you know what I have done? I have left Sunnyside and have come over here, and am just waiting for a telegram from mother giving her consent to my spending a great portion of my time with you. But if you go for the hammer and come back and break this window I shall go straight home to mother, whatever she says. Now, you can choose. Go away now, and behave yourself. It doesn't matter to me what you do. I sometimes think you are not worth saving."

"Oh, no, I am not," said Irene in a completely new tone. She went quietly down the ladder. The objectionable ladder itself was removed, and Rosamund continued her lunch in peace.

Half an hour afterwards the telegram arrived, which was quite cordial in its tone, giving a hearty consent to Rosamund's remaining for the present at The Follies; and saying that if all went well Mrs. Cunliffe herself proposed to pay a visit to Lady Jane within the next fortnight. In the meantime, owing to the sad circumstances at Sunnyside, she would send a box of clothes that very day from London for Rosamund's use.

"Now I will go and find Irene," said Rosamund. "You must have perfect confidence in me, Lady Jane, and if I do things that you do not quite approve of, you must nevertheless be satisfied that I am dealing with Irene as I think best. Oh, dear Lady Jane, how tired you look, and how sad!"

"This is a very sad day for me," said Lady Jane. "It is the anniversary of my most beloved husband's death. I cannot but feel it; but that child has no mercy. I am going now to visit his grave, in order to put a cross of beautiful flowers there. Any other girl would accompany her mother on such an errand, but of course Irene will not."

Rosamund did not reply for a minute; then she said gently:

"Perhaps she will come with you next year, dear Lady Jane. You cannot reform a nature like hers in a moment."

Lady Jane kissed Rosamund and left the room; and

Rosamund, being perfectly free to do exactly what she pleased, and being also refreshed and strengthened by her sleep and her good food, went in search of Irene.

She soon found her swinging in her favorite attitude in one of the beech-trees. The moment the girl saw her, she sprang to the ground, ran to her side, flung her arms round her neck so tightly as almost to throttle her, and kissed her over and over again.

"Your face looks as if you meant to stay."

"I do mean to stay just as long as you are good."

"Then, gracious me!" said Irene, "that won't be for long; because the utmost I can be good for is five minutes at a time. You see, I never was good at all—I never attempted to be—so it didn't enter into my calculations, and now to suddenly turn into a model of all the virtues is more than I can do even for your sake."

"I do not expect impossibilities. I only want you to try."

"Well, you are not so precious good yourself."

"I'm not at all good. We'll try to be good together."

"It will be fun our both trying," said Irene, looking at her with a comical expression. "How are we to begin? Shall we do penance like the old monks? Do you know, Rosamund"—here Irene linked her thin, almost steel-like little hand inside Rosamund's arm—"that I am a most voracious reader? Father was a great collector of books, and when I am tired of frightening the servants, and terrifying Frosty, and annoying mother, I spend days at a time in his library swallowing down the contents of his books. There is no other word for it.

So I know odds and ends of all sorts of things."

"You must know things properly henceforth. But what was that you said about penance?"

"Do you want us to do penance for our sins? The monks were very fond of standing out in the cold in their night-shirts. Do you want us both to do that to-night? It will terrify mother, and the servants will think we are a pair of ghosts. I should rather enjoy that."

"I don't want anything silly of that sort. Come along now, Irene. The very first thing you have got to do is to beg Miss Frost's pardon."

"I beg Frosty's pardon! But she is in bed. She says they are running up and down inside her."

"You know you were exceedingly cruel. It was a very low sort of trick to play. I can understand a girl being wild and doing all sorts of things that perhaps she ought not to do, and even neglecting her lessons; but to terrify a poor, harmless governess! And you have terrified more than one. You'll have to drop that sort of thing now, Irene."

"It strikes me you are a poor sort after all," said Irene, gazing at Rosamund attentively.

"Well, whether I am poor or not, I'm going to stay with you for a bit, and if you get any better I'll stay on; but if you get no better I shall go straight home to mother, for you will be hopeless. There now, you know."

"Oh, it is so delightful to have you! You don't know what you are to me. The courageous way you speak! I don't believe you'd be a bit afraid if I put a frog on your neck."

By almost sleight-of-hand Irene suited the deed to the word, for a cold frog of enormous size suddenly began to crawl along Rosamund's neck. Rosamund suppressed a shudder, for she would not for the world show the girl that she loathed frogs; but she took the creature and laid it gently on the ground.

"That is very silly," she said. "You are not to do it again."

"I am not to do it again?"

"No; not to me or to any one else."

"I thought I'd put a small toad just inside the teapot for James when he was going to make the tea this afternoon, for it would jump up and finish that affair of the wasps and spiders that occurred this morning."

"You are not to do it. It is ridiculous; there's neither sense nor fun nor anything else in it. It is downright, positive cruelty. You make your mother's life wretched, and you make the servants miserable. As to poor Miss Frost—oh, you can go to see her or not, just as you please. I am going into her room now."

"Are you indeed? But why should you take any interest in Frosty?"

"Because you are so unkind to her, and I want her to know that I at least am going to be her friend."

"Oh, dear, dear Rosamund, I do so earnestly want her to go! She doesn't suit me a bit. Can't you teach me instead? I'd learn from you."

"I don't know enough. I want to be taught myself. Miss Frost needn't teach you unless you like, but she shall teach me. I can't give up all my education even for you. Perhaps you understand that."

"I do—I do; but I am sure you know a great deal more than is good for you."

"Don't be silly, Irene. Now, I am going to see Miss Frost. You ought to come with me to beg her pardon; but perhaps when she is well enough to be up you will do so."

"You won't be long with her, will you?"

"If you will promise to beg her pardon at tea-time I won't stay long."

"I will, for I want us to go out in the boat, and I want to show you my pony, and to try to get you to ride him. I don't believe you will be able to conquer him. He'll stand no one but me. His name is Billy Boy, and I have made him as wild and vicious as ever I could; but he is like a lamb with me."

"Then you propose that he should throw me, and perhaps kill me? Thank you very much, Irene."

"Oh, I don't propose that really; only, you see, one must have larks. One couldn't live without them. I don't think there is anything quite so larky as frightening people."

"Now, once for all, Irene, if that is your idea of life, I will write at once to mother and tell her I am coming home."

"No, you won't. I won't let you. I love you. I will try to be a little bit good just to please you. I will say something to Frosty at tea-time. Oh! don't ask me any more."

L. T. Meade

Irene's queer eyes filled suddenly with tears. Rosamund saw that she was touched.

"Run away and do what you like. I don't want to be long with Miss Frost; but I am going to her now."

Rosamund entered the house. She was met in the hall by James.

"I am so sorry, James," she said, taking the initiative at once, "that you were so frightened this morning by Miss Irene. She is a friend of mine, and I have made up my mind to come and stay here for the present. Will you please tell the other servants, and remember yourself, that I shall do my utmost to prevent the sort of things occurring which have made you all so uncomfortable? I think you will soon see that Miss Irene has as kind a heart as any other girl."

"I'm sure, miss," said James, almost whimpering, "the trouble I've had already, and the anxiety and worry, not to speak of the pain, miss. Them wasps, their sting is very sharp, and even my lady's blue-bag did not remove them at once. And then the show I am, miss, in this respectable house! But that is nothing to what poor cook felt when the toad poisoned the bread. And there was Mary Ann, the second housemaid; Miss Irene caught her and put two spiders down her back. Mary Ann has such a horror of spiders as never was! Then, worst of all, there's poor Miss Frost, such a patient lady, and she has swallowed insects instead of pills. It's too awful to contemplate."

"It is very bad, but it won't happen again—at least I don't think so," said Rosamund. "Now, I want to see Miss Frost. Can you direct me to her room?"

James took upon himself to perform this office, and in a few minutes' time Rosamund was knocking at the door of Miss Frost's room. A very feeble, timid, suffering voice said:

"Who is there?" Then the voice continued, "If it is you, Irene, the door is bolted, and the blinds are down, and the shutters shut, so even if you break the glass you cannot get in."

"It is not Irene. It is I, Rosamund Cunliffe. I want most particularly to see you, Miss Frost."

Whereupon Miss Frost was heard getting out of bed and coming towards the door. She was a very cadaverous-looking person, about forty years of age, thin to emaciation, with small, light, frightened-looking eyes, a long upper lip, and a great many freckles on her face. Her hair was thin and dark, and was strained back from a lofty forehead. The moment Rosamund saw her she took her hand.

"Please don't keep the door locked," she said. "And please unbar the shutters and draw up the blinds, for it is a lovely summer's day, and Irene won't do you any harm. I want to talk to you. May I?"

"I don't believe, my dear young friend," said Miss Frost, "that I am long for this world. I feel those dreadful things even now creeping up and down. The doctor says they are dead; but how can he look inside me? I know they are alive. I know they are."

"I don't think they could be alive," said Rosamund. "I heard of that trick being played on some one once before, and nothing whatever happened, and I can assure you the person is quite well, and when the fright was got over the whole thing was forgotten."

"Are you sure?"

"Positive."

"Oh, I have lived through such a morning of agony!"

"You must forget your agony now."

"But how am I to endure that child?"

"Will you lie down again on your bed and let me talk to you for a minute or two?"

As Rosamund spoke she took the cold hand of the governess, led her to the bed, made her lie down, and covered her up. Then she drew a chair forward, and, still retaining her hand, she began to speak.

"I know quite well all that you would say about Irene; but please don't say it. I have come here contrary to rules, and at some trouble to myself, but also with my mother's approval, to be Irene's friend and guest for a time. You are all very much afraid of her. Yes, you are, from Lady Jane to the lowest servant in the place, and it is because you are afraid of her that she is so exceedingly naughty. Now, it so happens that I am not a scrap afraid of her, therefore I have some influence over her, and I know positively that she will not play any of her horrid tricks upon you again. For the moment she does so I shall leave her, and she doesn't wish me to do that. Therefore you needn't be at all afraid. What has happened gave you a nasty turn; but there, that's the end of it! You will get up, won't you, and come down to tea? I think perhaps Irene will be a little nicer to you. And to-morrow, or the next day, or whenever we are to begin, I want to know if you will teach me as well as Irene. I also want us to know other girls, and to have a good time all round. For Irene is only a young savage at present; but she has a warm heart, and I do believe that I can touch it."

"My dear," said Miss Frost when Rosamund had done speaking, "may I ask how old you are?"

"I am fifteen."

"Then you are three years older than the terrible Irene."

"Three years older, and I hope three years wiser."

"A thousand years wiser, my dear—quite a thousand years wiser. You don't know what I have suffered; and I am not the only one. Her one object in life when each new governess comes is to get rid of that governess. But I have a little brother and sister both dependent on me altogether for their daily bread, and Lady Jane gives me one hundred and fifty pounds a year, a very large sum for a governess who is not certificated. I simply daren't give it up. I try to, for I often feel that I must. Even the children do not seem worth the agonies I undergo. But then again I struggled on until now."

"You will have no more struggling, and if you teach me as well as Irene I know mother will pay you something, so your people will be better off than ever," said Rosamund in her cheerful voice. "Now cheer up. You have nothing to fear. Try to be courageous, and when you speak to the servants, get them to be courageous too. You have all let Irene get the upper hand of you, and it is exceedingly bad for her. Now, I promised to join her; but you will be with us at tea-time, won't you?"

"I will. You have put great heart into me. What a wonderful girl you are! When I saw you on Sunday I thought how remarkable you were, and now that you have spoken I see it more than ever."

"Perhaps you know what has happened at Sunnyside?"

"What is that, dear?"

"My own special friend, Jane Denton, is dangerously ill with diphtheria. I do not know if she will ever be better."

"Then is there any fear?" said Miss Frost.

"You mean of your taking it?"

"Oh, no, I don't mind for myself a scrap. I am not afraid of illness, and I had diphtheria when I was young, and people don't often have it twice; but it is that child—that queer child."

"I cannot give it to her," said Rosamund. "If she takes it she must have contracted the infection herself, owing to—But there, I won't say any more. Let us hope for the best. I must go to her now, however."

CHAPTER XIII

IN ANOTHER DRESS

When Rosamund went out, feeling both flushed and tired, she saw Irene waiting for her. She wore her favorite red dress, which was exceedingly shabby and by no means becoming. Rosamund felt just like St. George when he was about to slay the dragon. Irene at the present moment was the dragon. That dreadful part of her which was such a nuisance to her neighbors must be kept under by a firm hand. One person at least must have complete control of her.

"There you are!" said Irene, dancing up to her friend. "Oh, it is nice to see you, and how sweet you look! Do you know, I never noticed people's looks before. I always said to myself, 'They are all exactly alike—a pair of eyes, a nose, a mouth, a chin of sorts, eyebrows indifferent or not, hair dark or fair.' Oh, they're all alike—at least that is what I did think. Now I see you, there seems a difference."

"I hope I haven't got three eyes or two noses, or anything of that sort, to make you single me out for special observation."

"Oh, it isn't your features a bit—it's your way. You are different, and I like you."

"Do you know, Irene," said Rosamund very slowly and emphatically, and taking the little girl's thin hand as she spoke, "that you are the most wonderfully beautiful girl I have ever seen?"

"Am I?" said Irene, and a new light sparkled in her eyes. "People have always spoken of me as a horror, a terror, a nuisance, the wildest and most awful creature on earth. But if I am so pretty"—

"You could be lovely," said Rosamund. "I must say that red dress is rather trying, but your face is exquisite. Now, what do you say to going into the house and going quietly up to your own room? I will come with you and help you to choose another frock, which I think will make you look more beautiful than ever. Just let me dress you as I like for once."

"I trust it won't be tight, or too long," said Irene.

"I am sure you have abundance of frocks."

"I don't know. I dare say I have. I believe there is a wardrobe full; but I prefer my red dress because it annoys mother. When one is worn out, I ask for another made just on the same pattern, and just because they all hate it so."

"But you will change it for me. Come at once, Irene."

Rosamund took her friend's hand and led her upstairs to her room. Now, Irene's bedroom was not at all an attractive place to go into. In itself it was an exceedingly large and airy apartment, and the furniture was excellent. But the small bed was drawn up close to the window, and was more cot than bed, having iron bars all round it. Near the bed were several jars and basins containing toads and frogs and newts and water creatures of all sorts. Besides these, there was a box of caterpillars, most of which had escaped, and on the mantel-piece Irene proudly pointed to a bottle of leeches.

"I bought them, for a pound that I had given to me, from a chemist; and when any of the servants are quite determined to stick in the place I let the leeches loose, and that generally sends the housemaids away. I wouldn't part with my darling leeches for all the world. Do you see how they are dancing now? That means rain. When they lie quite sullen at the bottom of the glass, then I know we are going to have fine weather. That one on the stalk—do you see how he is wriggling, poor sweet pet?—that one I call Fuzz, and this one at the bottom of the glass is Buzz. Then there are their children, Thunder and Lightning, and the little Stars. The Stars are the tiny ones. I manage them myself. I love them better than any of my pets. Would you like me to take them out? You'll see how they crawl about on the floor; only they get rather dusty. Do you mind?"

"Not in the very least," said Rosamund.

"Well, you have spunk! You know, if you annoy me in any way, I should think nothing of putting either Fuzz or Buzz into your bed."

"Then I should leave the next day, that's all," replied Rosamund in a calm voice. "I shouldn't be afraid; but I should simply go. If you want me to be your friend you must not play tricks of that sort. But we needn't talk any more about leeches now. They seem happy and well. Let me see what dresses you have."

Rosamund herself opened the wardrobe and took out a quantity of beautiful dresses of all sorts and descriptions, mostly white washing silks and muslins and cambrics. She chose a neat white cambric, and insisted on Irene putting it

L. T. Meade

on. She fastened it on the little girl herself, and saw that it fitted her perfectly. She then brushed her hair and made her wash her hands, which this wild tomboy strongly objected to. But Rosamund was firm.

"I hope you're not always going to be like this," said Irene, stamping her foot.

"Oh, dear, no! because soon you will do it for its own sake. Now, here's a long mirror; come and see yourself in the glass. Can't you fancy what you are like?"

But Irene started away.

"No, no, no!" she said. "There's a pool at the bottom of the garden, and there are water-lilies all around it. We'll go, both of us, and look at ourselves there; that will be much prettier."

"As you please. I am quite indifferent; only I want you to respect yourself, Irene."

"Respect myself? But then, no one else does."

"Well, I intend to respect you, and I can only do it by your respecting yourself. Come along; let us look at ourselves in the pool. I am considered fairly good-looking—I don't pretend to deny it; but I am nothing to you to-day, for you gave me a very tiring night."

"So I did, you poor dear! This white dress is rather nice, but I wouldn't wear it for mother for all the world; I only wear it now. Now then, come along."

The two raced downstairs; the servants peeped out from different corners in astonishment. Miss Irene, who would make such a show of herself, was absolutely pretty in her shady hat of softest white, and her white dress to match, and that face, which, notwithstanding all her naughtiness, was and must ever be beautiful above ordinary faces.

By-and-by the girls reached the pool. They both fell on their knees, and Rosamund desired Irene to gaze at her reflection.

"Here are some forget-me-nots," said Rosamund. "I am going to make a wreath to put round your hair. Take your hat off."

She made a little wreath in a few minutes, and twined them through Irene's curling locks.

"Now look again. What do you see?"

"Why, she is somebody rather—I mean she is beautiful, very beautiful," said Irene in a low voice. "But she is not me."

"She is you. Look again. Don't you see that soft little mouth, and that nose, so beautifully formed, and those bright, bright eyes, and that hair, and the whole thing? It was God who made you, Irene, and He made you beautiful, and beautiful people have a great gift."

Irene ceased to look at herself. She flung off the forget-me-not wreath and turned to Rosamund.

"Now, what do you mean by all this lecturing?" she said.

"Beautiful people have a great responsibility," continued Rosamund in a stout voice. "They are sent into the world to make it better. As far as I can make out, up to the present time you have done nothing whatever but make the world worse. You have never, so far as I can tell, been kind to your mother. You have made the servants most unhappy. You have done your utmost to render your governesses' position impossible."

"Because I hate them, and don't want to learn."

"Not want to learn," said Rosamund, "with that forehead so full, so intelligent? Why, you could learn in a flash. You could get knowledge with the utmost ease, and you would love it when once you began. If I am to be your friend you have got to turn over a new leaf. There, I have said enough about yourself for the present. Just let us walk about until tea-time."

"No; I want to go in the boat."

"We won't go in the boat till after tea. I want to talk to you."

"I wonder why I am obeying you?" said Irene, slipping her hand inside Rosamund's.

"Because I mean you to."

"I wonder why I'm not hating you?"

"Because if you did I should leave you."

"I couldn't let you go. It seems to me the whole world is different since I got you. But do tell me, you are not very good yourself?"

"I am not at all so good. Ask the people at Sunnyside what they think of me. There is my dearest friend lying at death's door—that is not my fault, of course; but when I can smile at all when I remember her, you must see for yourself that there is a great deal that is very far from good in me. But there, now, I want to talk about Miss Frost."

"Now, why?" said Irene. "That horror! That dreadful stick-in-the-mud! Oh, she is detestable! I cannot tell you how I loathe her."

"You do, because you don't understand her."

"And pray do you?"

"I understand her more than you do; and in any case I could not be cruel to her."

"But she is so old, and so ugly."

"I thought you didn't mind about people's appearance. You said so a minute ago."

"Well, I didn't; but it seems to me that you have opened my eyes. If I am so beautiful I ought to be with beautiful people, like you, Rosamund; for, now I come to look at you, you are very beautiful."

"It is by no means necessary that you should be with beautiful people; but you should give pleasure to people who are not beautiful, because they would like to look at you, and hear your voice, and be refreshed by your kind actions."

"Good gracious me! Kind actions!" said Irene.

"In future I believe they will be kind. Now, please under-stand you have been exceedingly cruel to Miss Frost."

"I want her to go."

"She is not going."

"How do you know? I did think those wood-lice would finish

her. I thought and thought, and the happy idea came to me this morning. I was quite certain she'd give notice, just as Carter did. They could take her on at the Merrimans'. It seems to me that my governesses always find a berth near, so as to spread the fame of my dreadful character."

"Well, she is not going. She can't go. She has a little brother and sister, and she has got to provide for them."

"What do you mean by that?"

"She has got to feed and clothe them, and to put them to school, and do everything for them. If she left your mother's house she would have no money, and might find it difficult to get another post. So she is not going. I asked her to stay, and she is going to teach me as well as you."

"Dear me!"

"Yes; and we are going to make it exceedingly interesting. I mean you to learn a lot. I assure you, if I come here and give up the next few months of my life to you, I don't mean to do nothing in the time. I want to work hard, and you will have to work hard too. I am not bound to stay with you for a single hour. The moment your pranks begin, the moment I hear of any more toads being put into the bread-pan, or wasps and caterpillars descending on poor James's head, or spiders put down the housemaids' backs, or leeches being allowed to run about your bedroom, I shall just go off. If you want me you must refrain from that sort of thing."

"But won't I have any outlet?"

"Indeed you will have plenty."

"Of what sort?"

"You will see. But there is the tea-bell; let us go in."

Irene looked wonderfully thoughtful, for her. She walked slowly by Rosamund's side into the house. Still slowly, and with that thoughtful expression on her face; she passed along the hall until she reached the pretty parlor where tea was always served. Here Lady Jane herself was waiting in a state of nervous expectancy, and here was Miss Frost, very pale, shaky, and troubled, declaring stoutly to Lady Jane that "they" were running about inside her still.

When the girls entered there was a moment of silence, then a start of surprise, for Irene in white, and wearing her pretty shady hat, looked a totally different Irene from the untidy little creature who usually rushed about in her red frock at all hours and seasons. Rosamund gave Lady Jane a warning glance to take no notice of Irene, who flung herself, very much in her old manner, into a chair exactly opposite Miss Frost.

Of course she was going to be good. At least she supposed she must. It was horrid work, she so infinitely preferred being naughty; but then there was Rosamund, and Rosamund wished it, and she—oh, she did not really think she loved Rosamund, but she had a strange sort of longing to be with her, and Rosamund was free as air, and could go at any moment. Therefore, to keep Rosamund, she must be good. But that needn't prevent her staring hard at Miss Frost, which she proceeded to do with great alacrity.

Meanwhile Lady Jane poured out tea, and talked in her lady-like and refined tones to Rosamund, who replied in exactly the same style.

"Are they alive still?" asked Irene when there was a slight pause in the conversation; and she fixed her dancing eyes full on her governess's face.

"Oh, Irene, it was unkind!" began Miss Frost; but Rosamund hastily interrupted.

"Irene, you know what I mean. That subject is not to be alluded to. Miss Frost, I beg of you not to speak of it before Irene, and do for goodness' sake eat a good meal. Forgive me, Lady Jane, but I want us all to have a very good tea; and as it is such a lovely, lovely day, may we go for a little picnic afterwards, and take our supper with us into the woods? Will you come too, and Miss Frost? It would be so delightful!"

Lady Jane's plan had been to leave Irene entirely to herself. She was to have so many hours' lessons in the day, which generally resulted in not working at all, and the rest of her time she spent either in her boat or hatching mischief to annoy some inmate of the house. But now the idea of a picnic, with supper out-of-doors, on this most glorious summer's day, was altogether new.

"We might have the governess-cart, mightn't we, mothery?" said Irene, turning her eyes away from Miss Frost, and gazing at her mother with great anxiety and interest.

"Certainly, dear, but I"—

"Oh, you must come too," said Rosamund.

She knew very well that Lady Jane would say that she could not go out on the anniversary of her husband's death; but she felt at the same time that it was necessary for Irene's reform that both her mother and governess should accompany her.

"I want us all to go," she said. "I have got a plan in my head. You will let us, won't you?—Irene, you and I will choose what supper we will take, after tea is over. And now, will you kindly pass me the plum-jam—yes, and the butter too?"

What a masterful young person Rosamund Cunliffe was, and how Irene began to lean upon her! She no longer troubled herself even to glance at Miss Frost, who in consequence began to get back her courage and to make a good tea. "The creatures," as she termed them, were certainly less lively, and on the whole she felt better and more disposed to believe the doctor.

As soon as tea was over Rosamund took Irene out of the room, and they went together to the cook.

"Now, the very first thing you are to say to cook is this," said Rosamund: "'Cook, I am exceedingly sorry I put a toad into your bread-pan, and I am not going to do it again. I want you to give me the very nicest supper you can possibly collect at short notice.' You must put on your very prettiest manner when you speak to cook. Will you, Irene?"

"It will be horrid work, for she isn't a lady, you know."

"She is far more a lady than you were when you put the toad into the bread-pan."

"You are sharp, aren't you?" said Irene.

"Because you need it. I won't be sharp with you soon, for I know you are going to be a model girl, and the most beautiful creature in the whole country. You don't know how nice it will feel after being naughty for so long."

"I wonder if it will?" said Irene, beginning to dance along by Rosamund's side.

The necessary apology was made to the cook, who received it with dubious surprise, the other servants standing near; but when they saw Irene glancing in their direction they darted off in more or less pretended terror. Cook, however, was mollified by Rosamund's sweet face, and an excellent supper was packed in a hamper.

The governess-cart was brought round to the front door, and Lady Jane, to her own amazement and much against her will, took the reins and drove as far as Parson's Dale, a most lovely spot four miles away. Miss Frost felt the soft evening air fanning her cheeks and taking some of the nervousness out of her. Irene sat thoughtful, and looking exquisitely pretty. Rosamund chatted on all sorts of subjects. In short, such a day had never before been known to the younger girl.

CHAPTER XIV

SCHOOL AT THE FOLLIES

Jane Denton had a hard fight for her life. For days she hovered between this world and the next. Two or three doctors came to see her. She had two trained nurses; bulletins were put up at the door; no one was allowed to come in. The girls who were staying with Mrs. Brett were strictly forbidden to have any communication with the infected house; Rosamund and Irene were equally forbidden to go near Sunnyside.

But at last there came a day when there was a decided improvement. The diphtheria was gone, and the young patient began slowly to pass from danger to convalescence. Then a load seemed to be lifted from every one's breast; and Rosamund really turned, as she expressed it, to consider her future life. During the time of waiting she had a certain influence over Irene; not, perhaps, so much as on the first day, when that young lady, charmed, bewildered, and amazed by Rosamund's firmness, had followed her lead unflinchingly. Rosamund now had to consider herself. She wrote, therefore, a long letter to her mother.

"I could not do so," she thought, "while Jane lay between life and death, when there was a strong chance of the school at Sunnyside not existing any more. But now I must write to

L. T. Meade

dear mother and tell her the truth."

Accordingly, the following letter reached Mrs. Cunliffe on a certain morning early in July:

"MY DARLING MOTHER,—You know all about Jane, of course, and that she is now better—in fact, quite out of danger. In a short time they will take her away, probably to some seaside place, the house will be disinfected, and the girls will come back to their work. Miss Archer, the English governess, will be as strict and as unsympathetic as ever, and Mademoiselle Omont will teach excellent French, no doubt.

"Now, mother darling, you may have heard, or you may not have heard, that I am in disgrace at Sunnyside. I could not give up Irene, and in consequence the Professor says that I am not to return to the school. He means by that that I am to be in a sense expelled. I felt his words very acutely when he uttered them, for I didn't wish to do anything contrary to your desires; but I felt that I could not give up Irene. I was the first person who had any influence over her, and she was running wild and becoming a torment to her neighbors. I don't know what she would have come to in the end. So I elected, mother darling, to go straight to Lady Jane's instead of to Mrs. Brett, when dear Jane was so ill. Now I am established here at The Follies, and I am not allowed to go back to Sunnyside. Doubtless you know that, and perhaps you are angry with your own Rosamund. But I asked your leave to stay, and you gave it, although you did not know all the circumstances. Will you, dear mother, write to Professor Merriman and ask him to tell you exactly why he wishes to expel me? He will probably give you a very sorry story; but you must believe it or not as you please. I think you know your Rosamund better than he does. I am not going back to Sunnyside, for they would not accept me; but, at the same time, I do not feel at all a disgraced girl; and I should like the Merrimans to be friends with me, and I should still like sometimes to see Jane and Laura Everett, and some of the other girls—not Lucy Merriman, for she is not in the least to my taste; but even she does not greatly matter now that I am no longer living in the house with her. The fact is, dear mother, I could not have been a good girl had I stayed long in the house with Lucy, for she managed in some extraordinary manner to rub me the wrong way. She was so extra good, so punctilious, and so proper; she didn't suit me one bit, and I didn't suit her one little bit either. I was becoming quite a naughty girl. I never was too good—was I, mother dear? Perhaps, darling, I'd have become an awfully naughty Rosamund had it not been for Irene—poor little wild Irene; but she was really and truly much naughtier than I ever thought of being, and her example shocked me and pulled me up, and I resolved to try to be good for her sake.

"But I do like Professor Merriman, although I know he does not like me; and I believe they are very poor. So I wish you would find another pupil in my place—some ordinary kind of girl, who would pay about the same sum; or perhaps, mother, as you are so very well off, you might pay the money for her. What do you say to that? It is just a notion of mine. There is my cousin Anice: you know how her mother frets because she is not well educated. Well, she would be well educated at the Merrimans', for the two governesses, as well as the masters who come for occasional lessons, are first-rate. Now, just think that over, only don't let my name appear in the matter.

"Well, dearest, that's all about the Merrimans for the present. I am staying with Irene; but she knows that if she plays any very serious pranks I go. Meanwhile you must not suppose that I am letting my lessons alone. I am working very hard with Miss Frost. She is a dear creature when you get to know her, and she is very fond of me. I told you about those dreadful insects that that wicked child made her swallow. Well, she is all right again now, and isn't a bit afraid of them, and she believes the doctor, and is perfectly happy. As to Irene, nothing would induce her to do anything of the kind to Miss Frost now, for she would get it hot from me if she did. I should like to stay with Irene for the next few months at any rate, and if you want me to get on very fast indeed with my music, and to take up my drawing systematically, some of the masters who attend at the Merrimans' could come on here, couldn't they? I think that could be arranged. Dear Lady Jane is so fond of me, and I really think I am doing a little bit of good in the world, so you won't be angry even if the Professor writes you a horrid letter about your own

"ROSAMUND."

When this letter was despatched Rosamund felt quite light and happy, and she went out into the garden to talk to Miss Frost. Miss Frost looked already quite six or seven years younger than she had done on the day of Rosamund's arrival. She was no longer in terror of her life. Rosamund suggested to her that she should lock her door at nights, which the poor lady did very willingly. She told her there was not the slightest danger of anything happening, as nothing would induce Irene to give her any more frights.

"But if you are nervous, do lock your door," she said; "and if you really want pills for your indigestion, I will keep them for you, and see they are not meddled with."

Miss Frost had attended to all Rosamund's directions, for this masterful young woman was really ruling the entire house.

The servants, too, seemed very much brighter and better. Lady Jane was heard to laugh constantly, and was even induced to play some old-fashioned music on the old piano in the drawing-room.

As to Irene, she wore white dresses and blue dresses and pink dresses, and was not once seen in the obnoxious red.

"That dress you can put on the day I leave The Follies," Rosamund had said to her young friend. "No, I am not going to hide it or put it away. It can hang in your wardrobe; but you are not to wear it while I am here, for I dislike it. I want you to be pretty and beautiful, and an influence for good, as God meant you to be."

Now, all these things told upon Irene; but most of all was she amazed and lifted out of herself when both Miss Frost and Rosamund discovered that she had as quick and clever a mind as she had a beautiful face. It is true she hardly knew anything. She could read and write, and had read a great many books; but all the ordinary subjects of education had been set aside by the willful child.

Rosamund now suggested that they should both compete for a small prize. She chose a subject which she herself knew nothing about, therefore she said they were very nearly equal. They both did compete, and perhaps Rosamund did not exactly put forth her full powers; but, anyhow, in the end Irene won, and her delight was beyond bounds. She rushed down to her mother's boudoir and showed her the beautifully bound volume of Kingsley's *Water Babies* which was the prize she had won.

"I have got it through merit," she said. "Think of my getting anything through merit!"

Lady Jane very nearly cried, but she restrained herself, for Rosamund followed; whose face, with its slightly flushed cheeks and its eyes full of light and happiness, showed Lady Jane what a splendid character her young friend possessed. How could she ever thank God enough for having sent such a girl to her house?

Yes, lessons went on well, and Irene especially made great progress in her musical studies. She had always been fond of music as a little child. In her wildest moods, when Lady Jane had played for her she had become quiet, and crept close to her mother, laid her charming little head against her mother's knee, and listened with wide-open eyes. As she grew a little older she began to practice for herself, inventing her own melodies—nonsense, of course, but still with a certain promise in them.

Now Rosamund suggested that Irene should give up music with Miss Frost, for Miss Frost's style was by no means encouraging, and should take her lessons from the first-rate master who came twice a week from Dartford. It was amazing how quickly Irene made progress under this tuition. In the first place, Mr. Fortescue would not hear of any nonsense. He did not mind Irene's airs or her little attempts to subdue him; he simply desired her to do things, and when she failed he pounded her soundly on her knuckles.

"That is not the way to bring out that note," he would say; and then he would sit down to the piano himself, and ring out great melodies in the most splendid style, until the enthusiastic child almost danced with pleasure.

"Oh, is there any chance of my playing like that?" she once exclaimed.

"Every chance, and a great deal better, if you really take to it with all your heart and soul," was his response.

Rosamund was also intensely fond of music, and the girls were happy over their musical studies; in short, Irene, from having an aimless life, in which she did nothing but torment others, was now leading a full and happy existence. She had her distinct hours for work and distinct hours for play. She had a companion who delighted her; and toads, wasps, spiders, and even leeches lost their charm.

One day, to Rosamund's great delight, Irene suggested that Fuzz and Buzz and all their children should go back to the nearest chemist. This was no sooner thought of than done. Certainly it was a very great step in Irene's reform; but it must not be supposed that such a character could become good all of a sudden. It takes a lifetime, and perhaps more than a lifetime, to make any of us really good, and Irene was not by nature a very amiable child. She had been terribly spoiled, it is true, and but for Rosamund might have been an annoyance and a torment to every one as long as she lived. But she had splendid points in her character, and these were coming slowly to the fore.

Still, there were times when she was exceedingly naughty. Rosamund, having written to her mother, and so set her mind completely at rest, thought no longer of the sort of disgrace in which she was living as regarded the Merrimans. She was now anxious that Irene should make friends.

"There is no use whatever," she said, "in shutting a girl like Irene up with me. She ought to know the Singletons. I will ask Lady Jane if we may drive over some day and see them. Why shouldn't we go to-day? Irene has been quite good this morning. I dare say I could manage it. She won't like meeting Miss Carter; but she must get over that feeling. There's nothing for it but for her to live like ordinary girls. If

L. T. Meade

she refuses, I shall beg of Lady Jane to take us both from The Follies, to take a house somewhere else for at least six months, and to let us make new friends. But that does seem ridiculous, when The Follies is such a lovely place, and Irene's real home. Of course, I can't always stay with her, although I mean to stay for the present."

Rosamund ran up to Lady Jane, who was pacing up and down on the terrace. Irene, as usual, was in her boat. She was floating idly about the lake. The day was intensely hot. She wore a graceful white frock and her pretty white shady hat; her little white hand was dabbling in the water, and her graceful little figure was looking almost like a nymph of the stream.

Lady Jane turned with a beaming face to Rosamund.

"What is it now, my dear?" she said.

"Well, of course, you have heard the good news. Everything is all right at the Merrimans', neither Irene nor I have taken the infection, none of the other girls have taken it, Jane is getting well again, and I have written a full account of everything to mother."

"That doesn't mean, my darling Rosamund, that you are going to leave us? I really couldn't consent to part with you. I can never, never express all that you have been to me," said poor Lady Jane, her eyes filling with tears.

"Well, I can only part from you by going back to mother, for they won't receive me any more at the Merrimans'."

"But why not, Rosamund?"

"Because I have taken up with Irene. But we needn't go into

that now. What I want to know is, may Irene and I have the governess-cart, and may Miss Frost go with us, and may we drive over to the Singletons'?"

"Of course you may, Rosamund. But I am afraid it will be you and Miss Frost alone, for nothing would induce Irene to set foot inside that place. She has always refused, notwithstanding every effort of our dear clergyman to invite her to visit them. I have asked the children here, for they are nice children; but they are too much afraid of her to come. I do not think you will find the visit a success, even if you do induce Irene to accompany you."

"But I think I shall," said Rosamund calmly. "You know," she added, "Irene is not what she was."

"Indeed she is not. She is very different. I am beginning at last to enjoy my life and to appreciate her society. How beautiful she is, and how you have brought out her beauty!"

"Her beauty was given her by God," said Rosamund. "But, of course, now that she is learning, and becoming intelligent, and thinking good thoughts instead of bad thoughts, all these things must be reflected on her face. I want her to have other friends besides me, for I cannot always be with her, and I cannot tell you what a splendid girl I think Maud Singleton is."

"But then there is poor Miss Carter. Irene nearly killed her."

"Miss Carter is quite well and happy at the Singletons', and they just adore her, and Irene ought to apologize to her. I mean to make her when I get the chance. Perhaps not to-day. Anyhow, may we go?"

"You certainly may, and I wish you all success."

Rosamund danced away, and ran down the winding path to the edge of the lake.

"Irene, I want you to come in," she said. "I want to speak to you."

Irene rowed lazily back to the shore. She still sat in her boat and looked up at Rosamund.

"Will you get in?" she said. "There is a little breeze on the water; there is none on the land. What are you looking so solemn about?"

"I am not solemn at all. I want us to have fun this afternoon. It is rather dull here, just two girls all by themselves. I don't think that I can stay with you much longer unless you allow me to have other friends."

"Good gracious!" said Irene. "Perhaps I'd better get out. You look so very solemn."

"No, I'm not solemn exactly; but I want to have other friends. Will you get out, and may I talk to you?"

Irene jumped with alacrity out of the boat, and Rosamund helped her to moor it.

"Now, what is it?" said Irene.

"Well, Irene, it is just this: I want to go and see the Singletons this afternoon, and your mother says we may have the governess-cart, and if they ask us to stay to tea we may stay."

"We? What do you mean by 'we'?"

Irene backed away, her face crimson, her eyes dancing with all their old malignancy.

"I mean," said Rosamund, "you and I and Miss Frost."

"You mean that I am to go to the house where Carter is— Carter, whom I nearly killed?"

"I want you to come with me. Won't you, darling?"

"I wish you wouldn't speak in that coaxing voice. People don't speak in such a tender way to me. But no, I can't go. I really can't. I'd be afraid. I can't meet Carter."

"But if you come with me you needn't say much. We'll go together, and you'll find it quite pleasant. I do want to talk to other girls, for you know I've given up all my friends for you, or practically given them up for your sake."

"I wish you wouldn't throw in my face all that you have done for my sake. You had better go, and let me get back to my wild ways. I had great fun with my toads and frogs and spiders and leeches, and having everybody looking at me with scared faces. On the whole, I had much more fun than I have now. I was thinking about that as I was floating in the boat, and the thought of Frost came over me, and I wondered what she would do if I took her into a current in the middle of the lake and frightened her as I frightened Carter. Perhaps even the thought of her little brother and sister wouldn't keep her here any longer. Well, I was thinking those thoughts; but then I thought of you, and somehow or other I felt it worth while to be good just for the sake of your presence; and in many ways you have made my life more interesting. But if you want me to be friends with those Leaves; if you want me to see that dreadful, that terrible Carter again; and then if you want me to go to the Merrimans', and shake hands with that

L. T. Meade

Lucy, and be agreeable to all those people, I really can't."

"Very well, Irene, you can please yourself."

Rosamund turned on her heel and walked away. Irene stood and watched her. She stood perfectly still for a minute, her face changing color, her lips working, her eyes flashing. Then she took up a great sod of wet grass and flung it after Rosamund, making a deep stain on her pretty muslin dress. Rosamund did not take the slightest notice. She walked calmly back to the house, went up to her own room, and sat there quite still. Irene got back into the boat.

"I do wish Frost was somewhere near," she thought to herself. "I won't go and see those Leaves; nothing will induce me to. Horrid, affected creatures! And then to see Carter's frightened eyes looking at me! Haven't I seen them in my dreams until I am sick of the sight of them? And Rosamund wants me to go and see them again! Why, Carter, poor thing! would nearly die of fright, and every one of the Leaves would get into their native trees and disappear from view! Oh, Rosamund is all very well, but she isn't worth that! I wish I hadn't given those leeches back to the chemist. He wasn't a bit grateful, either, and I spent a whole pound on them. I can be just as obnoxious as ever. I know more than I did, and that will help me to be even more wicked than I used to be. I can clear the entire house now of every single servant, and I will, too, if Rosamund goes."

If Rosamund goes! Rosamund with the bright, resolute eyes, the cheerful, fearless face, the kind, soothing hand, and gentle manner; Rosamund, who was not in any way goody-goody, and yet had exercised such a softening influence on wild Irene!

"She will go. Of course she will go. She always keeps her

word," thought the child, and tears filled her bright eyes.

She ceased to paddle, bent slightly over the boat, and looked down at her reflection in the water.

"She says I am beautiful, too. I wish I wasn't beautiful. I don't want to be anything; only I like pleasing her. If Rosamund goes there'll be nothing worth knowing or caring for in Irene. If Rosamund goes!"

The girl suddenly dashed the tears from her eyes. What did the Leaves matter? Why shouldn't she endure a bad quarter of an hour looking at Miss Carter's terrified eyes? She couldn't live without Rosamund!

Accordingly, she pulled rapidly back to the shore, moored her boat, and rushed helter-skelter up to the house. Her mother met her in the hall.

"What is the matter, Irene dear?" she said.

"Nothing," said Irene. "Don't keep me. I want to speak to Rosamund."

Like a whirlwind, the wild little girl dashed through the house, up the winding stairs, down the corridor, until she burst into Rosamund's room. There she flung herself on the ground at her friend's feet, twined her arms round her waist, laid her head on her knee, and burst into tears.

"I will do anything you wish, for I can't live without you!" sobbed Irene.

CHAPTER XV

A DRIVE TO THE RECTORY

Rosamund was wonderfully wise for her years. She did not make a great fuss over Irene's tears. She did not soothe or pet her overmuch; she merely said, "I am glad you have come to your senses," and then she got up and began to prepare for lunch; so that Irene, feeling like a beaten child, and yet with a sense of happiness which she had never experienced before in the whole course of her life, went off to her own room, smoothed out her tangled hair, tidied her dress, and came down to lunch also, looking quite like a little ordinary Christian child—the sort of child who might have been first to a kindergarten and then at a good school—not the wild, obnoxious, terrible little creature whom every servant and every governess alike dreaded.

James was looking fat and strong, because for the last fortnight Irene had not taken the slightest notice of him. The other servants were becoming happy once more. They all worshiped Rosamund; and, truth to tell, Rosamund could not but enjoy her meed of popularity. Still, to-day she was feeling rather nervous. Nevertheless, she was quite determined to carry out her scheme.

As soon as lunch was over, therefore, she went up to Miss

Frost. Irene had danced away into the garden. She was the sort of girl who, having once made up her mind to do a thing, did it thoroughly. Now, she hated the Leaves beyond measure; she dreaded Miss Carter beyond measure; but she dreaded Rosamund still more. Accordingly, she secured a basket and a pair of scissors, and cut and cut from the choicest flowers until her basket was full. One of the gardeners came out and began to remonstrate with Irene on picking so many roses with buds attached to them; but Irene told him in a very tart voice to mind his own business, and in some fear the man withdrew. Then she went into the fruit-house and secured the earliest peaches which were coming into their finest bloom. And having collected what she considered her peace-offering, she sat down on a little wooden bench to wait for Rosamund and her governess.

Meanwhile Rosamund was having a talk with Miss Frost.

"Do you know where we are going to-day?" she asked.

"No," replied Miss Frost.

"Well, you have got to do exactly what I wish. I am most anxious that Irene should have other friends besides me."

"Oh, she will never, never under any circumstances have a friend in the very least like you," said Miss Frost. "You have made her! You have saved her! You are her idol! I am sure we all love you most dearly; but as to Irene, it is wonderful the influence you have over her."

"We needn't talk of that now," said Rosamund. "I can't give up every one in the whole world for Irene. Besides, although I shall always be a great friend of hers, I do not think it would be good for her to have me always by her side. I want her to make fresh friends, and I have been considering that in the whole neighborhood there are no people quite so nice as the Singletons for her to know."

"The Singletons! Why, it is there that unfortunate Miss Carter is—that poor woman who nearly lost her life in order that Irene might get rid of her. Oh, how often have I heard that terrible story! I have seen the girl in church. They look nice, but very stand-off and distant. You know Irene will never go to church. We cannot make her; but I go when I can in the evenings, and I always see the Singletons there with Miss Carter. But for my own little brother Hughie and my little sister Agnes, I would never have stayed here as I have done."

"But now it is all right, dear Miss Frost. Anyhow, Irene has consented to come with me to see the Singletons this afternoon, so don't make a fuss; and if you see Miss Carter, will you tell her that Irene is so much changed that you are able to stay? And, please, don't say anything against her, will you, dear Frosty?"

"I say a word against her? No, that I won't."

"And don't say too much about me. I want her to get all the credit she can. The fact is, she has become so exceedingly naughty because people talk so much of her naughtiness, and she is rather proud of it. Now, I want her to be thoroughly ashamed of it; and when that takes place, and she loses all sense of satisfaction in terrifying people to death and in getting rid of servants and governesses, she will become an ordinary girl—or rather, I should say, never an ordinary girl, but a girl very much above the ordinary. You know you must help me."

"I will, on one condition," said Miss Frost. "This expedition frightens me very much. I will do anything you wish on one condition."

"And what is that?"

"That you don't leave The Follies at present."

"I have no intention of leaving it before the holidays. The holidays will take place at the end of July, and then mother will be sure to want me to join her; but still we have a few weeks left, and there is already a great improvement in Irene. Now, please, go upstairs and get ready, for the governess-cart will be round in a few minutes."

The cart did come round, and, without a word, Irene herself stepped into it. She not only stepped into it, but she took the reins with a determined hand.

"I mean to drive Bob," she said. "I suppose no one objects."

She looked back with her bright, dancing eyes, first at Rosamund and then at Miss Frost.

"Certainly; he is your pony," said Rosamund. "You have every right to drive him."

Miss Frost did not speak. They both entered the governess-cart, and Irene, making a cracking noise with the whip, as she had learned from one of the grooms, started off at a break-neck speed down the somewhat steep avenue. Poor Miss Frost felt inclined to cry out, but Rosamund took one of her hands and pressed it.

After a minute Rosamund's hand was lightly laid on Irene's arm.

"Irene, pull Bob in; he is going much too fast for safety. You don't want his knees to be broken, and we don't want to be tossed out of the cart. Do what I wish you to do instantly."

Irene's eyes wore for a moment almost a wicked expression; then they softened. She put on a check with some vigor, and soon Bob was trotting along the country roads like an ordinary pony.

Many people looked at the three as they saw them in the cart. Never in the entire memory of man had Irene been seen driving with any of her family. There were times when she had gone herself to the stables, had harnessed Bob, who was a very wild and spirited little pony, and had driven off at a furious rate all by herself. She had then left the beaten track, and gone on the moors, bringing home the pony and cart much dilapidated from the exercise. But, strange to say, the wild child herself never seemed to come to any grief.

A mad desire to go right away from the Leaves, to dash on to the moors, and defy Rosamund and Miss Frost, had just for a moment taken possession of her. But again gentler thoughts had come to her, and by-and-by she found herself driving in at the gates of the Rectory.

Now, it so happened that on this very day Mr. Singleton was giving a feast to the poor children of the neighborhood; and when the governess-cart, containing Rosamund, Miss Frost, and Irene, arrived on the premises, there were no less than a hundred children enjoying tea on one of the lawns. In consequence, Maud, Alice, Bertha, Mary, Ivy, and Jasmine, and last, but not least, Miss Carter herself, were all busily engaged, when the sound of wheels caused them to raise their heads. Miss Carter gave utterance to one piercing scream, laid the cup which she had been filling from a huge urn hastily on the table, and disappeared from view. Maud, in some astonishment, her face rather pale, but her eyes bright and resolute as usual, came forward to greet her visitors.

"How do you do?" she said to Rosamund. Then she looked at Irene, whom she had never spoken to before.

"This is my great friend Irene Ashleigh," said Rosamund; "and this is her governess, Miss Frost. We have come to pay you a visit. I see you are busy. That is quite delightful. May we help you?"

"Of course you may, if you will."

Maud held out a gracious hand to Irene, whose little mouth, satirical enough at first, broke now into a gentle smile, while her eyes became tranquil and even happy. She had enjoyed a moment of exquisite bliss when she saw Miss Carter, after that first terrified glance, hurry into the house.

"I can stand the Leaves," she said to herself, "but I hope Carter will keep out of the way."

They all three got out of the cart. A groom came to take the pony to the stables, and the girls and Miss Frost were invited to help the Singletons to entertain their guests.

"We are ever so short of hands," said Maud, "and your coming is quite a blessing. You know, of course, that no one from Sunnyside can come near the place. Mrs. Brett won't allow the girls even to come over from Dartford, which father says is a pity; but still, one must err on the safe side. Isn't it jolly, Jane being quite out of danger? She is to go away at the end of the week, and next week the house will be disinfected, and then everything will be as it was before."

As she spoke she glanced at Irene, who dropped a little behind, keeping hold of Miss Frost's hand.

"Frosty," she said, "can you bear a little pain?"

"I suppose so, dear," said poor Miss Frost in a timid voice.

"I mean this: I must have some outlet for my feelings, and if a Leaf comes too near me I will just squeeze your hand. I won't really hurt you if I can help it, but if I can squeeze your hand I'll be civil to the Leaf; if not, I'll be awfully rude. Do you understand, and will you endure it?"

"I will try to," said Miss Frost; "but I have got very thin hands, Irene."

"Indeed you have, exceedingly bony and exceedingly ugly; but that can't be helped. Just let me hold this hand for the present."

"Do you mind," said Miss Frost after a moment's pause—"do you mind if I take off the rings I have on this hand and put them on the hand you are not going to squeeze? If you were to squeeze it with the rings on I might be forced to cry out, and then all would be up."

"You may do that, and then I'll be quite comfortable."

Miss Frost did so, and Maud and Rosamund walked on a little in front.

"I can't tell you how astonished I am," said Maud, dropping her voice, "to see her here. We heard of your extraordinary behavior—I mean your noble behavior, for father said you were most noble; but to think of your bringing her here! How did you induce her to come?"

"She will one day be a splendid girl, one of the best in the world," said Rosamund; "and the fact is, I wanted your help.

I can't quite manage her alone. I want your help, dear. Will you give it?"

Maud's frank blue eyes looked into Rosamund's dark ones, and over Maud's face there came a softened gleam.

"When I look at you I can believe almost anything," she said. "But to think of that girl ever being what you say! Did she not nearly kill our Cartery dear?"

"I know that; but remember she is very young, and could not realize what she was doing. However, I ask you to trust me, and to help me now with the task I have undertaken. I mean to reform her, and to give her back to her mother, not, as she considers herself, a changeling, but a beautiful, strong, and splendid character, the sort of woman God meant her to be."

"Then I think you are very noble," said Maud, "and I will help you all I can; but you must not expect poor Cartery to appear too. That is more than can be endured. She has rushed into the house, and is probably in hysterics. Yes, I am sure she is, for Bertha has disappeared too, and Bertha is her devoted slave."

"Never mind about Miss Carter now. Let us attend to our duties. I will manage Irene. Shall she and I take a table and help to give these children as much food as they want?"

This plan worked fairly well for a short time, until it was gradually whispered that the person who was helping them to slices of cake and bunches of bread-and-butter was no less than that dreaded creature Miss Irene Ashleigh of The Follies. Then the boys and girls shrank away, for had they not heard of her pranks, and might they not expect toads and frogs to come out of their mouths, and other horrors to happen if Miss Irene had anything to do with them? They therefore began to decline Irene's cake, and to say, "No, thank you, miss," in a very timid voice when delicious-looking pieces of bread-and-butter and jam were offered to them. On the other hand, when Rosamund offered any food it was gratefully accepted.

Rosamund felt the situation was growing critical. She by no means wanted an exhibition of Irene's wrath. The girl was really making a very great effort to control herself, and must not be tried too far. Accordingly, when one little girl refused a slice of bread-and-jam from Irene, and eagerly held out her hand to take it from Rosamund, Rosamund motioned Irene back again.

"That bread-and-jam is much nicer than this," she said. "If you don't take that you won't get any other;" and she insisted on the child taking a slice from the plate which Irene offered.

The little girl turned crimson. She put the bread-and-jam upon her plate, but evidently did not intend to eat it. Irene's face was changing color from moment to moment. She liked Maud; Alice, Mary, Ivy, and Jasmine were as nothing to her. Bertha was nowhere to be seen, and where was "Cartery dear"? That one glimpse she had caught of the terrified woman, who had disappeared like a flash into the house, had whetted Irene's desire to behold her again. Accordingly, when Rosamund's back was turned she slipped away toward the house. In a moment she was in the house, and in another moment she had climbed the stairs. Compared to The Follies, the Rectory was small, although it was really quite a large house. It did not take long for Irene to peep into each empty bedroom, until at last she found one occupied. It was occupied by a woman who was being devotedly attended to by Bertha Singleton. Bertha was bathing her head with aromatic vinegar, and soothing her with loving words. But the next moment the poor woman uttered a cry, for Irene herself was in the room.

"Oh, do go away! Don't, I beseech of you, do anything to me. Do go away!" cried the terrified woman.

Instead of going away, Irene marched straight to the bed.

"Look here, Miss Carter," she said; "you have been exceedingly silly in running away from me as you have done. As to me, I was a perfect fiend that time at The Follies. I wanted to get rid of you, and I could think of no other way. But now that Rosamund is here I see things from a different point of view. Will you trust me?"

"I don't know," said poor Miss Carter, looking at Irene with those absolutely terrified eyes which the girl detested. Perhaps she would have given up her efforts to make friends with Miss Carter had she not at that moment glanced out of the window and seen Rosamund resolutely doing her duty, and looking unlike any one else—even Maud, who was sweet enough to attract any one's attention.

"I am going to confess the simple truth," said Irene; and she came back and stood at the foot of the bed. "I have been a very wicked, bad girl. I used to think that I wasn't to blame, because I was a changeling; but Rosamund says I am not a changeling, and that I am just like anybody else, and ought to be good. I don't expect I'll ever be specially good; but anyhow, I want to be good. At least I sometimes want to be good. I once hated you all"—here she turned to Bertha. "I used to think you so affected, and I used to call you the Leaves. You don't mind, do you?"

"Not in the least," said Bertha; "it doesn't matter to us. But why should you call us Leaves?"

"Because you wear green. You have a green sash on now, and a green ribbon round your hat."

"Mother was fond of green, and mother is dead," said Bertha.

A kind of dewy moisture came to her eyes which did not amount to tears.

"Well, if that is the reason, *pax*!" said Irene.

Suddenly she held out her hand. Now, naughty as she was, there was no one who could be quite so charming as Irene when she chose; and the next minute, Bertha had not only shaken that hand, but had drawn Irene forward and kissed her on her lips.

"You are so very beautiful," she said. "I never saw you before. If you were good you'd be delightful. You'd be such a help to us all. We want some one lovely just to look at. Oh! wouldn't it be sweet, Cartery dear, to try and make pictures of her little face?"

"That will do. I hate people to praise me," said Irene. "I am not at all good at present; and if I am beautiful, why, there's an end of it. What I want to say now is this: Miss Carter, will you forgive me?"

"I—I'll try to."

"Are you still very much afraid of me?"

"I confess that I am."

"It's rather silly of you, isn't it? For you are quite protected from me."

"I know that; but you gave me a great shock."

"Dear Cartery," said Bertha, "she did, to be sure; but she is changed, and you never told us she was so beautiful."

"You don't think much of a beautiful face, my dear, when you are being dashed to pieces on the rocks," said Miss Carter.

"Oh yes! oh yes! but still, she is never going to do anything of that sort again. Are you, Irene dear?"

"I haven't any present intention of doing so, Bertha dear," replied Irene in a deliberate tone. "Now, Miss Carter, I want to know if you will forgive me. It will help me to be good if you will forgive me. Will you?"

"Then I will," said Miss Carter.

"Then there is only one way to prove it. You must get right up off your bed and come downstairs with me, and let me rest on your arm, and come out with me on to the lawn, where all the children are having their tea, and you and I between us are to offer them bread-and-jam and cakes and biscuits. Will you or will you not?"

"Of course you will, Cartery dear."

"Are you certain that you mean what you say?" said Miss Carter. "I have got a sort of headache."

"Oh no, you haven't," retorted Bertha. "You are always imagining things, Cartery dear."

"Will you come or will you not, Miss Carter?" said Irene. "Is it to be peace or is it to be war? I offer peace now. Do you accept it?"

"I do," said Miss Carter; and she got off her bed, and went downstairs by Irene's side.

CHAPTER XVI

AT HOME WITH "THE LEAVES"

Nothing could exceed the astonishment of the school children, the Leaves themselves, and even of Rosamund, when they witnessed this sight. Rosamund's first impulse was to fly up to Irene, kiss her passionately, and assure her that she was a darling, and that nothing would induce her ever to forsake her. But on second thoughts she decided that it was best to take no notice. Accordingly, the children pursued their games, for now tea was almost a thing of the past, and Irene found herself enjoying life as she had not yet enjoyed it. Never was any one more daring seen. She was the centre of attraction. From being dreaded, she was adored. Who but she could climb to the very highest branch of the tallest tree? Who but she could swing so high that she seemed almost to turn a somersault in the air before she came down again? Who but she could invent the most daring games? And then, when all other things failed, who but she could tell such weird stories? Her eyes shone; her lips were wreathed in smiles. She looked the very essence of beauty and happiness. Was this the ogre of The Follies, the terrible girl who kept every one away from the place, whom the servants dreaded, whom the governesses fled from?

Both Miss Carter and Miss Frost, standing side by side,

L. T. Meade

watched the young heroine of the hour as she won her way to popularity. What was the matter? What was wrong? Or, rather, who had put wrong right?

Rosamund, who was herself a very gay, resolute, determined girl, kept more or less in the background on this occasion. She wanted Irene, as she said afterward, to win her spurs. The two governesses stood together and talked.

"Of all the wonderful things I have ever seen, the behavior of Irene Ashleigh beats them," said Miss Carter, turning to Miss Frost. "How do you account for it?" she added.

"How do I account for it?" replied Miss Frost. "I account for it because a blessed angel came to the house in the shape of Rosamund Cunliffe, the most splendid girl I have ever met. She came, and showed not a scrap of fear, even though that child—that terrible child—took her into the middle of the stream, just where she took you, you poor thing!"

"Don't speak of it. Don't mention it," began poor Miss Carter, trembling all over.

"Well, she took Rosamund there, and Rosamund was strong and got the upper hand with her at once, and from that hour Irene has been different. It is true she has done terrible things. She behaved almost as badly to me as she did to you."

"Shall we walk down this shrubbery?" said Miss Carter. "The children are all quite happy. Every one who comes to the Rectory is happy, and you can hear by the shouts of the village children that they are in the very acme of bliss. Shall we walk down here and talk together? I have always been so amazed at your remaining on at The Follies, Miss Frost."

"I have a little sister called Agnes, and a little brother Hugh,

and they are the dearest little children. They are only my step-
brother and sister, of course; but they are to me just as though
they were my very own. They depend on me altogether for
their maintenance. I buy everything for them. I spend my
holidays with them, and they love me. My darlings! They are
like my own children. Were I to give up so good a situation
my little ones would starve. You understand, Miss Carter, do
you not, that under such circumstances one would endure a
great deal?"

"But even under such circumstances," said Miss Carter, in
astonishment, "I do not think people would put up with Irene
Ashleigh as she used to be. Oh, never, never shall I forget
how the boat dashed against the rocks! I thought my last
moment had come."

"How did you escape drowning, dear?" said Miss Frost. "I
never heard that part."

"It is more than I can tell you myself. I suppose I lost
consciousness. When I came to myself I was on dry land,
and Irene was dragging me back to the house; and then I had
a terrible—most terrible—interview with Lady Jane. I told
her that I would go at once, that nothing would induce me to
stay. She was nearly in despair, and, metaphorically
speaking, went on her knees to me. But I remembered my
promise to that dreadful child, and stuck to my word. Go I
would. I never saw Lady Jane in a temper before, but she
was then. She refused to let me have a carriage. She said
Irene's conduct was past bearing, and that I ought to stay if
only to support her. But I couldn't, for my nerves were
frightfully shattered. I went away as quickly as ever I could
that very afternoon, intending to send a porter from the
railway station for my luggage. Before I got half-way there I
nearly fainted, and the dear, kind rector found me on the
road. I told him my story, and he brought me home—yes,

L. T. Meade

home, for this is indeed a complete and absolute home to me. I cannot tell you how kind they have been."

"I have lived through *my* horrors too; but I will not speak about them to-day," said Miss Frost. "Irene is immensely improved. I believe as long as Rosamund remains with her she will be a really good girl. She is making great efforts."

"She is; that is the astonishing part of it," said Miss Carter. "She came up to my room—I will confess to you that I was hiding from her, absolutely hiding, and shaking from head to foot, scarcely knowing what to do—and she came in as bold as brass, and yet with a new sort of humility about her, and she said to me, 'Will you forgive me? And if you forgive me, will you come downstairs and let me put my hand inside your arm?' And somehow, although it was the very last thing on earth that I wanted to do, I did it; and now here I am, and I don't feel nearly so much afraid of her as I used."

"It is all owing to Rosamund," said Miss Frost again. "She is the most wonderful girl I have ever met. I know one of her objects now is that you and I, Irene, herself, and the Singletons should be friends. She means Irene to invite you all over to The Follies to-morrow or the next day, and I hope you will have the courage to come."

"Indeed I don't know how I can. It is one thing to have Irene here; it is another thing to look at that terrible lake and reflect that the boat is at hand. Oh, of course, she will excuse me."

"But I don't think she will. If you come I will look after you, and we will both firmly refuse to go in the boat. It wouldn't hold us all, so there is no fear of that."

"But she is very ingenious. There is no end to her resources."

"At present her mood is different. You and I, who are so much older, ought to try to encourage her; for, after all, she has been a most sadly mismanaged child, allowed even from her earliest days to see that people were afraid of her, and thus the spirit of cruelty gained a strong hold; but there is a great deal of good in her nature."

Miss Carter was called loudly by Maud, who requested her to help the little ones to play Puss-in-the-corner. The group broke up into different detachments, and by-and-by the time came when Rosamund whispered to Irene that it was necessary to order the governess-cart so that they might go home.

"But I am so happy," said Irene, who had been helping some of the little girls to climb up and tumble down cocks of hay, and otherwise disport themselves. "I didn't know other children could be so nice; but I find poor children are much nicer than rich ones. They have no manners, which I detest, and just say what they think. They have been telling me some home-truths, and I have been laughing like anything. I didn't know I was such an ogre; but it is great fun to hear it from the lips of the children."

"We must go home; it is time," said Rosamund. "But before we go, Irene, will you kindly ask the Singletons to come to see us on Thursday? They might come to lunch, and spend the time until after tea. Thus we should have a long afternoon."

"But if they must come, why not to-morrow?" said Irene. "I didn't know that other children could be so charming."

"They can't come to-morrow. We have our music lessons with Mr. Fortescue to-morrow."

"Can't we put him off?"

"Of course we can't. His time is all engaged. Ask them for Thursday, or, if you prefer it, for Saturday. Anyhow, will you ask them?"

"Oh yes, I'll ask them, and for Thursday."

Irene's flushed face, her speaking eyes, her lips apart in smiles, looked such a different creature from the somewhat pale, queerly dressed little inmate of the woods, that Mr. Singleton, who came out at that moment, did not know her.

"Who is this little lady?" he said, going straight up to her and holding out his hand.

"I am the ogre," was Irene's instant response.

This answer amazed Mr. Singleton, but he kept looking at her and smiling.

"I am sure, my dear, that is not your name. You look more like an angel than an ogre."

"But I am the ogre—the ogre of the whole place. I am Irene Ashleigh."

The clergyman's astonishment was seen now on his face. Rosamund hastened to interpose.

"Irene is my friend," she said, "and I think she is going to turn into a very fine sort of woman, if not into an angel. Anyhow, here she is, and I hope you bid her welcome."

"I do most heartily," said Mr. Singleton. "You must come and see us often. I am very glad you have broken the ice at last. What good news," he continued, turning to Rosamund, "this is about your young friend! It is such a relief to the Merrimans that she is getting on so well."

"And a great relief to me," said Rosamund.

Irene moved away to talk to three little red-haired girls, who made a charming group, standing under an oak-tree. She soon had them in fits of laughter; and Mr. Singleton, just glancing at her, spoke again to Rosamund.

"What a miracle you have performed!" he said. "She is a changed creature. But I suppose there is a great deal of the old Adam in her still."

"Yes; but she will change still more. The fact is, she was so terribly naughty because people used to be afraid of her."

"And you are not?"

"I certainly am not."

"My dear, there is something I want to say to you. Do you know that I have had a conversation with Professor Merriman, and he gave me a very queer account of your conduct? He seemed greatly distressed at the way you have behaved."

Rosamund shrugged her shoulders.

"The Merrimans did not suit me," she said. "Life at The Follies does suit me. At the Merrimans' I was growing to be a very naughty girl myself. I could not stand Lucy, although I liked the Professor; and I liked Laura Everett and one or two of the other girls. But at The Follies, you see for yourself, rector, I have done no harm."

"Harm! Indeed, you have done most blessed good. I never could have believed in such a change in any one. Why, that child is quite lovely."

"And by-and-by she will have a lovely mind," said Rosamund. "But, Mr. Singleton, it is only right to tell you that I am practically expelled from the Merrimans' school."

"That is a very grave matter. It ought not to be allowed," said the rector. "The Professor cannot understand. His eyes must be blinded. You have done a noble work."

"But I don't mind; and, besides, I could not go back."

"But you could if it were just and right, could you not?"

"I don't really think I could."

Just then the pony-cart came round. The rector said no more for the time being; and a few minutes later, the young Singletons and Miss Carter having promised to arrive at The Follies on Thursday, Irene, Rosamund, and Miss Frost took their leave.

"Well, now, wasn't I a darling? Didn't I behave well?" said Irene. "Aren't you pleased with me, Rose—dearest, sweetest, red, red Rose?"

"Yes, on the whole, I am quite pleased with you," said Rosamund; but she leaned back in her seat. She felt tired and sad. She had done a good work, and she knew it, and yet she had injured her reputation; and her mother would be annoyed, and her father displeased. What was to be done?

There was some one else who was very much troubled on Rosamund's behalf, and that was the Rev. John Singleton. It was not his habit to consult any of his children, not even Maud, whom he relied on almost as he had relied on his wife; but he went straight over that very evening to the Merrimans' house; and although he could not go inside for fear of infection, he had a conversation with the Professor in the garden. There he spoke with such verve and enthusiasm with regard to Rosamund, and the marvelous change she had already wrought in the naughtiest girl in the entire district, that he induced that gentleman to change his mind.

"If you think it absolutely necessary, I will give her a chance."

"You must give her a chance. It would be culpable to allow such a girl to enter on the world with such a stigma as being expelled from school would mean. You must give her a chance, sir. I hope you will not hesitate to do so."

Professor Merriman explained that his pupils would not return for at least another fortnight, that Jane would be sent away in a little over a week, that the house would be thoroughly disinfected, and the school would continue.

"Perhaps it would be best for Rosamund to remain where she is for the present," he said, "and come back to us at the beginning of next term. I acknowledge that she is a fine girl; very good-looking, too, and with a most taking way. But she must learn obedience. She would not obey when she was with us. It was for the sin of disobedience that I dismissed her. She also broke her word of honor."

"Give her a chance. Believe me, there are circumstances which overcome all ordinary conditions," said the good clergyman; and he went away feeling assured that Professor Merriman would keep his word.

L. T. Meade

CHAPTER XVII

NEW RESPONSIBILITIES

This was the beginning of July. Towards the end the school would break up and the holidays would begin. The young Singletons were going to the seaside, and every one was about to have a merry-making of one sort or another.

In the past Irene and her mother had lived on in a dull sort of fashion at The Follies. Lady Jane had never the heart to leave home, therefore Irene knew nothing of the delights of traveling. But as the time approached for the holidays Rosamund spoke once or twice of the fun which ought to be before them.

"Where would you like to go?" she said to her young friend. "There are ever so many places where you can have amusement—you and Lady Jane."

"You want to tame me down," said Irene. "I don't think I can be altogether tamed. There is something in me here"—and she put her hand on her breast—"a wild sort of thing that will assert itself now and then. I can't help myself. I can't, for instance, sit still in a drawing-room, or be a very good little girl in church, finding out the hymns and the lessons for the day, and the right psalms. I could not teach in the

Sunday-school—no, I couldn't, for all the world. I could do none of those things, because I have a wild living creature that seems to be inside me. I don't know what it means; I don't understand it myself. It is rampant when you are not here; but when you are present it stays quiet mostly, just because I love you. That is the whole reason."

"Aren't you very much happier since I came to you?" said Rosamund.

The two girls were pacing up and down in front of the lake, about a week before the holidays were to begin.

Meanwhile, at Sunnyside, school had recommenced. It is true that Jane, far too delicate to resume her lessons, was away at the seaside; but Lucy, Laura, Annie Millar, Phyllis Flower, and Agnes Sparkes had all returned to their studies. Miss Archer and Mademoiselle Omont were also very much to the fore. The kind Bretts had found rooms for the two governesses at Dartford; but they could not manage to take them in themselves. The girls had therefore gone, after a certain manner, through their lessons; but now the holidays were approaching.

"What a queer term it has been!" said Rosamund, talking to Irene as they walked by the water-side. "I, who belonged to the Merrimans' party, spending all my time with you; you working hard at your daily lessons and enjoying them; Miss Frost and Miss Carter the best of friends, and meeting Sunday after Sunday; and you having quite a fancy—yes, and more than a fancy—for Maud Singleton!"

"I am fond of her," said Irene, "just because she is like yourself, so brave. I wanted brave people. I never came across a brave person until I met you."

"Well, now we have to think of the holidays," said Rosamund. "I have something to tell you, Irene. You have been good— very good; but all our goodness is worth nothing until it has been tried. Yours has not been tried yet."

"What do you mean by that?" said Irene, in some terror, raising her lovely, wild, bright eyes to Rosamund's face.

"Well, it hasn't, darling—has it?"

"I don't understand. I can't tell you what an effort it has been not to collect worms and toads, and frogs and newts, and wasps and bees, and blue-bottles and spiders. I did so adore frightening the servants, particularly James; and there are such heaps of darling wasps this season. I just longed to stick one down his neck; but I refrained when I looked at you."

"You ought not even to speak of these things; they mean downright cruelty, and aren't the least bit funny."

"Aren't they, now? Are you sure? They used to seem very funny to me—the way James used to start at table; because I generally managed, when he attended, to put a spider on my plate when I handed it to him. I used to keep a little collection of them in my handkerchief, and generally popped one on my plate; and he used always to say 'Oh!' and he would generally drop and break the plate, which was a valuable china one, and mother was quite annoyed."

"Well, all those things are past. We needn't talk of them any more. I want to know what you are going to do in the holidays."

"What are you going to do, Rose?"

"I am very sorry, Irene, but I am afraid I must go away from you. I have to visit my parents; and there is something else they want me to do. They want me to go back to the Merrimans' school in the autumn, and stay there for at least a term. They say that in no other way can I get over the disgrace of having, as it were, run away from school. I don't mind a bit having done that, for I know that you wanted me; but I think I ought to go back to the Merrimans' for at least a term."

"Even with Lucy, odious creature?"

"Well, now, you don't know her."

"But you do; and do you like her?"

"I can't honestly say that I do."

"It is Sunday to-morrow; can't we both go to church, and then I can look at Lucy in the distance and see what I think of her?"

"You ought not to go to church in that spirit."

"Well, perhaps something else will happen. Maud Singleton is always asking me to go to church. I think I will, if you will come with me. We can go to the evening service. I have never been. Maud says I wouldn't feel so like a changeling if I could pray like other people, and sing hymns like other people. But then I'm sure I can't. May we sit near the door, and if I feel it impossible to remain quiet any longer, do you mind if I rush out?"

"We will certainly go to church, and we can sit near the door, and you shall rush out if you feel inclined, and I will come with you," said Rosamund. "But this is rather starting away from our question. What do you want to do during the holidays? You wouldn't, for instance, think of spending them with the Singletons at the seaside?"

"I will tell you another time," said Irene. "I can't make up my mind on that point quite so soon. Now, let us come in, and you shall read me some more from those wonderful *Arabian Nights* fairy-tales. They are so beautiful; I feel they were written for me. Afterwards we will have Hans Andersen."

"For my part, I like Hans Andersen best," said Rosamund.

The two girls went towards the house. Rosamund read, as was her wont, for half-an-hour to Irene, during which time that young person grew very sleepy, and soon afterwards went away to bed. Rosamund was about to follow her when Lady Jane came into the room.

"My dear Rose," she said, "I have had a letter from your mother. She says that you are to join them in Switzerland during the first week of the holidays. I suppose you wouldn't think it possible that Irene and I should accompany you?"

"I should like it very much," said Rosamund. "But I don't know that mother would think it quite fair. Mother is not accustomed to a girl like Irene, and although she is wonderfully good to what she used to be, you can scarcely call her a good girl yet—not an ordinary good girl, I mean."

"I suppose not, but she is quite sweet to me. Only I feel certain that when your influence is withdrawn we shall have the old dreadful things occurring again."

"I don't think so, indeed. But do tell me what mother has said."

"She says that you are to go back to the Merrimans' for the

next term; but after that you can come and live with us if we want you. She suggested that we should take a house for the winter in town, so that you and Irene should have the advantage of the best masters possible to be obtained, and the best literature classes, and the best concerts. I am quite agreeable, for I am tired of living at The Follies."

"You ought to take Irene away for the holidays, and of course Miss Frost will go with you," said Rosamund. "I wish I could stay. I would with a heart and a half; but I know father and mother would be terribly put out."

"I feel very despondent," said Lady Jane; "for although Irene is very much improved, there is a lot of the old nature in her still; and when you are gone, even the Singletons will be away, for they are going to the seaside for the month of August—to Herne Bay, I believe. We shall have no one at home, and Irene and I alone at the seaside would make a terrible pair."

"I will write to mother. Something ought to be done," said Rosamund very thoughtfully. "Leave it to me," she continued. "What I have been thinking is this: that Irene ought to come with me to the Merrimans' for one term."

"You mean that I am to part with her—that she is not to live with me? Besides, would the Merrimans take a child with such a character?"

"She is quite a good character now, and it would be just the very thing. It would be the making of her. Then, perhaps, afterwards we might go together to a good foreign school and learn languages properly. I am sure it would do her a lot of good. But I will think about the holidays."

Rosamund felt rather old and worn. A very heavy burden had

been laid on her young shoulders. She, a girl of only fifteen years of age, was more or less responsible for the entire life, the entire future, of a brilliant little sprite like Irene Ashleigh.

The next day was Sunday, and it arose in great beauty and majesty. The sun shone out of a cloudless sky, the flowers bloomed everywhere, the birds sang, the heat was excessive, the gardens looked their best. Visitors came and went. Irene, no longer in the objectionable red frock, but now dressed as a pretty young girl of her age ought to be dressed, walked by Rosamund's side and chatted about books, about music, about all sorts of things, the existence of which she had scarcely known a few weeks ago. Her intellect was of such a keen and brilliant order that she grasped knowledge almost as easily as she imbibed her food. Rosamund felt more and more proud of her.

"With such talent and such beauty, what might she not aspire to?" thought the elder girl. The younger looked at her with a light in her eyes.

"What are you thinking about, Rose?" she said.

"I was wondering about something. You have promised to come to church with me this evening. I will tell you after church."

Rosamund went away to her room, and there she sat down and wrote a long letter to her mother. She did not tell any one the contents of that letter; but it took her a long time to write, and when she had finished her cheeks were flushed and her eyes brighter than ever.

At last the sweet bells ringing out the time for evening service smote upon the summer air, and the two girls, in their white dresses, started off to walk to the pretty church, which was in reality not far away. Irene had not been in church since she was a tiny child, when she had screamed loudly, uttered naughty words, declared that the clergyman had no right to come in in his night-gown, and, in short, disgraced herself so thoroughly that she was carried out amidst a tempest of tears and protestations.

Now the older and wiser Irene, beautifully dressed all in white, looking more like an angel than a naughty, wayward, disagreeable girl, entered the old building and sat down near Rosamund in a pew at the end of the church. One of the churchwardens invited the two young people to come up higher; but Rosamund requested to be left where they were, and presently the rest of the congregation streamed in.

Irene was all excitement. She was, in fact, trembling all over. The quiet grayness and the age of the building impressed her, she knew not why. Then the boys in their white surplices excited her wonder; then she watched the congregation. The Singletons, as usual, were in their simple white and green; as usual their beautiful fair hair flowed down their backs; as usual they walked up the old aisle in pairs, two, and two, and two; and last of all came Miss Carter.

"She doesn't look nice at all," said Irene to herself.

"How well I remember all about her: that rather crooked back of hers, those sloping shoulders, that ill-made dress, and that hat put on always at the wrong angle. She is rather like Frosty. I wonder why I never had a stylish governess? But I'd have hated her worse than ever. Well, now I have got Rosamund—my dear, darling Rosamund—and she is beautiful as well as good."

Irene gazed with adoring eyes at her friend. Miss Frost was not present at the evening service.

By-and-by the Merriman party made their appearance, and took their seats in the large square family pew. There was the Professor, with his slightly bent figure and his white hair; there was Mrs. Merriman, round and cherubic, looking as though no care had ever troubled her; and there was Lucy, fair almost as the Singletons, with that particularly prim face which aggravated Rosamund, and which would certainly drive Irene to distraction. None of these three even glanced at Rosamund Cunliffe and her friend; but when Laura Everett and one or two other girls appeared, they did see the pair seated in a pew all alone at the end of the church, and Laura nodded with a bright glance at Rosamund, who colored with pleasure in reply.

"Is that stiff un, all prunes and prisms, Lucy?" whispered Irene in a loud voice.

"I'll talk to you afterwards," said Rosamund. "The service is going to begin. This is the right place. I will find all your places for you to-night. You will find the service so nice. Remember, we are here to pray to God, and not to think evil of our fellow-creatures."

"You're getting quite too goody-goody," laughed Irene in an excited voice.

The service began; the music, of the simplest kind, but quite sweet and true, filled the little church. Irene fidgeted, turned first white, then red, and finally, grasping Rosamund's arm, said in a choking voice, "I don't like it. I can't stand the music. The wild, wild thing in me is just as though it would tear me in pieces. I must get out. Come! You promised to come with me."

Rosamund took her eccentric young friend outside the church.

"What is the matter, Irene? You ought to try to control yourself."

"I do as a rule. I am much better as a rule; but it came over me in church how proper people were, and they all of them talk about being miserable sinners, and every one looks so good and righteous, and knowing down deep in their hearts that every single one of them is a miserable sinner, except your darling, precious self; and they all repeat the words, not feeling them a bit. I couldn't be like that. If they'd all lie flat on their faces, and cry and tear their hair, or do anything to show that they were really sorry, I could sympathize with them. But I can't sympathize with the proper sort of people who fill a village church."

"They have learned to control themselves. They very likely do feel that they are miserable sinners in the sight of God. We must learn not to judge people. Oh, Irene, what am I to do with you? What will you do when I am gone?"

"I know what I will do when you are away," said Irene. "I have thought it all out. I'll have a wild, wild time. I have been good long enough. I'll go back to my frogs and toads and leeches, and spiders and wasps and bees. I'll terrify the servants again, and scare mother, and send Frosty off her head. That's what I'll do; and I'll wear my little red dress, and I'll get Frosty into the middle of the lake, and I'll make her promise to go away, and if she refuses to go—I know she won't, for even those children won't keep her when such a thing as that is thought of"—

"Oh, I have such a splendid thought!" said Rosamund suddenly. "Suppose you make Frosty happy instead of miserable? You can if you like. Suppose you allow her to ask the two children, Agnes and Hughie, to spend the holidays at The Follies?"

L. T. Meade

"The two children—Frosty's two children?"

"Yes, her little brother and sister. She was telling me the other day she didn't know what to do with them. It would be such a splendid opportunity, and there is really no necessity whatever for you to leave The Follies. You could be there, and they would look up to you. They don't know that you are naughty—they need never know. I would be with you for the first two or three days, for their different schools break up before most schools, so they could come next week, and I could help you with them. What do you think? You wouldn't be without companions, and it would be a tremendous trust to repose in you, Irene. Do you think you would be worthy of it?"

"These were those words the clergyman said—Mr. Singleton, I mean—'I will arise and go to my Father, and will say unto Him: Father, I have sinned.' They made such a lump come in my throat; and when you talk to me a great lump comes in my throat too, and I feel that I have done nothing but sin all my life. Oh, I can't be sure of myself; that's about the end of the matter, Rosamund."

"I know—I know!" said Rosamund. "I know it is very hard; but then, anything worth living for is hard; and you have done so much that is wrong, it would be a splendid thing to turn over a new leaf now. Do you know what I have further in my mind? You know that I am to go back to the Merrimans' next term, but only till Christmas, and I want your mother to let you come with me. The Merrimans want another governess, so Frosty could come; and perhaps her little sister Agnes could be another pupil. Everything can be arranged if only you will promise to be good."

"But you weren't good yourself while you were at the Merrimans'. How can you expect me to be?"

"We'll keep each other good. When I am inclined to be naughty you shall correct me, and when you are inclined to be naughty I will correct you. We will arrange to sleep in the same room. Shall we try it, Irene—shall we?"

Irene paused for a minute. There were tears in her eyes. After a moment she said, "How long is it since I have known you?"

"About six or seven weeks."

"It seems like quite that number of years. I never can believe that there could have been a time when I didn't know you. I know you, oh, so well now, and I love you so much! You have done a great deal for me."

"I don't pretend that I haven't, Irene. But I must do what my father and mother want during the holidays. I do think it would be a splendid plan to ask little Hughie and Agnes to spend August at The Follies. I wonder what Frosty would say? Let us ask her after supper."

Irene flung her arms round Rosamund's neck.

"I don't quite promise to be good," she said; "but I'll do my best. I will do it for your sake, more particularly if you will promise that you will be with us for the first few days."

"Yes, I'll be with you for the first week. They could come early next week, and I am not going away until the week after."

"Oh! don't talk about it; it is too horrible. Let us come into the fields and talk about ourselves."

The two girls did walk together, and it was Irene's turn to tell

Rosamund some of the wild and fanciful fairy-tales which she was always making up. But she could never be still very long, and in the midst of her most earnest and fascinating stories she would rush from one end of the field to the other, or turn a somersault, or climb a tree and look down at Rosamund with her laughing, mocking face from the midst of the branches. But then again she would be good, and come back and say that the wicked little living thing inside her was quiet for the time being.

"I wonder if it will ever go away?" she said. "If it were gone I'd be much like other girls; but as long as it is there I can't be like any girl—I can't."

"There is such a thing as praying to God to take it away. But perhaps it is never meant to go," said Rosamund.

"What do you mean by that?"

"Perhaps it is a very beautiful gift that God has given you— something that you can't quite control at present, but something which will make you by-and-by different from others: more earnest, more enthusiastic, more full of spirit, more full of zeal. You have set your face steadily towards everything that has been naughty. You don't know yourself. Just tell that thing, as you call it, inside you that you are going up, not down, in future, and see if it won't behave itself and help you all the time."

"I wonder if it will?" said Irene. "It is a good thought."

CHAPTER XVIII

FROSTY'S DARLINGS

Miss Frost's alarm, surprise, and delight when Rosamund had an earnest talk with her on the following morning can be better imagined than described.

"Of course, you can understand," she said, "that nothing would give me greater pleasure than having the darlings here with me; but how am I to trust Irene? Agnes is rather a timid little thing. Hughie is brave enough. I should not be afraid of him. He is fourteen; Agnes is only eleven. I am so afraid that Agnes, who has a little bit of me in her nature, will succumb utterly and show Irene that she is afraid of her. Then all would be lost."

"Nothing will be lost," replied Rosamund. "It is the very best plan possible. You must make Irene the guardian of Agnes from the very first. You must make her take that position with her; it is the only thing to do. The mistake has been that people were terrified of her. Her character, which is really very fine, has been spoiled by such a course. Give her a little tender thing to love, and make her guard that creature, and she will fight for her to the very death. I do believe it. Trust me, I have studied her character so carefully."

"I do indeed trust you, dear," replied Miss Frost, with tears in her eyes. "Well, then, if Lady Jane approves"—

Of course Lady Jane approved. She said at once that she did not wish to leave The Follies.

"I like to go away sometimes in November," she said, "or at the end of October, when the leaves are falling. But I love my own beautiful home in the summer weather best of all places on earth, and I am afraid of taking Irene to fashionable places. I tried her once at the seaside for a week; but her conduct was scandalous, and I was forced to bring her home at a minute's notice. I needn't repeat what she did; but she really was unbearable to every one in the house. Of course, Miss Frost, if your little brother and sister can be happy here, I shall be delighted to receive them."

"Then I will write this very day," said Miss Frost; and Rosamund took care that she kept her word.

In consequence, just as the holidays at the Merrimans' began, on the very day that Mrs. Merriman walked all the way to The Follies in order to see Rosamund, the little Frosts also made their appearance on the scene.

Mrs. Merriman came an hour before the children. She was dressed in her usual prim and proper style, and Rosamund could not help owning to a distasteful feeling when she saw her. She and Irene were walking about in a considerable state of excitement. Irene had been planning every hour of the day for her visitors.

"You know I have never had visitors before," she said. "I don't exactly count you as a visitor. You are dearer to me than I am to myself. You are all the world to me; but these are visitors. If I could only forget that they belonged to

Frosty all would be well."

"But you must on no account forget it. You must think of Frosty's pleasure as well as your own. You know you have promised—yes, you have promised me, you who don't tell lies—to go up, not down, in future. Oh, there is Mrs. Merriman! I must run and speak to her."

"That prim, dumpling sort of woman? Oh, all right, go; but don't stay long with her. I want you. I am beginning to count the minutes now. I feel so terribly anxious at your leaving me."

Rosamund almost wished that she were not obliged to leave The Follies at this juncture; but her own father and mother would not hear of her staying away from them. She accordingly left Irene on the present occasion, and walked across the lawn to meet Mrs. Merriman.

Mrs. Merriman paused when she saw her.

"How do you do, Rosamund?" she said. She spoke coldly, and did not hold out her hand.

Rosamund replied in as prim a voice as the little lady had used:

"How do you do, Mrs. Merriman? I hope you are all quite well at the school. How was Jane when you heard from her last?"

"Almost quite well, I am glad to say. She will be able to return to her lessons in the middle of September. I have something to say to you, Rosamund, and as we have met here in the avenue, I need not go up to the house."

"Just as you like about that," said Rosamund. "Wouldn't you like to have a cup of tea? I am sure Lady Jane would be pleased to see you. Are you not tired? The walk is a some-what long one."

"I am never tired," replied Mrs. Merriman. "If my dear husband, my beloved Professor, had even half my strength, we should not be obliged to keep a school full of troublesome girls at all."

"Indeed! are the others troublesome?" asked Rosamund, her eyes sparkling.

"I cannot say that they are particularly troublesome now that you are away."

Rosamund lowered her lids, but her eyes danced. She looked on the ground.

"If I am to go back to the school next term, and take Irene with me, I don't know how I shall bear it," she said to herself.

Mrs. Merriman, however, was nothing if not to the point.

"My dear," she said slowly, "it is my husband's lot and mine to have to earn money in a way which is in no way congenial to either of us."

"But you are always so kind! You never gave any trouble of any sort," was Rosamund's response. "You seemed to understand us in a sort of fashion. It was—Lucy!" she added with a burst.

"Lucy is my darling, beloved, and only child. You must not say a word against her. I cannot stand it."

"Very well, I will try not to; but you know she does not like me."

"She certainly doesn't; but has she any reason for liking you, Rosamund?"

"Perhaps she has not; that is quite probable. I know I was not particularly good when I was at Sunnyside."

"And do you think you are particularly good now?"

"I do not. Perhaps I see my faults more plainly than ever. But I have helped Irene, and Irene is worth helping."

"I hardly dare to think of what I have come about to-day; but the Professor has sent me. He has received a letter from your mother, and he has also seen Mr. Singleton, and Mr. Singleton has suggested an extraordinary thing. He wants both you and Irene—yes, the dreaded, the feared Irene—to come to our beautiful house for next term. You were practically expelled from the school; but he wants you to come back again, and the Professor has sent me to say that he is willing to receive you both, on condition that you will not disturb the peace of the house."

"As far as I am concerned, I will not disturb it; but I cannot answer for Irene."

"I dread her unspeakably," said Mrs. Merriman. "Do walk with me for a little down this path, my dear. You, of course, are only an ordinarily naughty girl. You have been very disobedient, but I can overlook that, and perhaps understand it; but she—some people say she is not quite right in the head. Do you think that is true?"

"I know it to be false. She has cleverer brains than most of us."

L. T. Meade

"Then, if that is the case, she is just extraordinarily wicked—wicked beyond most people."

"You may think that if you like, Mrs. Merriman, but it is also untrue. I will tell you quite frankly what has been wrong with Irene. People have been afraid of her. I was the only person who ever came across her path who showed no fear at her presence. I simply conquered her by having a stronger will than she has. Now, if all your girls will behave in that sort of fashion to her, not minding her when she does what she considers clever little tricks, she will soon stop them. I don't believe she will even attempt them, for I shall do my utmost to prevent it. But if she does, your only plan is to take no notice of her. If people show no fear, then her fun is gone—her wings are cut, in short. That was the way I got an influence over her, and it is the way in which others may get an influence over her. I want her to sleep in my room, instead of dear Jane, whom I am so fond of."

"Oh! that will be quite easily managed, for no other girl would endure her as a room-fellow."

"I will do my very best to keep her tame. More I cannot say."

"I suppose you are very kind; but do tell me, is it true that she puts wasps down people's necks? Does she put leeches into the beds without any one knowing anything about it? It is perfectly awful to think of."

"I am not going to tell tales out of school," said Rosamund, laughing. "I can only say that Irene is greatly improved; and if your girls, your Lucy included, will behave themselves, and not show the slightest fear—and why should they fear?—I think she will come out of the ordeal a brave and strong and good girl. They all ought to help, and I wish I could see them all and tell them so."

"I do believe you are quite a good girl," said Mrs. Merriman, turning her eyes in some amazement and looking at Rosamund. "I have been very angry with you, and so was Lucy; my poor dear Lucy will never quite forgive you; but I see now that you meant right, although you went the wrong way about it."

"It seemed the only way at the time. I am very sorry if I have troubled you," said Rosamund.

"Well, then, I will expect you and Irene at the beginning of the term. You shall share the same room, and I trust you to keep Irene within bounds. Now, good-by."

Mrs. Merriman turned and walked down the avenue, and was soon lost to view.

Irene, who had been watching this interview from the top branch of a tall tree, now quickly descended and came up to Rosamund's side.

"So she has gone!" she said. "So she is to be my head-mistress in future. But never mind her now. It is a long way off school-days, and the holidays have hardly begun. Frosty has gone off to fetch the children. I am dying with excitement to see them. But it was great fun to watch you, Rosamund. I could not hear what your words were; but I saw that you were pleading for me, and promising to be my sponsor, my godmother. As if I could be good there!"

"You must be good. I have declared it; I have almost staked my reputation on the fact. You will not disappoint me," was Rosamund's reply.

The girls walked about for some little time together, and by-and-by there came the sound of wheels, and they knew that the travelers had arrived.

"Come along, Irene," said Rosamund; and they went down the avenue to meet Miss Frost, who was herself driving the governess-cart. Her thin face was flushed with excitement, her eyes were bright; she looked ten years younger, and almost pretty. An exceedingly pretty little girl, with dark eyes, and a quantity of fair hair tumbling about her face, sat close up to her half-sister. A boy, plain, with freckles, sandy hair, and light-blue eyes, was ejaculating in a lordly tone:

"I tell you, sister, you are not holding the reins right!—Oh, hullo!" he exclaimed as he saw Irene and Rosamund. "Won't you tell my sister that she is not to hold the reins like that? She is nagging at the pony's mouth all the time, and hurting him."

"Of course she is," said Irene, springing forward.

Hugh jumped from the governess-cart. Miss Frost also descended. Hugh and Irene had an earnest harangue on the subject of pony-driving, and Miss Frost, much relieved at such an unceremonious introduction, turned her attention to little Agnes.

"Agnes is tired, and has a headache, and would like me to take her into the house. May I?" she said, looking appealingly at Rosamund.

But Rosamund was not going to shirk her duty. These children were to be Irene's guests, and they must be immediately put into their right position. She turned, therefore, to her little friend and touched her on the arm.

"Irene," she said, "you ought to have a proper introduction to Agnes. This is Agnes Frost."

Little Agnes came shyly forward and looked straight up with her big dark eyes at Irene. She was a smaller girl, and if possible still more delicate-looking, but very pretty and interesting. Hugh, who had been having such an interesting debate with Irene, now stepped up to Agnes and flung his arm round her neck.

"She is tired, poor baby!" he said. "She wants to go in and go to sleep for an hour. You have a headache, haven't you, little un?"

"Yes," replied Agnes. "My head aches rather badly. It is the train—it always makes me feel sick."

"Then shall I take you into the house?" said Irene.

She forgot Hugh, to Hugh's own amazement. She took Agnes' tiny hand and led her toward the house. Miss Frost longed to follow; but Rosamund held her back.

"No, no. On no account go with them," she said. "Let Irene feel that she has got possession of the little one at once. You see how confidently Agnes gave her hand. That is the best possible sign. Let her take her to her room and see after her comforts."

Irene—who never before in all her life had any creature to look up to her, who was looked down upon with terror and shunned by her fellow-creatures, with the exception of Rosamund, who ruled her, although with the weapons of love—felt an altogether new sensation now as the little creature, not so old as herself, clung to her confidently.

"I shall be glad to lie down," said little Agnes. "Have you ever gone long journeys by train, and does your head ache?"

"No, I haven't gone long journeys by train; but I will take you to your room and draw down the blinds, and you can go to sleep."

"May I? That is what I want more than anything else. If I could sleep for half-an-hour I should feel better."

"You shall, of course," said Irene.

She walked slowly through the house, holding this small, dependent creature by the hand. Was she not her guest? She forgot all about poor Miss Frost, whose heart was devoured with jealousy; for little Agnes, in the olden times, had clung to her. Now she clung close to Irene.

"You are so nice," she said, "and so pretty! I am glad I am coming to spend the holidays with you."

"Are you?" said Irene, with a queer look.

James the footman saw them as they went upstairs; and Lady Jane stood at the drawing-room door, but made no sign.

Irene presently reached the small but very prettily arranged room which the little girl was to occupy.

"This room opens out of Frosty's," she said.

"Who is Frosty?" asked the child.

"My governess, of course, and your sister."

"Oh! but I'd rather sleep in a room opening out of yours. Can't I? Of course, I'm very fond of my dear sister Emily; but you are so fresh, and I think you will take care of me."

"There is a tiny room which you could have next to mine, and we could have the doors open, and I promise to be awfully careful of you, if you really like it best," said Irene, who felt more and more charmed at the dependence of this small creature.

"Yes, I know I'd like it best. But may I lie down here just for the present?"

"Of course you may."

Irene herself helped to remove Agnes's boots. She laid her on the bed and put the coverlet over her, and then rang the bell. One of the housemaids appeared.

"I want some tea," said Irene in a lofty tone, "for little Miss Agnes Frost. You can bring it up on a tray with cakes, and I can have some at the same time. And please arrange the pink bedroom opening out of mine for Miss Agnes to sleep in to-night. Do you hear? Do you understand?"

"Yes, miss, of course," said the girl, retiring in a great hurry in the utmost amazement; for over Irene's curious, expressive little face had come a new look—a look of protection, almost of motherhood.

She bent down and kissed little Agnes; and Agnes put her thin arms round her neck, and said, "Oh, you are so beautiful, and so—so kind to me! Of course, I love dear sister Emily; but she is old, and you are young. I want somebody young—somebody like you—to be kind to me, for I am such a timid little girl. Will you take care of me?"

"I vow I will," said Irene.

"Then you will hold my hand if I do drop asleep—for this is

such a big, strange house, and I may feel frightened?"

"No one shall frighten you while I am here," was Irene's answer.

The housemaid, the veritable Susan who had once spoken such harsh things to Irene, presently came in with the tea-tray. Irene herself poured out the tea and brought it to little Agnes, who drank it feverishly, and then lay down; but she was too tired and too ill from her journey to care to eat any cakes. Just as she was dropping off to sleep, Miss Frost put in an anxious face.

"Run away, Frosty; run away at once. She is my charge," said Irene; and Miss Frost, smothering the jealousy which could not but arise in her heart, left the room.

This was a position she had not expected. Nevertheless, there was no help for it.

"Now, I am going to munch cakes, and you shall sleep. Would you like me to tell you a story while you are dropping off to sleep?"

"If it isn't at all frightening—if it is nice."

"I will tell you about the little princess in Hans Andersen. My darling, my noble, my beloved Rosamund told it to me, and I will tell it to you. Now then, listen."

Irene began. She could tell that marvelous tale with all the grace and unction and passion which her genius inspired her with. Little Agnes listened and listened, and forgot her terrors. She clung closer and closer to her companion, and when the story came to an end her starry eyes were brimful of tears.

"Oh, that is very sweet!" said the little girl. "And now the little princess is one of the spirits of the air, and she has won something"—

"She has won her soul," said Irene in a strange, strangled sort of voice; for it occurred to her that, after all, the little princess might have a greater resemblance to herself than ever she had thought. For was she not fighting for her own soul all this time?

While little Agnes slept, Irene sat in the room by her side still and quiet. There were voices heard in the distance; the manly voice of Hughie, who was somewhat dictatorial, and was ordering people about, and telling this person or the other that they were doing things wrong, and was terrifying his sister by his manly ways. There was Rosamund's voice, who was quite delighted at the turn events had taken. There was Miss Frost's voice, anxious about Agnes, and quite sure that Irene must end by terrifying her. There was Rosamund again persuading and soothing, and doing all she could to allow the present order of things to take a natural course. But upstairs in the pretty little bedroom the child slept peacefully; and Irene looked at her and felt new sensations, new hopes, new desires struggling in her breast. She had loved Rosamund because she was so strong. She was beginning to love little Agnes because she was so weak. What a strange tangle the world was! What was happening to her? And why was that curious living thing within so satisfied, so happy, so sure of itself?

It was between six and seven o'clock when Agnes, neatly and tidily dressed, came downstairs, accompanied by Irene, who led her straight into the drawing room.

"This is Agnes Frost, mothery," said Irene; "and you are on no account to tire her. She is better now. Are you not, Agnes?"

"Yes, I am better," replied the little girl. "But who is this grand lady you are introducing me to?"

"This is my mother—Lady Jane."

"I never knew anybody called 'Lady' before."

"Well, my mother is Lady Jane—Lady Jane Ashleigh."

Little Agnes held out a timid hand.

"How do you do, dear? I hope you have got over the fatigue of your journey."

"Oh, yes, mothery, she is quite well now. Don't worry her," said Irene almost rudely. "I am going to take her out in the boat on the lake."

"Be sure you are very careful."

"I will be careful enough."

Just then Miss Frost came in.

"Agnes, I hear Irene wants to take you out in the boat. You are not to go."

"But she has promised," said little Agnes.

She raised confiding dark eyes to her new friend's face.

"You must trust me, Frosty. Don't be a perfect goose," said Irene; and taking Agnes' hand, they went down across the summer lawn to the place where the boat was moored. By-and-by Irene was seen by those who watched, gently rowing among the water-lilies, with little Agnes at the other end of the boat.

"What a beautiful girl you are!" little Agnes kept saying; "and how happy my sister ought to be, living always with you!"

"Don't ask her if she is happy for a day or two. I have given directions about your room. You shall sleep in the little pink room next to mine."

L. T. Meade

CHAPTER XIX

A SORT OF ANGEL

Irene pulled with swift, sure strokes across the summer lake. The lake was one of the great features of the place. It was a quarter of a mile wide, and half a mile in length, and had been carefully attended to by owner after owner for generations; so that groups of water-lilies grew here, and swans arched their proud white necks and spread out their feathered plumes. Little Agnes had never seen anything so lovely before, and when she bent forward and saw her own reflection in the water she gave a scream of childish pleasure.

"Oh, how happy sister Emily must be!" was her remark.

Again Irene made the strange answer, "Don't ask for a day or two."

Then little Agnes raised grave dark eyes to Irene's face.

"But any one would be happy with you," she said. "To look at you is such a comfort."

"Tell me about yourself," said Irene suddenly, shipping her oars, bending forward, and fixing her intensely bright eyes on the child.

She did not feel at all like a changeling now. That wild thing in her breast was still. She felt somewhat like a mother, somewhat like an ordinary little girl might feel towards a loved baby-sister, or even towards a doll. This new sense of protection had a marvelous effect upon her. She would not have minded if little Agnes had crept into her arms and laid her head on her breast.

"Tell me what you did before you came here," she said.

"But don't you know?" said Agnes. "Sister Emily has been living with you for a long time. She must have told you about me."

"I am ashamed to say I never asked her anything about you."

"I suppose that is because you are very thoughtful. You were determined—yes, determined—not to give her pain. She is always so sad when she thinks of us; but Hughie and I are not really unhappy. We don't mind things now."

"What do you mean by 'now'? Tell me—do tell me."

"Oh, we are at school. Hughie is at a pretty good school, although it is rather rough. He is learning hard. He is to be apprenticed to a trade some day. Dear sister Emily cannot afford to bring him up as a gentleman; but she is saving every penny of her money to put him into a really good trade. Perhaps he will be a bookbinder, or perhaps a cabinetmaker."

"But people of that sort are not gentry," said Irene. Then she colored and bit her lips.

Little Agnes had seen so much of the rough side of life that she was not at all offended.

"Sister Emily says that she could not afford to bring us up as a lady and gentleman, and so we are to be trained for something else. I think she is going to put me into a shop."

"Indeed she won't," said Irene fiercely, "for I won't let her."

There was a new tone in her voice which frightened little Agnes. She sank back among her soft cushions.

"You mustn't be angry with her, for she is the best sister in all the world. No one else would work so hard to support us. You know, when father and mother died there wasn't a penny-piece to keep us, and we were both very young; and if it hadn't been for Emily I might have been sent to one of those dreadful charity schools. But as it is, I am being taught, and now I am staying at this lovely place for the holidays, and I have met you, and I think you are a sort of angel."

Irene burst into a ringing laugh.

"You're the very first person who has ever called me that," she said. "Now look here, Agnes; there's just one thing I want to ask you."

"What is that?" asked little Agnes.

"Don't speak to the servants about me, nor even to your beloved Emily, nor much to Rosamund. You think certain things about me. Other people may not agree with you."

"I should like to fight them if they differed," said the little girl.

"Well, that's all right; you can fight them by-and-by if you like; but at present say nothing about me. I am your friend; it will depend on whether you keep silence or not whether I continue to be your friend. As long as I am your friend you are safe and happy here, so that is all right."

Little Agnes, never having heard anything about Irene except that she was her sister Emily's pupil, believed these words, and continued to look with a fascinated gaze at the white-throated swans, at the beautiful water-lilies, and at the calm reflection of the boat and their two selves in the water. She saw nothing whatever of the rapid stream in the centre of the lake, where poor Miss Carter had almost met her death, nor did she see any fierce or turbulent side to Irene's erratic nature.

By-and-by the bell sounded, and Irene exclaimed, "I declare it is time for us to go in. You are much too young to sit up to dinner. I will see that you are put to bed, and have something very nice for you to eat, and I will sit with you until you fall asleep."

"But you will want your own dinner," said little Agnes.

"My own dinner doesn't matter in the very least. I will have a snatch of something when I go downstairs. Now come along."

She began to ply her oars again, and in a minute or two they had landed, the boat had been moored, and the two children went up to the house.

Hughie was standing on the steps, blowing a loud whistle through his fingers.

"Hullo, Aggie!" he cried. "Why, you are looking as fresh as possible; and Miss Irene—the wonderful Miss Irene"—here he gave a mocking bow to Irene—"has taken you under her wing. I can tell you sister Emily is pretty jealous."

Irene looked at him with small favor.

"Will you please let us pass?" she said.

The boy made another sweeping bow, and Irene and little Agnes passed into the house. They went upstairs. Irene took her little friend to the pink room next to her own. Here all her things had been unpacked already by Miss Frost herself, who had now, however, vanished. Agnes, tired, happy, pleased with her new friend, fearing nothing, trusting all things, was soon got into bed, and Irene sat by her until she dropped asleep. Then she laid a light kiss on her forehead, closed the door softly, and went downstairs.

Dinner was a thing of the past. Hughie and Miss Frost were pacing about in one of the corridors. Irene ran into the drawing-room. Lady Jane was lying on one of the sofas, half-asleep. She started up when she saw her daughter, and said in a quiet tone, "You will want some dinner, won't you?"

"Yes; I have desired James to give me something. He is getting it ready."

"I will come and sit with you while you eat it," said Rosamund, who was also there, jumping up and tossing down the book she had been looking through somewhat restlessly.

The two girls moved off. Irene satisfied her appetite, and then Rosamund asked her to come with her into one of the greenhouses.

"Well," said Irene, her eyes sparkling, "I suppose you are satisfied with me to-night. I have behaved well to little Agnes, have I not?"

"In one sense you have behaved well enough; but you have quite forgotten one thing."

"I do hope you are not going to scold me, I feel so wonderfully virtuous. She is a dear little soul, and I have promised to take her under my protection—that is, if no one will interfere. But I see you mean to begin at once. It is exceedingly unkind of you. What is wrong now?"

"Only Miss Frost—poor Miss Frost! You seem to have taken the little sister quite away from her. She has not been able to speak to the little thing since she arrived, and she has done everything for her."

"It doesn't matter what Frosty has done in the past. I mean to do everything for little Agnes in the future—that is, if I am not bullied. If I am, I—What is it, Rosamund?"

"Dear Irene, I quite know what you feel. It is the first time you have found some one absolutely to trust you. Little Agnes trusts you; but you ought to remember that she is Miss Frost's little sister. You ought not to hurt her feelings. You ought to let Miss Frost do something for her, too. If you had been supporting somebody very precious and very dear for a great many years, and then quite a fresh person came along and took that treasure from you, how would you feel?"

"I'm sure I don't know. I can't understand the position. I only know that I like little Agnes, and as long as she is left with me I shall be good to her. The best possible thing for Frosty and yourself and that horrid, tiresome boy to do is to go away, I'll look after little Agnes."

"You were very sweet to her to-day, I will admit that; but what I want to say is, do try and remember that Miss Frost will want to see something of her too. Don't let Miss Frost become too jealous, for she is devoted to her little sister."

"Well, I hate the boy," said Irene. "He was so rude when we came off the lake, and he whistled in such a defiant way. He isn't one bit a gentleman. Little Agnes told me that he was going to be a sort of tradesman. We oughtn't to have those people coming to the house. You shouldn't have insisted on my inviting them; you really shouldn't, Rosamund."

"I thought you were quite above that sort of thing," said Rosamund in a lofty tone. "But never mind. Do what you wish; only remember that both the boy and girl are your guests, and that I am going away next week."

Irene suddenly felt that Rosamund, much as she adored her, was a little too dictatorial that evening. She had expected great praise for her conduct, instead of which she had been blamed. She ran out into the cool night air, notwithstanding the expostulations of her mother, and came in late, feeling fagged and wearied. She did not invite Rosamund, as was her custom, to come to her bedroom; but she went there alone, locking the outer door, and then softly opening the door between herself and the new treasure she had found. Yes, little Agnes was a treasure. She was something more precious than gold. She was like a doll of the most beautiful order.

Now, Irene had always despised dolls; but this living doll, with the pink cheeks, and the black eyelashes, and the soft hair, and the sweet little face, was altogether a different matter. The little one stirred in her sleep and breathed a name softly. Irene bent to listen—the name was her own.

"Irene darling!" murmured little Agnes.

"Oh, she is a pet! I am so glad she has come! I'd almost die for her!" thought the girl.

She went back to her own room after gazing once again at the sweet little face. That night, for the first time for years, Irene deliberately dropped on her knees and uttered a prayer full of thankfulness to God. "I thank Thee, great good God, for having given me a darling little girl to protect and love. Please don't allow Frosty to be jealous, and please let her stay with me, for she is just the person to quiet that horrid living thing inside me," whispered the child. Then she got into bed and fell fast asleep.

She was awakened by cries before morning dawned. In a moment she started up, sprang out of bed, and rushed into the next room. Little Agnes was sitting up in her bed, puzzled and terrified.

"Where am I? Oh, what has happened?"

"Are you frightened, darling?" said Irene. "Are you really frightened? Would you like to come into my bed? Have you had a bad dream?"

"I have. I thought I was at school, and that Mrs. Treadgold, one of our mistresses, had beaten me. I fancied that she was beating me hard, and that made me wake. Now I remember that I am with you. Oh, yes, I should like to come into your bed."

"Then you shall come at once," said Irene.

She lifted the little girl out. She herself felt quite old and motherly beside the little one. During the remainder of the

L. T. Meade

night they slept in each other's arms, and much of the hardness and the wildness of Irene's nature melted away during that sleep, and some of that motherhood which is the most blessed gift God can give to a girl visited her.

She herself insisted on helping Agnes to dress in the morning, and then they went down to breakfast hand in hand.

CHAPTER XX

A SORT OF WITCH

Hughie was a dictatorial, troublesome sort of boy; but Rosamund took him in hand from the first, and kept him somewhat in order. Miss Frost, looking very patient, followed her brother and sister and Irene about. Once little Agnes was all alone in a bower, where she was waiting for Irene to come to her. This was Rosamund's opportunity. She went straight up to the child, took one of her hands, and sat down near her.

"I am so glad, Agnes," she said, "that you love Irene. But now I want to say something to you."

"I love you, too," said little Agnes, who was the gentlest and most affectionate creature under the sun.

"And don't you love your own dear sister Emily?"

"Oh, of course I do! I love her very much indeed."

"Then I wish you would go and tell her so, for she is sitting not far away crying very bitterly."

"Crying?" said little Agnes.

"Yes—because you haven't been with her at all to-day, and hardly yesterday; she can't make out what it means, and it troubles her a good deal. Do go and put your arms round her neck, and tell her that although you love Irene, you can never love any one like you do her."

"But I think," said little Agnes, who was the soul of truth, "that I do love Irene quite as much as I love Emily."

"Then you oughtn't to, for Miss Frost is your own sister, and she has done so much for you—far more than you can in the least understand at present."

"Anyhow, I do love her very much, and I'll tell her so," said the little girl.

She flew away from Rosamund, who sat down on the seat which Agnes had occupied. She had not been there more than a minute or two before Irene, carrying a basket of fruit in her hand, entered in great excitement.

"Where is Agnes? Where is my dear little pet? Oh, you are there, Rosamund!"

"Yes, Irene, and I hope you are glad to see me."

"Of course I am, Rosamund. I am always that. But where is my little Agnes? I want her to have some of these ripe plums. She is so fond of plums."

"Well, she oughtn't to have any more, for she ate too many yesterday, and Miss Frost says they don't agree with her."

"As if Frosty knew anything about the matter! I am the person who is going to take care of Agnes in the future. I have settled all that with myself. As to mother, she will do as

I wish. I am going to adopt Agnes; I call her my adopted child."

"But that is rather ridiculous, isn't it, Irene, seeing that you are almost the same age?"

"There are two years between us; but then, Agnes is so very small, so *petite* in every way, and so—so sweet and so defenseless."

"I always thought you did not care for defenseless people, nor for weak people, nor timid people."

"Oh, I like her sort. You see, she believed in me from the first."

"I hope she always will," said Rosamund.

"Well, where is she now?"

"She has gone to talk to her sister. You cannot expect her to give up all her time to you."

"But indeed that is just what I do. What can she have in common with that tiresome, frowzy old Frosty?"

"Only she happens to be her sister, and that tiresome, frowzy old Frosty, as you call her, has looked after her since she was a little child, when her mother died."

"Oh, yes, I've heard all that story. I suppose it's very noble; but, all the same, little Agnes is fonder of me."

"You have no right to steal her heart from Miss Frost."

"Rosamund, I don't know what to make of you. You always

have a great influence over me; but what is the matter now? Do you want to take Agnes away from me? If you wish to, you may; but I shall follow, for I don't intend to give her up, and nobody living will make me. I am sure you can do what you like with that detestable Hugh, and Frosty can go for her holidays. It would be a very good idea. Agnes and I would be quite happy at The Follies, with dear mother, of course, to take care of us."

Just at that moment there came a whoop and a spring, and Hughie, his red face redder than ever, his freckles more marked, his carroty hair sticking up all over his head, and his light-blue eyes wearing a most mischievous expression, entered the little arbor and sat down at one side of Irene.

"I say," he remarked, "I want to ask you a direct question."

"What is that?" she said, moving slightly away from him.

He edged a little nearer.

"Is it true that you gave sister Emily horrid live things that curled themselves up into so-called pills, and she swallowed them and nearly died afterward? Is it true—tell me?"

"It's quite true," said Irene, all the dancing wickedness coming to the front at once, and her eyes blazing with anger.

"Then you are a really wicked girl. You might have been had up by the police and put into prison."

"And what if I had, you wicked boy—for you are about the wickedest and rudest boy I have ever come across? Much do I care! I wanted her to go, and I thought that would be a good way to get rid of her."

"Oh, that's all right!" said Hugh. "I'll just go and tell Agnes. I'll tell her that you'll do things of that sort to her, that you are a sort of witch, and will show your true colors before long. Now, what is the matter?"

"You sha'n't tell her. You daren't!" said Irene.

She caught both his hands as though in a vise. He was amazed at their strength, also at the beautiful, extraordinary passion of her face. Rosamund started up to interfere.

"Come, children," she said, "don't quarrel. Hughie, you do extremely wrong to speak in that tone to Irene. Come and have a walk with me. You know I am going away to-morrow, and I wouldn't have asked Irene to invite you both to this beautiful house, and to give you such a splendid holiday, if I hadn't thought you were going to be quite good. Ah! here comes Agnes."

Agnes was seen flying across the lawn. She was wearing a pretty white dress, and her whole dainty little figure, with her light hair flying wildly behind her, made her a most charming little picture. She dashed up to Irene, flung her arms round her neck, and kissed her passionately.

"Oh," she said, "it seemed hours while I was away from you! I was with Emily, and Emily says that perhaps I had better not eat plums—at least not more than one or two."

"Then I'll pick out the ripest in the basket for you," said Irene, her voice trembling.

"You take care there are no—no live things"—

"Hush, Hughie! Come with me," said Rosamund; and she pulled the reluctant boy out of the summer-house.

"Now, Hughie," she said when she had got him quite by herself, "I want to know, in the first instance, exactly how old you are."

"I was fourteen my last birthday," he said, drawing himself up to his full height.

"You suppose yourself to be a good bit of a man, don't you?"

"Well, I'm not far from being a man, am I, Rosamund? You don't mind my calling you Rosamund, do you?"

"You may call me anything in the world you please."

"Well, I'll call you Rosamund, because all the rest of the people here do; but by-and-by perhaps I shall be behind a counter, and you will come in and ask for stationery—I want particularly to go into a stationer's shop—or any other article you fancy, and I'll have to say, 'Yes, miss.' That is, unless you're married. You'll be much too grand to notice me in those days, won't you, Rosamund?"

Rosamund turned and looked calmly at him.

"Hugh," she said, "I'll never be too grand to take notice of you if you turn out the sort of boy I expect you to be."

"And what is that?" he asked, touched and astonished at her words.

"Well, now, I want you to undertake a rather difficult office."

"Oh, I say, and these are holidays!" grumbled the boy.

"Nevertheless, even in holidays a true boy, who means to be a true man, will act according to the best of his abilities; and what I want you to do now is to help and not hinder me with regard to Irene."

"That horrid, spiteful, handsome little witch?" said the boy.

"You admit that she is handsome?"

"I should rather think so. I never saw such eyes or such a face. But she's a horrid little thing for all that. Last night I was in the pantry, and James told me a lot of things about her; how she used to get wasps to sting him, and how she frightened away such a lot of servants from the place with leeches and toads, and all sorts of horrors. He said he didn't believe she was a girl at all, but that she was a sort of half-witch; and she is having that effect now upon our dear little Agnes, for Agnes doesn't care a bit for any one but her. She likes to spend all her time with her. She even insists on sleeping in her bed at night, and poor old Emily never gets a sight of Agnes, nor do I; and if it weren't for you I don't know where we'd be."

"Well, I'm leaving to-morrow," said Rosamund; "and it is just because I am leaving—and I am forced to go—that I intend to put a trust in you. I intend to tell you all about Irene—there is no other way to manage a boy like you; but I intend to tell you in such a way that you must give me your word of honor you will never repeat what I say."

"You have a queer way of talking," replied the lad, "and you do look wonderfully handsome, and unlike any other girl I ever saw. Little Aggie is a poor sort, you know. She is very sweet and pretty, and gentle and easily influenced."

"She is a dear little soul," said Rosamund, "and I don't wonder that you and your sister love her so much."

"Of course we love her; that is just what I say to Em. Of course we love her, and I don't think it is right of Emily to spend all her time crying. Her eyes are as red as anything. I never saw anything like it; and whenever she talks to me it is to say something of the way Agnes has forsaken her; and Agnes is quite unsuspicious."

"That is just it, and I want her to be unsuspicious. You must be kind to poor Frosty—forgive me, we always call her Frosty; but at the same time she must exercise the wonderful and healing influence she possesses over Irene."

"What do you mean by that?"

"You see, Irene is a very fine character"—

Hugh whistled.

"A fine character!" he said. "What about the toad in the bread-pan? What about the horrid live things she made poor dear Emily swallow? If Em had died, she'd have been had up for murder."

"It was a cruel and wicked thing to do; but I am sure she would never do it now—that is, unless you goaded her to it. You are in the mood to torment her to do wrong things. It is exceedingly wicked of you, and I tell you plainly I don't know what I shall do if all my hard work of the whole summer will be overthrown, unless you make me a solemn promise before I leave."

"Well, it is good of you to trust me," said Hughie, softening in spite of himself, for such a bold, handsome, independent girl as Rosamund had never addressed him in such a way before; and, like all lads, he was susceptible to a girl's influence.

"I am at a horrid common school," he grumbled. "All the fellows there say horrid common things; but it is the best that poor old Em can afford, and I ought to be content. Some day I'll be a tradesman—not a gentleman. But now Aggie and I are both staying here with gentry of the first class in every way, and you say you'll be my friend even if I am a tradesman?"

"My hand on it," said Rosamund suddenly; and she held out her little white hand, which the boy grasped heartily.

"Now then," she continued, "I am going to tell you my story."

She did tell it, very simply, describing her influence from the very first over Irene, and contriving to put Irene's character into altogether a new light to the boy.

"There is the making of a splendid woman in her," she said; "but if you taunt her now you will undo all the good that I have done. Instead of doing this, suppose you take my place when I am away, and help Frosty not to be jealous, and help Irene and Agnes to enjoy themselves. Just show Irene that you are not a scrap afraid of her; but at the same time do not rouse her passions. Will you do this, and for my sake? If so, I do really believe all will be well."

Hughie was amazed at his own sensations.

"I declare," he said, "you'd turn any fellow into a brick. If there were more girls like you in the world I shouldn't be surprised if there were a lot of good men too; and the world could be oiled on all its hinges, so to speak, so that it wouldn't creak and jump and fret one at every turn as it seems to have an unpleasant habit of doing at the present moment."

"Will you promise, Hughie? I think you are the sort of boy who would keep your word at any and all times."

Hughie mumbled something that Rosamund took for a promise. In truth, he could not raise his eyes to her face, for they were full of tears, which he was ashamed to show.

"I wish you'd let me go away all by myself for a minute. I'll come back before lunch," he said. "You make a fellow feel like a gentleman, and that's the truth of it."

Then he dashed out of sight among the flowers.

Rosamund's last day at The Follies was spent in trying to soothe all parties. She tried to make Miss Frost rather less miserable. Hughie kept a good deal out of sight. Irene was so absorbed with Agnes—her new toy, as the servants called the little girl—that she did not even remember that Rosamund was to leave on the following day.

But when the next morning came, and she saw the carriage arrive at the door, and perceived Rosamund's trunks being put on the roof, she suddenly woke to the fact that the strong influence of her life during the last couple of months had come to a complete end; that Rosamund, the strong, the vivacious, the daring, the noble, was leaving her. All in a minute even little Agnes seemed distasteful to the excited girl. She flew up to Rosamund's side and flung her arms round her neck.

"Oh, you are going! You are going, and what is to become of me without you?"

Rosamund drew her into a little room leading out of the hall.

"Just one word, Irene," she said. "I know you are very fond

of Agnes, and you are behaving splendidly to her; but you will think of Miss Frost and of Hughie. You will write to me once or twice a week, and afterward, you know, it is settled that you and I are both to meet at the Merrimans', where we are to spend one term together."

"Oh, dear, how am I to endure that?"

"You will endure it when I give you a piece of news. It is arranged that little Agnes comes also, and"—

"Oh, have you settled that, you darling?"

"Partly. And Miss Frost comes, too, as they want another governess; and your dear mother, who needs change, will spend the time with one of her sisters in Scotland. Now you know exactly what is before you, and I must be off. I trust you, Irene. You won't disappoint me? If I thought you could, I don't really know what would become of me."

CHAPTER XXI

A REAL ROUSING FRIGHT

Wonderful to relate, the holidays passed smoothly enough. Hughie was the sort of boy to be touched by Rosamund's words. No one had before appealed to him just in Rosamund's way. He found, too, considerable pleasure and interest on his own account at The Follies, for Lady Jane was singularly kind to him, and gave him a pony to ride, and he was permitted the rare indulgence of going with the game-keeper into the woods to take his first lesson in partridge-shooting; but this came later on.

Meanwhile Miss Frost made a great effort to recover her self-control; but such an agony of jealousy had taken possession of the poor lady that she could scarcely bear to be in the society either of her pupil or her little sister. Irene exercised more and more influence over Agnes, and for a long time that influence was altogether for good. When the child asked simple questions Irene replied simply. She felt ashamed of her own want of knowledge on many particulars. She went regularly to church twice every Sunday because little Agnes thought that no living person could do otherwise. She did not at all want to go, and she trembled as much as ever when the choir sang, and when the place became hushed and people called themselves "miserable sinners," and looked so unconcerned and so well-dressed. But for the sake of Agnes she restrained herself, for Agnes' little, pale, calm face appeared not to think at all about the matter.

Nevertheless, it was scarcely possible that such a cloudless state of things could continue. As to Hughie, he and Irene were more or less neutral, neither speaking much to the other. They were both absolutely different, but both were absolutely without fear.

There came a day, however, when Irene took it into her wild little head that Hughie needed a lesson to be taught him.

"I know by his looks," she thought, "that he hates my loving Agnes so much."

Accordingly, she made up her mind to administer a lesson, and to make it as stiff a piece of terrorism as she could devise.

"He thinks he knows a great deal; but I'll teach him!" thought the girl.

Some of her old wicked spirit had come back to her. She had no longer any lessons to employ her time; she had no longer Rosamund's wholesome influence—Rosamund who was in Switzerland, and whose letters, delightful as they were, could not take the place of her constant presence.

The day was a sultry one toward the end of August. Miss Frost, pale and dejected, was seated in one of the arbors. She was doing some needlework, and little Agnes was sitting on a low stool at her sister's feet. Miss Frost looked up when Irene suddenly entered.

"I wonder," she said, "if you and Agnes would go to town for me after lunch? Mother says you may have the pony-trap and drive in. I want you to get"—

She produced a list of all sorts of materials, including a new doll for Agnes.

"I want Agnes to have a doll, and a cradle to put it in at night, and she shall make the clothes for it. Between you and me, we can show her how. Would you like it, Agnes darling?"

"Oh, shouldn't I just love it!" said little Agnes. "Fancy my being your baby, and then having a baby of my own! Oh, it seems altogether too beautiful! Isn't she sweet, Emily?"

Miss Frost looked with her nervous eyes at her pupil. Irene's own bright eyes looked back in reply. They were full of dancing mischief.

"Mothery will give you some money to buy the necessary things," she said. "I have spoken to her about it; indeed, she is going with you, and lunch is to be a quarter of an hour earlier."

"But would you—would you," said Miss Frost, who was trembling all over with delight at the thought of having her beloved little sister all to herself for a whole afternoon— "wouldn't you like to keep Agnes? I would buy the things for her."

She felt herself very noble as she made this remark.

"No," said Irene, shaking her head. "No; I want Agnes to choose her own doll. You can have a boy-dolly or a girl-dolly," she said, "just as you please. There is a beautiful shop at Dartford, in the High Street, where you can buy everything you want. It is called Millar's. You know all about it, don't you, Frosty? Now, there is the luncheon-bell."

The luncheon-bell sounded. Miss Frost, little Agnes, Irene, and the rest of the party all assembled in the cool dining-room.

Soon after lunch, Lady Jane, Agnes, and Miss Frost started for Dartford, and Irene turned and faced Hughie.

"Hughie," she said, "would you like to come for a row on the lake with me?"

"If you wish," he replied.

He had kept his promise to Rosamund so far. He had made no further inquiries with regard to Irene. He had tried, as he expressed it, to wash his hands of her. He did not like her. He felt that he never could like her. There was something to him repugnant about her. He had a kind of uncanny feeling that she was a sort of changeling; that she could do extra-ordinary, defiant, and marvelous things. Now, as she looked full up at him, trying to steady her face, and trying to look as like an ordinary girl as possible, he endeavored to conceal a queer sort of fear which stole suddenly over his heart. He remembered the old stories; the servants who shrank from her, the wild creatures that seemed to be her constant companions, and the tricks she was capable of playing on any one.

"I will go with you, of course," he said. "Do you want me to row?"

"No; I want you to sit in the stern and steer. Will you come? Just wait a minute. I'll be ready in no time."

She flew upstairs, and came down in the obnoxious red dress, which she had not worn for such a long time. It made a queer change in her, giving her a more elf-like appearance than usual.

"Why do you wear that? It isn't pretty," said Hughie.

"Never you mind whether it is pretty or not," retorted Irene.

"Well, I'll try not; but a fellow must make remarks. You know, you look ripping in your white dresses, and that silk thing you wear in the evening; but I don't like that."

"Don't you? Well, I do. Anyhow, I'm going to wear it to-day while we are having our fun on the lake. It's just a perfect day for the lake. Do you know, there's a storm coming on."

As Irene spoke she fixed her bright eyes on the sky. It was blue over the house; but in the distance, coming rapidly nearer and nearer, was a terrible black cloud—a cloud almost as black as ink—and already there were murmurs in the trees and cawings among the birds, the breeze growing stronger and stronger—the prelude to a great agitation of nature.

"I suppose we won't go on the lake to get drowned," said Hughie. "That is a thunder-cloud."

"Never mind; it will be all the greater fun. I am in my red dress, and you can put on any shabby clothes you happen to have. If you are going to be a counter-jumper you must have got some very shabby things."

"Why do you speak to me in that tone?" said Hughie.

"Oh, I don't know. I didn't mean anything. You can put on

anything you like, and you needn't come if you don't want to; but I thought you were a plucky sort of chap."

"You may be quite sure I am. Of course I will come with you. Let us run down to the boat-house. Perhaps," continued Hughie, struggling with the promise he had made to Rosamund, "the storm may go off in another direction, and we sha'n't have it."

"I see you are awfully afraid of it, and it mayn't come here at all," said Irene, who knew perfectly well that it would, for the cloud was coming more and more in the direction of the house each moment.

In a very short time the two children were in the boat, Irene taking both the oars, and giving Hughie simple directions to steer straight for the stream in the middle of the lake.

"Now I will give him a real rousing fright," she said to herself. "After that perhaps he will be my slave, the same as Carter was. Anyhow, I have a crow to pluck with him; and the storm, and my knowledge of the water, and his absolute ignorance will enable me to win the day."

Aloud, she said in a gentle voice, "Perhaps you'd like to take the oars?"

"I will if you like," said Hughie; "but the fact is, I'm not very good at rowing. I have never been much in a boat."

"Ah! I thought as much. But I can teach you. Come and sit here."

They had just entered the stream, which made the lake dangerous even on a calm day. Hughie stumbled to his feet; Irene sat in the stern, took the ropes, and skillfully guided the

L. T. Meade

boat into the centre of the stream. It began to rock tremendously.

"Now pull! Pull hard!" she said to the boy.

Just then a blinding flash of lightning came across their faces.

"Oh!" said Hughie, "the storm is on us. It will rain in a few minutes. Hadn't we better get back?"

"What a coward you are!" said Irene. "It is the most awful fun to be out on the lake in a storm like this. Ah! do you hear that growl?"

"But I can't manage the boat a bit."

"I thought all boys could manage boats. You don't expect a girl to do it—a girl out in the midst of a storm of this sort? Besides, I must put up my umbrella or I shall be soaked."

"But I told you it would rain. You shouldn't have come out," said Hughie, who felt more annoyed, distressed, and angry than he had ever felt in his life before. He felt that suddenly the boat was quite unmanageable, that it was rocking and racing and taking them he did not know where.

All of a sudden Irene sprang to her feet.

"Get back into the stern," she said. "Sit quite still, and let me take the oars. I wanted to see if you could row. I see you can't. There is another flash of lightning. Don't be frightened. I know you are; but try to keep it under. I have something to say to you."

She seated herself, and the two children faced each other.

The flash of lightning was followed by a crashing peal of thunder. The trees bowed low to meet the gale; the frightened birds, the swans and others, took shelter where they could best find it; but as yet there was not a drop of rain.

"How hot it is!" said Irene. "Let us fly down the stream."

"What do you mean by that?" said Hughie, whose freckled face was deadly white.

"I will tell you if you like; but don't speak."

He looked at her with fascinated eyes. In her red dress, with her witch-like face and glancing, dancing, naughty eyes, she became to him for the moment an object of absolute terror. Was this the gentle and exceedingly pretty girl whom little Agnes so adored? He was alone with her, and they were, so to speak, flying through the water, although she scarcely touched the oars, allowing them to lie almost idle by her side.

Suddenly she shipped them and bent toward him.

"We needn't row any more," she said. "We are in the current. The current will take us. Hughie, can you swim?"

"I don't know anything about swimming," he said.

"Well, that is rather bad for you; for in about five minutes of this sort of thing we go right down the cascade at the end of the lake and among the breakers. The boat will be upset, and you will have to fight for your life, unless I choose to save you. I could save you, for I have perfect control of myself in the water."

"But you don't mean to say you are going to do anything of

L. T. Meade

that sort! Can't we get into the calmer part of the lake? I don't understand you," said Hughie.

"But I understand you. You don't like me, and I don't like you. From the very first you have been disagreeable. I like your little sister, but you don't want me to like her."

"Well, I think you are a bit rough on old Em," was Hughie's remark.

"What a flash that was!" said Irene; and her eyes danced with cruel pleasure. "Ah! here comes the rain."

A terrific hail-shower drenched the two children as they sat within the rocking boat. For the first time in her life Irene was really slightly frightened. Had she dared too much? Even she might not be able to get the boat out of the current just at present; and if she did not, and they really got among the breakers and over the cascade in the present storm, it might be beyond her power to save Hughie. As to herself, she was not at all afraid. She felt she could swim through anything and over anything; but she was not certain that she could swim and support a boy so big and strong as Hughie.

Then there rose before her vision the face of Rosamund— Rosamund's face with its noble expression, its clear, steadfast, dark eyes—Rosamund with her ringing voice. Oh, what influence for good she had exercised over Irene's wild, worthless, almost terrible life, and yet she was disobeying all her precepts now, and frightening poor Hughie almost to death!

"I tell you what it is," she said in a husky voice; "we will both try to get out of this current if you will make me a promise."

"It seems to me that I am spending my whole life in making promises," said Hughie. "But I will make any promise if that will help you now. Oh, what a flash that was! I expect we shall both be struck by the lightning."

"I suppose that doesn't matter. I suppose you are not afraid to die, are you?"

"I haven't thought of it," said the boy. "People of fourteen don't think much about dying, do they? But I don't think I'd be specially afraid. It might be a sort of relief to poor old Em to have only one of us to keep. But for you there is your mother and little Agnes."

"Yes; I wouldn't like to die on account of little Agnes," replied Irene very gravely. "I love her just as though she were my own little child."

"Well, I am her brother. I suppose you ought to be pleasant to me because I happen to be her brother, and Emily happens to be her sister," retorted the lad.

"That is true enough. I will tell you why I did this. I brought you out into the current to test your courage. If I do nothing, if we both sit still as we are now, in all probability you will be drowned; but if you will exert yourself and help me with all your might and main, then I will respect you as a truly courageous person, and perhaps we'll be better friends than we have hitherto been."

"What do you want me to do? I will do anything," said the boy.

"Well, look here. I will take one oar and you take the other, and we must get out of this current whatever happens. As soon as we are out of it we are safe. Oh, never mind the lightning, and don't listen to the thunder."

"It almost blinds me," said Hughie, passing his hand across his eyes as he spoke, dazzled by the vividness of the ever-increasing storm. Irene gave him strict directions.

"You are strong," she said. "When you see me pull, you must pull, too, and you must be very quick, for the nearer we get to the cascade the swifter runs the current. On a calm day I could save you, there wouldn't be a bit of fear; but on a rough day, in a storm like this, I mightn't be able to manage it. Now then, a strong pull, and a pull all together!"

The boy obeyed her directions. Whatever she might have thought of him a minute ago, he was indeed no coward. He pulled with all his might and main. Irene did likewise, and in a few minutes' time they were out of the dangerous current, in smooth water. But it was a close shave, and the girl's hands trembled and for a minute she dropped her oar.

"Never mind," she said to Hughie.

"But you look as white as death, just as though you would faint. Did that last flash touch your hair? It seemed to me that it was almost hot on my cheeks."

"No, it wasn't that; and the storm is going off," said Irene. "Somehow I am ashamed of myself. I oughtn't to have been so mean."

"Please tell me."

"I have tested you, and you are brave. You are not a coward like poor Carter."

"Who is Carter?"

"A governess I once had. I took her on to the lake, and into the central current, and she was in such terror! I wanted her to go away, and I wouldn't get out of the current, however hard she implored. But I promised to save her when we got among the breakers if only she would go afterward. She promised, and I did save her, and she is all right now; and Frosty—your dear Emily, I mean—and she are the best of friends. And I am friendly with her, too. I have been much better lately—much better since dear Rosamund came—only somehow I felt that you defied me, and I wanted to test you. I have tested you, and I respect you, for you weren't really frightened that time, and you did row all right. What a strong arm you have! I wish I had an arm like that."

Hughie colored with absolute pleasure.

"You are a plucky un," he said; "but I didn't know that you really wanted to drown me."

"Of course I didn't want to drown you. I knew a storm was coming on, and that it would be very rough in the current to-day, and I wanted to test you; and you have proved worthy of the test, and we are in safe water now. The storm is dying away, too; and shall it be *pax*? Shall we be friends for the remainder of your stay at The Follies?"

"I think you are a splendid girl, although you are quite the queerest I ever came across," said the boy.

"And you are awfully plucky. Now, I tell you what it is. Mothery and I will do our best to make you a gentleman by and by. You won't be too proud if mother and I help Frosty—your Emily, as you call her—to make you into something better than a counter-jumper?"

"Would you indeed?" he asked, his eyes glowing, and the

L. T. Meade

color coming into his cheeks. "You know, I always hated the thought of it, for my people were gentry. My mother was such a refined woman, something like sweet little Agnes, and it always cut me to the very heart to think that I was going down in the social scale."

"You sha'n't," said Irene. And now the pair, dripping wet, landed at the little landing-stage.

Hughie helped Irene to put the boat into the boat-house, and then they stood there together until the storm died away, and the rain had ceased, and the birds were singing once more. Then they silently shook hands each with the other, without uttering a word.

CHAPTER XXII

NOT A COUNTER-JUMPER

The holidays came to an end on the whole satisfactorily. Irene was by no means perfect; even Agnes showed signs of being spoiled owing to the new *regime*. Hughie expressed a strong desire to be back at school. Miss Frost never ceased to watch the two, and the struggle within her breast did not die out. Lady Jane alone was thankful for the marked improvement in her child. Not that she saw very much of Irene, for Irene and Agnes were together almost all day long; Agnes the petted darling of the elder girl, Irene yielding to her every whim, delighting in the daring spirit which slowly but surely began to awaken in the little one. Nevertheless, the servants were unmolested, Miss Frost had a peaceful time, Lady Jane began to breathe freely, and even Hughie turned to other occupations and more or less forgot Irene and his little sister. He had never told any one of that awful time which he had spent with Irene in the boat. That secret he kept confined within his own breast; but he never could forget it; the moment when his young manhood seemed to forsake him, when the spirit of cowardice arose before him, and he felt certain that he should die; the longing which arose to his lips to implore Irene at any cost to save him; the way he kept back the words. Then her test and his acceptance of it, the victory he had really won over her, the knowledge that in the

L. T. Meade

future she would treat him with respect.

Irene, with all her faults, was true to her word, and one day just when the long summer holidays were coming to an end, and when every one was talking and thinking again of school life and school affairs, and its joys and sorrows, Irene went and sat down on a low stool by her mother's side.

"You are sending me next week to the Merrimans'," she said. "I don't at all know whether I shall be able to endure it. You think me greatly improved, but I don't know that I am improved. Be that as it may, however, I want to ask you a great favor, mothery."

"What is that, my darling?" asked Lady Jane.

"You, of course, mean to go away. Rosamund said that you would. She said you would take a rest, and forget all the worries that your naughty, naughty child has given you all these years. You will do that, won't you, mothery darling?"

"Yes, I will go away," said Lady Jane. "I have arranged it. But what is your request, Irene?"

"Well, it has something to do with Hughie. You know about Miss Frost?"

"I know she is an excellent creature."

"She is; and you know how fond I am of little Agnes."

"No wonder. She is a sweet little soul," said Lady Jane; "although, sometimes, Irene"—

"Please don't!" said Irene, putting her hand to her mother's lips. "I have made a resolution. Agnes is to be my child in the future. She is to live with me always and always, mother. I couldn't do without her. She is my doll, my baby, my plaything—the creature that keeps me human. With Rosamund on one side and Agnes on the other, I can be good, mothery. But if you were to take either or both of them away, I should be worse than ever. Miss Frost must give Agnes up to me."

"I don't think she will be able to stand that. I don't see how you can expect it."

"Well, I do expect it, and I don't mean to discuss the point now. Agnes comes with me, does she not, to Mrs. Merriman's school?"

"She does. Rosamund's mother is paying for her during this term."

"And Miss Frost goes, too?"

"Yes, dear, certainly."

"Well, now, there is Hughie. Miss Frost says that she cannot give him the education sufficient to make a gentleman of him. But, mother, he is a nice boy—he is, really."

"He is quite a plain boy," said Lady Jane—"very different from his little sister—a little rough, I call him."

"But he is quite nice, all the same. Anyhow, mother, I wish it—I want him to be made a gentleman. I want him to be sufficiently educated, and I want us to help Miss Frost. We needn't take all the burden off her shoulders, for I know you pay her very well indeed; but I want him to be left at school until he is old enough to take up some profession. I don't know what he would like. I'll run and ask him now; may I?"

"But, first of all, let me consider. Why should I have this on me? I have—although you never seem to remember it, you naughty little Irene—a great many expenses."

"Yes, but you are rich, and I am your only child. I want Hughie, just because he is Agnes's brother, to be a gentleman. Agnes's brother can't be a counter-jumper, can he, mothery?"

"What a horrid expression! Where did you learn it, Irene?"

"Oh, I picked it up from one of the servants; her cousin was a counter-jumper. She always made me laugh when she spoke about it. She described how he doled out yards of ribbon, and she said that his figure was all gone to nothing, but he was very genteel-looking. I used to make her tell me about him, because I used to frighten her with spiders and wasps if she didn't. But I don't do that sort of thing now. I'll take to it again, though, if you don't do what I wish."

"Then I am sure I will do what you wish, although I am rather puzzled."

"Well, we'll settle it, and at once," said Irene.

She ran out of the room and met Miss Frost, who was crossing the hall.

"Frosty," said the little girl, going up to her governess, "I want to ask you a question. How much money do you pay a year for Hughie's schooling?"

Miss Frost turned painfully red.

"That is scarcely your affair, is it, Irene?" she said.

"I am not naughty, really; I want to know for a most serious, important reason. Do you pay much, or do you pay little?"

"I pay what is really very little. I pay fifty pounds a year. It is not a good school, but it is the best I can afford. It is a commercial school. I trust to get Hughie a place in a shop when he is sixteen—that is, in two years' time. I think I can manage his school for the present."

"Thank you, Miss Frost. That is all I need."

Irene then went out, and whistling in a boyish fashion, presently brought Hughie to her side. He was quite at home with her now, and walked willingly along the gravel path listening as she spoke to him.

"Hughie, you know the promise I made to you?"

"Yes, I know," he said, his eyes dancing. "I am to be a gentleman. You said so."

"You are; but I must know all about it. Your sister pays fifty pounds a year to keep you at school."

"It's an awfully low sort of place," said the boy. "I mean the fellows there aren't gentlemen, and it is frightfully difficult to be a gentleman when no one else is."

"Well, it ought not to be. A gentleman ought to be a gentleman through everything," said Irene. "However, that is not the point. What profession would you like best if, supposing you were rich, you could have your choice?"

"I'd like best in all the world," said Hughie, "to be educated to become a lawyer—I mean a barrister. But there's no chance of that. I like arguing and disputing, and proving that other people are wrong, more than anything else in the world."

"You are not particularly amiable, Hughie," said Irene, with a laugh; "but I think I understand."

"Well, that is all right. Have you anything more to say?"

"Not just at present, only I want to speak to mother."

Lady Jane was sitting just where Irene had left her. Irene went and laid her head on her mother's lap.

"Frosty pays fifty pounds a year," she said, "and it's a horrid commercial school, so we'll have to pay a quarter's fees, for I think that is what is done generally, and Hughie must go to a proper school at once—a really good one—and we will pay the difference between a really good school and Frosty's fifty pounds. Then, if Hughie is clever and gets a scholarship, he can go to one of the 'Varsities, and afterward he must study for the Bar. You see, I have read up all about it, and I know. You must help me to do it, mother. I dare say he will make a very clever barrister, for he looks quite disagreeable enough to be so."

Lady Jane struggled against Irene's whim. But Irene, as she knew quite well, had the victory; for the next morning there was a serious conversation with Miss Frost, who left Lady Jane's presence in floods of grateful tears, the result of which was that Hughie was sent to a first-class school on the very day that Rosamund, Irene, Agnes, and Miss Frost went to the Merrimans'.

"Now, indeed, the world is beginning to go in the right direction," said Irene, who considered herself one of the most important people in the whole of creation.

CHAPTER XXIII

AT SCHOOL AGAIN

It is a curious fact that there are some weak but loving people who are not loved in return. If they are sincere and honest they always inspire respect. If they are at the same time unselfish, that noble quality must also tell in the long run. But to look at them is not to love them, and consequently they go through life with a terrible heart-longing unknown to their fellow-men, only known to the God above, who will doubtless reward these simple and earnest and remarkably beautiful souls in His own good time in another world.

Such a person was Emily Frost. She was very patient, very brave, very unselfish; but no one particularly cared for her. She knew this quite well; she had a passionate hunger for love, but it was not bestowed upon her. She was well educated and could teach splendidly, but she could never arouse enthusiasm in her pupils. A far less highly educated woman could do twice the amount poor Miss Frost could ever achieve, simply because she possessed the gift denied to the latter.

Now, Agnes Frost was much of the same temperament as her half-sister. She also was timid, easily frightened, very easily subdued, but sympathetic, loving, and unselfish. Agnes, however, had the great power of inspiring love in all those with whom she came in contact. Miss Frost herself worshiped that little delicate and beautiful face, those sweet lips, that tender and dainty form. She felt she could almost die for the child. But the child, although she loved her half-sister, did not love her in the passionate way that Miss Frost desired. Irene was the first person to whom Agnes had given all her strong powers of affection. For Irene she would have done anything. She did not care nearly so much for Rosamund, although she admired her, and Rosamund herself was drawn to the child and attracted by her. Agnes had been perfectly happy while at The Follies; never a fear had she of the much-dreaded Irene. It is true she had not heard the dreadful stories of the toads and wasps and leeches; but whether she heard them or not, it would be difficult now to remove her affection from the girl who adored her, and whom she in return so worshiped.

Miss Frost looked on, tried to be satisfied, tried to believe that Rosamund was right when she told her that nothing in all the world could happen more advantageously for little Agnes' future; but nevertheless she carried an unhealed sore at her heart.

This was the state of things when the three girls arrived at the Merrimans'. The house had truly been swept and garnished. The room where Jane had been ill was re-papered and painted, the place looked spick-and-span and beautiful, and Mrs. Merriman came out with a smiling face to welcome the arrival of the party from The Follies.

"Welcome back, my dear!" she said to Rosamund, kissing her affectionately, and just as though there had never been any ill-feeling between them. "How are you, you dear little thing?" she said, addressing Agnes in that petting tone which almost all women assumed toward her. "How do you do?" she said more stiffly to Miss Frost.

Then she turned and addressed Miss Archer, who happened to be not far away.

"Miss Archer," she said, "this is our new teacher, who will assist you in every possible way. Will you take her to her room now? And Rosamund, you know where to find yours. Irene and Agnes are to sleep in the same room, and it is next to yours. You can go upstairs, therefore, all of you, and get tidy for supper—at which you will meet the rest of your school-fellows, Rosamund."

Rosamund smiled; she had come back from her holidays in Switzerland feeling very brave and determined to do what was right. She felt that she was a sort of person who had begun a crusade. Her crusade was against the crudities, the cruelties, and naughty conduct of one little girl of the name of Irene Ashleigh; but she had little idea how complex was the task set her, and how difficult it would be even now to perform it. Nevertheless, she was feeling courageous and happy for the time being; and if Lucy Merriman had not belonged to the school so effectually and so thoroughly as to make it impossible to have any school at all without her, Rosamund might have been perfectly happy at Sunnyside. As it was, she knew she would have a hard fight with herself in the midst of her present surroundings.

Irene took her hand affectionately, guessing little of her thoughts.

"Do come and show us round, Rosamund," she said. "I know Aggie is tired. Aren't you, darling?"

"Oh, no," said Agnes. "I'd like to go out presently and have a walk all alone with you, Irene."

"Then of course you shall, dear."

"But there's no time to-night," said Rosamund. "We have barely time to get our things unpacked and get ready for supper. You know this is school, and I told you what school meant."

"You did," said Irene, raising her bright, wild eyes to her companion's face; "but I confess I had forgotten it. This house seems like any other house, only not so handsome. It isn't nearly as big as The Follies, and the people don't seem so rich; and I have seen fat Mrs. Merriman all my life driving about with the cob and the governess-cart; and I have seen Professor Merriman, too, with his bent back and long hair. But I never chanced to come across Lucy except that time in church, and then I thought her horrible. Why should I alter my plans because of the Merrimans? I don't intend to do it."

"You must, Irene. You promised me that you would try to be good. Come, look at Agnes."

Agnes was gazing up at her chosen companion, at the girl she loved best in the world, with wonder in her dark eyes. It was not a reproving look those eyes wore; it was a sweet, astonished, and yet slightly pained gaze. It conquered Irene on the spot. She bent down and kissed the little one.

"You never thought I should be naughty, did you?" said Irene, lowering her voice.

"You couldn't! you couldn't! You are the best girl in all the world," whispered Agnes.

"Then I will make a tremendous effort to be good for

your sake."

These words were also said in a whisper, and by this time the girls had reached their own room, which they were to share together. A door opened into Rosamund's room, and thus the three who were to be so closely united during the greater part of their lives were more or less in the same apartment.

"It does seem strange not to have dear Jane Denton here," said Rosamund; "but she seems to be still so delicate that she won't come back to school this term. Now, shall I help you to unpack, Irene? And shall I help you to put on a pretty frock for supper? I want you to look as nice as possible. All the girls are just dying to see you."

At that moment there came a knock at Rosamund's door. Rosamund flew to open it. Laura Everett stood without.

"So you have come back, Rosamund! How glad I am to see you! May I come in?"

"If you don't mind, not for a few minutes," said Rosamund. "May I have a chat with you after supper, or one day after lessons?"

"Of course to-night. We can walk about in the corridors if it is too cold to go out-of-doors. But is it absolutely true—I only heard it as a whisper—that you have brought Irene Ashleigh, the terror of the neighborhood, here?"

"She will be a terror no longer if you will all be kind to her," said Rosamund. "I have a great deal to say to you; but don't keep me now. She has come, and so has dear little Agnes Frost, and—oh! do ask the other girls to be kind, and not to take any special notice. You will, won't you?"

"I'm sure I'd do anything for you," said Laura. "I think you were splendid all through. I cannot tell you how I have admired you, and how I spoke to mother about you in the holidays; and mother said that though you had not done exactly right, yet you were the finest girl she had ever heard of or come across, and she was very glad to think that you and I might be in a sort of way friends."

"Well, let us be real friends," said Rosamund affectionately. "Now, don't keep me any longer. I have as much as I can do to get my couple ready to make a respectable appearance at supper."

Laura ran off to inform her school-fellows that the noted, the terrible Irene was in very truth a pupil at Mrs. Merriman's school. The girls, of course, had heard that Irene was coming, and that Rosamund had been forgiven, and, notwithstanding her disobedience, was returning to the school. But although they believed the latter part of this intelligence, they doubted the former, thinking it quite impossible that any sane people would admit such a character as Irene into their midst. But when Laura came downstairs and told her news, the girls looked up with more or less interest in their faces.

Annie Millar, who was Laura's special friend, said that she was glad.

"She needn't suppose that I'll be afraid of her," said Annie.

"And she needn't think that I'll be afraid of her," said Phyllis Flower. "She may try her toads and her wasps if she likes on me; but she won't find they have much effect."

"Oh, do stop talking!" said Laura. "Can't you understand that if Irene is to be a good girl we must not bring things of that sort up to her? I believe she will be good, and I think

Rosamund is just splendid. Yes, Lucy, what did you say?"

Now, Lucy had up to the present been one of Laura's great friends. Their mothers had been friends in the old days, and the clever, bright, intelligent Laura suited Lucy to perfection. But Lucy had imbibed all the traditions with regard to the willful Irene, and was horrified at the thought of having her now in the school. She was also angry at Rosamund's being reinstated; in short, she was by no means in a good temper. She thought herself badly treated that the news of the advent of these two young people had been kept from her, and was not specially mollified when her mother came into the room and told her that her father wished to speak to her for a minute or two in his study.

The girl ran off without a moment's delay, and entering the study, went straight up to the Professor, who, gentle, patient as of old, laid his hand on her shoulder.

"Well, Lucy," he said, "and so school begins, and the old things resume their sway."

"I don't think they do," retorted Lucy. "It seems to me that they are giving place to new. Why is it, father, that a girl whom you expelled has come back again to our dear little select, very private school? And why has she brought the very naughtiest girl in the whole neighborhood to be her companion?"

"I can only tell you this in reply, Lucy: Rosamund, although she was naughty, was also noble."

"That is impossible," said Lucy, with a toss of her head.

"It is difficult for you to understand; but it is the case. She was actuated by a brave motive, and has done a splendid work. I confess I was very angry with her at the time; but dear Mr. Singleton—such a Christ-like man as he is—opened my eyes, and told me what a marvelous effect Rosamund was having on little Irene Ashleigh, whom every one was afraid of, and who was in consequence being absolutely ruined. It was at Singleton's request that I reinstated Rosamund in the school, and it was further at his request and that of Lady Jane Ashleigh that I decided not to part the two girls, but to allow them to come here for at least a term. So Rosamund and Irene are both members of the school, and I desire you, Lucy, as my daughter, not to repeat to any of your fellow-pupils the stories you may have heard in the past with regard to Irene. I desire you to be kind to her, and if you cannot be friends with her, at least to leave her alone. You have your own friends, Laura Everett"—

"Oh, Laura has already gone over to the enemy," said Lucy. "Why, she was talking and preaching as hard as ever she could just now, when mother came in and said that you wanted me."

"Well, my dear, I did want to speak to you. I wanted to say just what I have said. You will attend to my instructions. You understand?"

"I understand, father," said Lucy; and she left the study with her fair head slightly bent.

There was a puzzled expression on her face. What was the meaning of it all? Never in her life, which would soon extend to sixteen years, had Lucy Merriman consciously done a wrong action. She had always been obedient to her parents; she had always been careful and prim, and, as she considered, thoughtful for others. She adored her father and mother. She herself had been willing to sacrifice her position as a happy only girl to become a member of the school, just to help her father out of his difficulties, and to enable his health to be restored, and now she was reprimanded because she could not see that wrong was right. What was the matter with Rosamund? Who could consider her conduct in any other but the one way? And yet here was Mr. Singleton inducing her father to overlook her fault.

"I felt dissatisfied when father expelled her," thought the girl. "But now he has taken her back again; and that awful ogre, that terror, has come here. What does it all mean? It's enough to turn a good girl naughty; that's all I've got to say."

There was a pretty sort of winter parlor where the girls always waited until the meals were served. Lucy re-entered it now, and found most of her companions waiting for her. She was scarcely there a moment before the gong sounded, and at the same instant Rosamund, followed by Irene, who was holding little Agnes's hand, entered the room.

Now, report had said a great deal in disfavor of Irene Ashleigh. She was the queer girl who wore the unkempt red dress, who did the strangest, wildest, maddest things, who terrified her governesses, who was cruel to the servants, who made her mother's life one long misery. But report had never mentioned that there was a charm in her wild face, in those speaking eyes; and that the same little figure clothed in the simplest, prettiest white could look almost angelic. No, angelic was hardly the word. Perhaps charming suited her better. Beyond doubt she was beautiful, with a willowy, wild grace which could not but arrest attention, and all the other girls immediately owned to a sense of inferiority in her presence. But Irene was so endowed with nature's grace that she could not do an awkward thing; and then the child who accompanied her, the small unimportant child, was as beautiful in her way as Irene was in hers. So charming a pair did they make, those two, each of them dressed in the purest

L. T. Meade

white, that Rosamund, who was considered quite the handsomest girl in the school, seemed to sink into commonplace in comparison. But no one had time to make any remark.

Irene said lightly, "Oh, so you are the others!" and then nodded to one and all; and turning to Agnes, she said in a low tone, "These are the rest of the girls, Aggie; and I'm ever so hungry. Aren't you, Aggie?"

Mrs. Merriman came in and conducted her young group to the room where supper was laid out, and here the first cross occurred to disturb Irene's good temper; for Agnes was placed at the other side of the table, between Phyllis Flower and Agnes Sparkes. Agnes Sparkes was bending toward her and talking in her lively way. She was remarking on the similarity of their names, and little Agnes was looking up at her older companion and smiling back, not at all frightened; for, as she said to herself, people were so kind to her.

Miss Frost, anxious, pale, and miserable, was watching her treasure as she gave a little bit of her heart, at least, first to one girl and then to another, and poor Miss Frost's face looked anything but inviting. Her nose was red, her cheeks pinched and hollow, her eyes somewhat dim. She felt inclined to cry.

Rosamund, however, boldly asked Laura Everett to change places with her, and sat next to Irene.

"Why have they taken Agnes away?" said Irene. "I don't like it. I have a great mind to walk round the table and to snatch her away from those two horrid creatures at the other end, and to bring her to us. Why shouldn't she sit between us? I know she wishes it, poor little darling!"

"We had better leave her alone for the present, Irene; supper won't take long. Don't take any notice. I'll ask Mrs. Merriman to let Agnes sit next to you in future; but don't make a fuss now."

"I hate being good. I don't think I can stand it," said Irene in a most rebellious tone. And then she scowled at Miss Frost in quite her old ferocious way, so that the governess looked more anxious and unhappy than ever. But this was nothing to the scowl she presently gave Lucy Merriman. She fixed her bright eyes on Lucy's face, and not only a frown came between her brows, but the frown was succeeded by a mocking laugh, and then she said in a low tone, which yet was clear as a bell, "I saw you in church one Sunday, and you frightened me so much that I had to go out."

This remark was so strange and unexpected that most of the girls gave utterance to a nervous laugh; but Professor Merriman raised his voice.

"Irene," he said, "that is not at all a polite thing to say. I must have a little talk with you when supper is over, for you are not to say unkind things to your neighbors, or of them, as long as you are in my house."

The firmness of his voice and the dignity of his bearing had a slight effect on Irene. Rosamund began to talk rapidly to her on different subjects, and by and by the meal came to an end.

That evening nothing very extraordinary occurred; but Irene, without waiting for any one, rushed down to the room and seized little Agnes's hand.

"Come, Agnes," she said, "it is time for you to go to bed."

"I am the person who has charge of putting the little ones to bed," said Miss Frost, going up and speaking in a trembling tone.

"You may put all the other little ones to bed, as far as I am concerned," said Irene; "but you don't put my Agnes to bed."

"But she is my Agnes, too."

"No; she is mine. Agnes, say at once that you belong altogether to me; that you are my darling, my doll, my baby."

"I do love you," said little Agnes; "but of course I love Emily, too—dear old Emily!"

She laid her hand on her elder sister's arm and looked up affectionately into her face.

"I thought, Irene, I said I wished to speak to you," remarked the Professor then; and before Irene could reply he had taken her hand and led her into the study.

He made her sit down, and seated himself opposite to her.

"Now, my dear," he said, "you are going to be under my roof for a few weeks. The term as a rule lasts about twelve weeks—that is, three months."

"An eternity—impossible to live through it," said Irene.

"I hope you may not find it an eternity; but, anyhow, it is arranged that you are to stay here, and during that time you must be subjected to the rules of discipline."

"What is discipline?" said Irene.

"One of the rules of discipline is to obey those put in

command of you."

"In command of me? But there is no one in command of me!"

"I am in command of you, and so is my wife, and so are your three governesses."

"And what do you mean to do now that you are in command of me?"

"I, for one, hope to help you, Irene, to be a good girl."

"I think," said Irene steadily, "that I'd rather be a naughty girl. When I was at The Follies I used to do what dear Rosamund wished; and then sweet little Agnes came, and she loved me, and I loved her and did kind things for her, and I felt ever so much better; but I am not at all better at your horrid school."

"Did any one ever happen to punish you, Irene?"

"Punish me?" said Irene, opening her eyes.

"Yes, punish you."

"Well, no. I don't think anybody would try to do it a second time."

"I don't wish to punish you, my dear child." The Professor rose and took one of Irene's little hands. "I want to help you, dear—to help you with all my might and main. I know you are different from other girls."

"Yes," said Irene, speaking in her old wild strain; "I am a changeling. That's what I am."

"Nevertheless, dear—we won't discuss that—you have a soul within you which can be touched, influenced. All I ask of you is to obey certain rules. One of them is that you do not say unkind things about your fellow-pupils. Now, you spoke very unkindly to my daughter at supper to-night."

"I don't like her," said Irene bluntly.

"But that doesn't alter the fact that she is my daughter and one of your school-fellows."

"Well, I can't like her if I can't. You don't want me to be dishonest and tell lies, do you?"

"No, but I want you to be courteous; and ill-feelings are always wrong, and can be mastered if we apply ourselves in the right spirit. I must, therefore, tell you, Irene, that the next time I hear you speak, or it is reported to me that you speak, unkindly of any of your school-fellows, and if you perform any naughty, cowardly, childish tricks, you will have to come to me, and—I don't quite know what I shall be obliged to do, but I shall have a talk with you, my dear. Now, that is enough for the present."

"Thank you," said Irene, turning very red, and immediately leaving the room.

The Professor sighed when she had gone.

"How are we ever to manage her?" he said to himself.

In truth, he had not the least idea. Irene was not the sort of girl who could be easily softened, even by a nature as gentle and kind and patient as his. She required firm measures. Nevertheless, he had made a deeper impression than he had any idea of; and when the little girl went up to her room presently, and saw that Agnes was in bed, but wide awake and waiting ready to fling her arms tightly round her companion's neck, some of the sore feeling left her heart.

"Oh, Aggie, I have you! and you will never, never love that other horrid Agnes, or that dreadful Phyllis, or that hateful Lucy, or any of the girls in the school as you love me."

"Oh, indeed, I never could, Irene—I never could!" said little Agnes. "But you don't mind Em putting me to bed, do you, for it makes her so happy? Her hands were quite trembling with joy, and she said she had not been so happy for a long time."

"Well, she is your sister, and she's a good old sort. But, Agnes, how are we to live in this school? Tell me, can you endure it?"

"I was at another school, and this one seems perfectly beautiful," said little Agnes. "I think all the girls are quite nice."

"You had better not begin to praise them overmuch, or I shall be jealous."

"What is being jealous?" said the little girl.

"Why, just furious because somebody cares for you, or even pretends to care for you. I don't want anybody to love you but myself."

"I don't think I should quite like that," said little Agnes. "Though I have promised to love you best, I should like others to be kind to me."

"There you are, with your sweet little eyes full of tears, and I have caused them! But I'm dead-tired myself. Anyhow, it will only last for twelve weeks—truly an eternity, but an eternity which has an end. Shall we sleep in one bed to-night, Agnes? I won't be a moment undressing. Will you come and cuddle close to me, and let me put my arms round you and feel that you are my own little darling?"

"Yes, indeed, I should love it!" said little Agnes.

CHAPTER XXIV

GUNPOWDER IN THE ENEMY'S CAMP

Miss Archer was a most splendid director of a school. She was the sort of woman who could read girls' characters at a glance; and as her object was to spare Mrs. Merriman all trouble, and as she was now further helped by Miss Frost, a most excellent teacher herself, and Mademoiselle Omont took the French department, there was very little trouble in arranging the lessons of the different girls.

Irene, on the morning after her arrival, awoke in a bad temper, notwithstanding the fact that sweet little gentle Agnes was lying close to her, with her pretty head of fair hair pressed against the elder girl's shoulder. But when she went downstairs, and took her place in the class, and found that, after all, she was not such an ignoramus as her companions evidently expected to find her, her spirits rose, and for the first time in her existence a sense of ambition awoke within her. It would be something to conquer Lucy Merriman—the proud, the disdainful, the unpleasant Lucy. After what Professor Merriman had said, Irene made up her mind to say nothing more in public against Lucy; but her real feelings of dislike toward her became worse and worse.

Now, Lucy's feelings towards Irene, which were those of

L. T. Meade

contempt and utter indifference until they met, were now active. She was amazed to find within herself a power of disliking certain of her fellow-creatures which she never thought she could have possessed. She was not a girl to make violent friendships, but she did not know that she could dislike so heartily. She hated Rosamund with a goodly hatred, but now that hatred was extended to Irene. Why should Irene be so pretty and yet so naughty, so lovable and yet so detestable? For very soon the peculiar little girl began to exercise a certain power over more than one other girl in the school; and except that she kept herself a good deal apart, and absorbed little Agnes Frost altogether, for the first week she certainly did nothing that any one could complain of. Then she was not only remarkable for her beauty, which must arrest the attention of everybody, but she was also undeniably clever. Laura Everett was greatly taken with her, so was Annie Millar, so was Phyllis Flower, and so was Agnes Sparkes. Rosamund assumed the position of a calm and careful guardian angel over both Irene and little Agnes. She had a talk with both Mrs. Merriman and the Professor, and also with Miss Frost, on the day after their arrival.

"I will promise to be all that you want me to be if you will allow me to have a certain power over Irene and over little Agnes Frost, a power which will be felt rather than seen. I want little Agnes to sit next to Irene at meals; and I want this not for Agnes' sake—for she is such a dear little girl that she would make friends wherever she was placed—but for Irene's sake, for I don't want her to become jealous. At present she has a hard task in conquering herself, and my earnest desire is to help her all I can."

"I know that, dear," said Professor Merriman; and he looked with kind eyes at the fine, brave girl who stood upright before him.

Mrs. Merriman and Miss Frost also agreed to Rosamund's suggestion, and in consequence there was a certain amount of peace in the school. This peace might have gone on, and things might have proved eminently satisfactory, had it not been for Lucy herself. But Lucy could now scarcely contain her feelings. Rosamund exceeded her in power of acquiring knowledge; she excelled her in grace and beauty. And now there was Rosamund's friend, a much younger girl, who in some ways was already Lucy's superior; for Irene had a talent for music that amounted to genius, whereas Lucy's music was inclined to be merely formal, although very correct. There were other things, too, that little Irene could pick up even at a word or a glance. Agnes did not much matter; her talents were quite ordinary. She was just a loving and lovable little child, that was all; but when Lucy sometimes met a glance of triumph in Rosamund's dark eyes, and saw the light dancing in Irene's, she began to turn round and plan for herself how she could work out a very pretty little scheme of revenge.

Now, there seemed no more secure way of doing this than by detaching little Agnes from Irene; for, however naughty Irene might be, however careless at her tasks, one glance at her little companion had always the effect of soothing her. Suppose Lucy were to make little Agnes her friend? That certainly would seem a very simple motive; for Lucy, in reality, was not interested in small children. She acknowledged that Agnes had more charm than most of her companions, and, in short, she was worth winning.

"The first thing I must do is to detach her from Irene. She does not know anything about Irene at present, but I can soon open her eyes," thought Lucy to herself.

The school began, as almost all schools do, toward the middle of September, and it was on a certain afternoon in a very sunny and warm October that Lucy invited little Agnes Frost to take a walk with her. She did this feeling sure that the child would come willingly, for both Irene and Rosamund were spending the half-holiday at The Follies. Miss Frost was busily engaged, and beginning to enjoy her life, and little Agnes was standing in her wistful way by one of the doors of the schoolroom when Lucy came by.

"Why, Agnes," said Lucy, "have you no one to play with?"

"Oh, yes, I have every one," said Agnes, raising her eyes, which appealed to all hearts; "only my darling Irene is away, and I miss her."

"Well, you can't expect her to be always with you—can you?"

"Of course not. It is very selfish of me; but I miss her all the same."

"Now, suppose," said Lucy suddenly—"suppose you take me as your friend this afternoon. What shall we do? I am a good bit older than you, but I am fond of little girls."

Agnes looked at Lucy. In truth, she had never disliked any one; but Lucy Merriman was as little to her taste as any girl could be.

"There's Agnes Sparkes. Perhaps she wouldn't mind playing with me," said she after a pause.

"As you please, child. If you prefer Agnes you can go and search for her."

"No, no, I don't," said Agnes, who wouldn't hurt a fly if she could help it. "I will go for a walk with you, Miss Merriman."

"Lucy, if you please," said Lucy. "We are both school-fellows, are we not?"

"Only I feel so very small, and so very nothing at all beside you," replied Agnes.

"But you are a good deal beside me. It is true you are small; but how old are you?"

"I was eleven my last birthday. I am two years younger than dear Irene; but Irene says that I am ten years older than she is in some ways."

"Twenty—thirty—forty, I should say," remarked Lucy, with a laugh. "Well, come along; let's have a good time. What shall we do?"

"Whatever you like—Lucy," said the little girl, making a pause before she ventured on the Christian name.

"That's right. I am glad you called me Lucy. We all like you, little Agnes; and it isn't in every school where the sister of one of the governesses would be tolerated as you are tolerated here."

"I don't quite understand what you mean by that."

"Well, your sister is one of the governesses."

"Yes, I know."

"And yet we are all very fond of you."

"It is very kind of you; but they were all fond of me at Mrs. England's school; and when I was at that sort of school at Mrs. Henderson's, where there were boys as well as girls, the girls used to quarrel with the boys as to who was to play with me. People have always been kind to me. I don't exactly know why."

"But I do, I think," said Lucy; "because you are taking, and can make people love you. It is a great gift. Now, give me your hand. We'll walk along by the riverside. It's so pretty there, is it not?"

"Yes, lovely," said little Agnes.

Lucy walked fast. Presently they sat down on a low mossy bank, and Lucy spread out her skirt so that Agnes might sit on it, so as to avoid any chance of taking a chill.

"You see how careful I am of you," said the elder girl.

"All the girls are careful of me like that," said little Agnes. "I don't exactly know why. Am I so very, very precious?"

"I expect you are to those who love you," said Lucy, coming more and more under the glamour of little Agnes's strange power of inspiring affection.

"When you look at me like that you seem quite kind, but sometimes you don't look very kind; and then, you are not fond of my darling Irene and my dearest Rosamund. I wonder why?"

"Shall I tell you?"

Lucy bent close to the little girl.

"Oh! if it is anything nasty I would rather not know."

"But I think you ought to know about your Irene. Nobody

loved her at all—nobody could bear her—until—Why, what is the matter, child?"

"Don't—don't go on; I won't listen," said little Agnes.

Her face was as white as death; her eyes were dilated.

"But I will tell you," said Lucy. "She was the dreadful girl who nearly drowned poor Miss Carter, one of her governess, who is now at the Singletons'. She was the terrible, terrible girl who made your own dear sister swallow live insects instead of pills; she was the awful girl who used to put toads into the bread-pan; and—oh! I can't tell you all the terrific things she did. She is only biding her time to do the same to you. Some people say she isn't a girl at all, but a sort of fairy; and fairies always fascinate people, and when they have made them love them like anything they will turn them into wicked fairies, or something else awful. What is the matter, child?"

For little Agnes was trembling all over. After a minute she got up and made a great effort to steady herself.

"I don't think you should have told me that story," she said. "And I don't believe you."

"You don't believe me, you little wretch!" said Lucy, reddening with anger. "How dare you say such things? Do you think I, the daughter of Professor Ralph Merriman, would tell lies?"

"Well, you've told one now," said Agnes stoutly; "for I don't believe my darling Irene ever did such naughty—such very naughty—things."

"You ask Miss Frost—your dear Emily, as you call her. Here

she comes walking along the bank. You go up and ask her, and if she tells you that I am wrong, then I will confess that some one told me lies. There, go at once and do it."

Miss Frost approached the pair to take little Agnes off Lucy's hands, for it did not occur to her as possible that a girl of Lucy Merriman's type could be really interested in her little sister. When she saw the white face and trembling lips, and the anxious eyes, she stopped suddenly, her own heart beating violently.

"What is it, Aggie? What is wrong, darling?" she said; and she bent down and touched the little one on the shoulder.

"Oh, Emmie, it isn't true—it can't be true!" said little Agnes.

"I have been telling her one or two things," said Lucy. "I have thought it best to put her on her guard. You have done an exceedingly silly thing to allow her to sleep in the room with that changeling sort of girl, Irene Ashleigh. Some day little Agnes will get a great fright. She says that she doesn't believe me; but you can tell her the truth, can't you? You did swallow wood-lice, did you not?"

"I—I would rather not speak of it," said Miss Frost. "It is all over now." But she shuddered as she spoke.

"Nevertheless, you must tell her. The child will not believe me."

"It was a long time ago, darling. Oh, Lucy, what have you done? What mischief you have done! How could you be so unkind?"

For little Agnes, in a perfect agony of weeping, had thrown herself into her sister's arms.

"I—I don't believe it!" she said. "Irene! Dearest, dearest Irene! She couldn't do anything of that sort."

"She couldn't now, Aggie. Oh, Lucy, do go away! Leave her to me—leave her to me," said Miss Frost, in the greatest distress.

Having accomplished her mission—and, as she said to herself, brought gunpowder into the enemy's camp—Lucy retired, wondering that she did not feel more satisfied. Agnes and her sister had a very long talk, the end of which was that they returned home a short time after Irene and Rosamund had come back from The Follies.

Irene began at once to call for Agnes.

"Aggie! Where's my Aggie? Aggie, I have brought you something back—something ever so pretty!"

But there was no response, and Irene felt a queer sensation at her heart.

"Where is the child?" she said. "Where is my little Agnes?"

After a time Agnes was seen running towards her. She did not come quite as fast as usual, and there was a change in her face. Irene did not know when she saw that change why a sudden sense of fear stole over her. It was as though some one had snatched the heart out of a gem, the glory out of a flower. It was as though little Agnes was no longer the beautiful Agnes she loved. She could not analyze her own feelings. She herself had returned in the best of spirits. Rosamund had been so bright, so cheery, so brave; her mother had been so pleased at the reports which Irene's different masters and mistresses had given her. All seemed going prosperously and well, and on the way home

L. T. Meade

Rosamund had spoken of Agnes, and said how glad she was that Irene should have the little one to look after, to love and to guide and to cherish. Altogether, Irene was in her most softened mood, and she had brought back to Sunnyside several old toys of her own which she had rooted out of a cupboard in the long-disused nursery. They would charm little Agnes; they had never had any fascination for her.

She thrust the parcel into the child's hands.

"They are for you," she said.

Little Agnes took the parcel, but not in her usual frank, enthusiastic, and open delight, but timidly.

"They're not—they're not toads?" she said.

"Toads!" cried Irene; and then she colored crimson. "Don't take them unless you want them," she said; and she snatched the parcel away from the child.

Little Agnes burst out crying.

"Irene, what do you mean?—Surely, Agnes, you are not silly!" exclaimed Rosamund. "See, let me open the parcel."

"I don't want her to have it unless she really wishes for it," said Irene. "I wouldn't force my gifts on any one, not even little Agnes." But there was an imploring note in her voice.

Little Agnes, however, was still full of the horrors with which she had been crammed. Rosamund went on one knee and opened the ungainly parcel. It contained a Noah's Ark, a box of bricks, some soldiers (the very best of their kind), and other toys of the sort that would ravish children. At another moment little Agnes would have been all delight, but now she seemed to see—behind the marching soldiers, and the fascinating bricks which could raise such marvelous architectural edifices, and the Noah's Ark with its quaint animals—toads and lizards and newts, and wasps and bees. Oh, why was she so frightened, she who had never really been frightened before? And she did love Irene. She looked up into her face now with piteous terror, and yet a piteous love mingling in her eyes.

"I will take them; they are beautiful," she said; and she clasped them in her arms. Then she put her face up for Irene to kiss, and then she went away staggering under the weight of her new treasures.

Irene turned to Rosamund.

"What is the matter?" she said. "Something has happened to the child. She was so jolly when we went out—so like her dearest, sweetest self—and now she is quite altered. What can have happened?"

"I can't tell," said Rosamund. "You had better take no notice, Irene."

Irene could scarcely promise to do that, and she was sulky and disturbed during the rest of the evening; and although little Agnes sat in her usual place at supper, she hardly spoke to her.

After supper Agnes flew up to Miss Frost and whispered something in her ear.

"May I—may I—sleep in your bed to-night? I want to," she said.

"Certainly," replied Miss Frost, intensely gratified. "But

what will Irene say?"

"I can't help it. I daren't stay in her room. I am frightened."

Miss Frost whispered again to the child, who went off presently to her studies, which always took about a quarter of an hour before she retired to bed. Miss Frost insisted on always seeing her little sister to bed herself, and after the first night or two at Sunnyside no one interfered with this arrangement. Irene had her own happy time afterwards, when she went to bed herself, and could look at the dear little face smiling in its sleep, when she could now and again hear the happy murmured words, "Dear Irene! darling Irene!" and when she knew she had constituted herself the little one's guardian—a sort of guardian angel over her—to fight to the death for her against all that was evil, all that was frightening. She was busy as usual to-night over her tasks, and took no notice when little Agnes and Miss Frost left the room together. Agnes, being the youngest pupil in the school, was always put to bed before the others. By-and-by the time came when all the girls were to retire for the night. Lucy had made herself delightfully inconspicuous this evening. She had scarcely spoken to any one. Even Mademoiselle Omont, with whom she had struck up a sort of friendship, developing rapidly a very sound knowledge of the French language, had scarcely been addressed by the loquacious young lady; while as to Miss Archer and Miss Frost, Lucy disdained even to speak to them.

By-and-by Rosamund too went up to her room. It was next to the room occupied by the two girls, Irene and Agnes.

"I won't come into your room to-night," said Irene. But she hesitated for a moment. "Have you found out anything to account for little Agnes's strange behavior?"

"No—nothing. If I were you I would take no notice. Perhaps the child was tired."

"Perhaps some one has told her things that she ought not to know," was Irene's response.

Rosamund was silent. She had much the same fear at her heart.

"Did you, or did you not, notice how quiet Lucy Merriman has been all the evening—a sort of hush about her which is not usual? I expect her conscience has been pricking her. Well, if she dares to interfere with me and Agnes she'll rue it, that's all I can say. Goodnight, Rosamund. I am sleepy."

Irene went into her room. She longed beyond words to find Agnes sufficiently awake to put her arms round her neck and kiss her as of yore. She wanted to tempt the little one to come into her bed. She felt, more than she cared to own, the acute pang at her heart with regard to little Agnes when she brought back the toys. Now, these were placed tidily away on a shelf just beside little Agnes's bed, but the bed itself was empty. The little night-dress had been removed; the brush and comb that always stood on the small dressing-table were also conspicuous by their absence. The little blue felt slippers which looked so sweet on her tiny feet were gone, as was also the blue dressing-gown. But none of these things mattered. It was the absence of little Agnes herself that Irene noticed. Agnes was not in the room. She stood quite still, clasping her hands, while a sensation of rage such as she had never before experienced—such as, with all her tempestuous nature, she had never believed could sweep over her—now visited her.

"Agnes!" she said once, and she went up to the empty bed and turned down the clothes as though she might even find

Agnes beneath.

But the bed was quite empty; the child was gone.

Scarcely knowing what she was doing, Irene burst into Rosamund's room.

"There's something up, and you might find it out. I won't go to bed until I know. They have taken Agnes away from me. She is not in my room. What is the matter? You must find out."

"I will," said Rosamund very gently. "Just sit down and keep as quiet as you can. I will go at once and see Miss Frost. She can't have gone to bed yet."

"Let me come with you."

"No, no; stay where you are, dear; and try to be calm, I beseech you. By your love for me, and by your love for Agnes, try now to control yourself."

Irene made a mighty effort. She sank into a chair. Tears came close to her eyes, but they did not fall, though she was trembling from head to foot.

Rosamund went quickly down the corridor. At the farther end she met Lucy, who was returning to her own room. Rosamund stopped her.

"What have you been doing to little Agnes Frost while we were away?" she said.

"I?" said Lucy, starting and turning very pale. "Nothing. What should I have done?"

"You know you have done something. You have frightened her, telling her dreadful stories about Irene. You know it. You are mean and cowardly. You ought not to have anything to do with any respectable school. I cannot tell you how I despise you. Think how much I have given up to save Irene, who never had a chance until she knew me, and yet you now destroy every effort that I have made for her good. Oh, I despise you! I cannot help it."

Lucy was absolutely speechless. Rosamund walked along the corridor until she came to Miss Frost's room. She tapped very gently with her knuckles. Miss Frost came out.

"Frosty dear, is little Agnes sleeping with you to-night?" she said.

Miss Frost shut the door and came on to the landing. She put her finger to her lips.

"Hush!" she said. "She is with me; she is in my bed. She is very nervous, starting every moment. Lucy Merriman told her dreadful stories while she was out to-day. The child told me about them. Lucy had no right to tell her. She is afraid of Irene now."

"She need never be afraid of Irene. I wonder if she has pluck enough to go back to her? If she has, all will be safe. If not, Irene's character will be spoiled for ever. Is she asleep?"

"Scarcely asleep; very nervous and restless. You won't take her back to Irene to-night? You know what the effect of nervous fear is upon a delicate, tenderly nurtured child. You could not be so cruel."

"Agnes is not so delicate as all that. She can stand it. When I think of Irene, who has almost been saved, who has almost been turned into the paths of goodness and righteousness, and mostly by little Agnes herself, and when I think of that cruel, wicked, unscrupulous girl, I have no patience. Frosty, I have helped you—you must let little Agnes help Irene now. Don't be frightened. I shall be next door to them, and nothing can possibly happen to the child; but she must come back."

Miss Frost stood aside.

"Really, Rosamund," she said, "I do admit the strength of your words. I know how good—how more than good—you have been; but, at the same time, I feel she is my little sister, and Irene has taken her away."

"For the present, I grant it, and I am sorry; but not for always. Let her have her back now, for a time at least—to-night at any rate."

"Very well, you must manage it your own way."

Poor Miss Frost wrung her hands in nervous terror. She thought of that awful moment when she had swallowed the wood-lice. She thought of the terrible appearance of James when the wasps had stung him. She remembered another occasion when she had found a leech in her bed. Oh, how terrible Irene had been! And there was Miss Carter, who had nearly lost her life in the boat. Then there was Hughie— something very queer had happened to Hughie on one occasion, only Hughie was no coward. He was brave and practical. But then, again, there was Irene herself—Irene so altered, so sweet to little Agnes, so kind about Hughie. Poor Miss Frost was so torn between her diverse emotions that she scarcely knew what to do.

Meanwhile Rosamund had gone into the room. She made a slight noise, and Agnes, only half-asleep, opened her dark eyes and fixed them on Rosamund's face.

"What is it? Is there a toad in the room?" she said.

"Don't be silly, Agnes," said Rosamund. "I really have no patience with you. Now, what is the matter? Sit up in bed and tell me."

Rosamund did not mean to be unkind, nor did she speak in an unkind way, although her words sounded somewhat determined.

"I want to speak to you, Agnes," she said. "You were told stories—and very exaggerated they doubtless were—by Lucy Merriman when Irene and I were at The Follies to-day."

"I was told frightful stories all about Irene."

"Then do you mean to tell me you don't love her any more?"

"I shall always love her; but if she were to do such a thing to me it would kill me."

"She would never do such a thing to you. Now, I will tell you something about her. She used to be a wild and very naughty child. People were afraid of her, and she had nothing else to occupy her time but to add to their terrors. Then I came across her path, and I was not a bit afraid of her. In short, I think I helped her not to be so naughty. But I did not do half the good you have done."

"I?" said little Agnes, in amazement.

"Yes, you, Aggie—you; for you loved her, and you helped her to be good by simply trusting her, and by clinging to her and thinking her all that is good and beautiful. Between us—you and me—we were softening her, and she will be a splendid woman some day, not a poor, miserable wretch, half-wild, but good and true and noble."

"I like women of that sort," said little Agnes, in a fervor of enthusiasm.

"And that is what your own Irene will be, provided that you do not give her up."

"I give her up?" said little Agnes. "But I never will."

"You gave her up to-night when you refused to sleep in the room with her. She is in my room now, trembling all over, terrified, grieved, amazed. Oh, Aggie, why did you do it?"

"I was frightened," whispered Agnes. "I suppose I am a coward."

"You certainly are a very great coward, and I am surprised at you, for Irene would no more hurt you than a mother would her own little child. You have got to come back to her in my arms, and you have got to tell her that you love her more than ever, and that you trust her more than ever. Now, will you or will you not? If you will not, I believe that all our efforts will be fruitless, and Irene will become just as bad as ever. But if you do, you will have done a brave and noble act. You are not a coward, Agnes; you are a girl with a good deal of character, when all is said and done, and you ought to exercise it now for your friend. Just think what she has done for you. Think what she has done for your sister, and"—

"It was to Emmie that she gave the awful wood-lice," said Agnes.

"She did it as an ignorant girl, not in the least knowing the danger and the naughtiness of her own trick. I do not pretend to defend her; but she would not do such a thing now to anybody, and certainly not to you. And yet, because you hear a few bad stories about her, you give up the girl who has sheltered and loved and petted you; who has influenced Lady Jane to make your brother a gentleman, not a shopman; who will help you all through your life, as you, darling, are helping her. Oh! I know you are a little girl, and cannot understand perhaps all that I say; but if you give Irene up to-night I shall be in despair."

Tears came to Rosamund's bright eyes. She sat quite still, looking at the child.

"I won't give her up! I won't be frightened at all. I will run back to her now."

"There's a darling! Go this very second. Where are your slippers? Here is your little blue dressing-gown. You will find her in my room. I won't go back for a minute or two, for I will explain to Frosty. Now, off with you, and remember that I am close to you; but you needn't even think of that, for Irene herself would fight the fiercest and most savage creature to shield and protect you, little Agnes."

It seemed to little Agnes as Rosamund spoke that the terrors that Lucy's words had inspired rolled away as though they had never existed. The brightness came back to her pretty dark eyes. She put her small feet into her little felt slippers, wrapped herself round with her little blue dressing-gown, and ran down the corridor. It was too late for any of the girls to be up, and the corridor was deserted. Lucy had gone to bed, to wrestle and cry and wonder by what possible means she could revenge herself on Rosamund Cunliffe.

L. T. Meade

Irene was sitting in Rosamund's room, feeling more and more that wild living thing inside her—that wild thing that would not be subdued, that would rise up and urge her to desperate actions. Then all of a sudden there came the patter of small feet, and those feet stopped, not at Rosamund's door, but at her own. It was opened and a little face peeped in. Irene, in Rosamund's room, could not see the face, but she heard the sound, and her heart seemed to stand still. She rose softly, opened the door of communication between the two rooms, and peeped in.

With a cry, Agnes flew to her side.

"Oh, Irene! I have come back. I couldn't sleep in Frosty's bed. I thought—I did think—oh, don't ask me any questions! Just let me sleep with you to-night. And oh, Irene, don't be angry with me!"

"I angry with you?" said Irene, melted on the spot. "No, I won't ask a single question, you sweet, you dear, you treasure! Yes, we will sleep together. Yes, little Agnes, I love you with all my heart for ever and for ever."

CHAPTER XXV

REVENGE

After this incident there was peace in the school for some time; Lucy was defeated. Agnes was more Irene's chosen chum and adored little friend than ever. The child seemed to have completely lost her terrors, and she gave Miss Frost rather less than more of her society. Rosamund watched in silent trepidation. If only Lucy would not interfere! But she did not trust Lucy, nor did she trust another girl in the school, Phyllis Flower, who—small, thin, plain, but clever—had suddenly become Lucy's right-hand. At first Phyllis had rather shrunk away from Lucy, but now she was invariably with her. They talked a good deal, and in low tones, as though they had a great many secrets which they shared each with the other. On one occasion, towards mid-term, when all the girls had settled comfortably to their tasks and life seemed smooth and harmonious once more, even Irene being no longer regarded with dislike and terror by the rest of the girls, Lucy Merriman and Phyllis Flower took a walk together.

"I am very glad we have this chance of being alone," said Lucy, "for I want to speak to you."

"What do you want to say?" asked Phyllis. She was flattered

L. T. Meade

by Lucy's confidence, for some of the girls admired this prim though rather handsome girl very much. Besides, was she not the daughter of their own master and mistress? Had she not a sort of position in the school which the rest of them would have envied a good deal? Lucy was beginning to exercise her power in more than one direction, and she and Rosamund between them really headed two parties in the small school. Of course, Phyllis Flower belonged altogether to Lucy's party.

"Well, what is it?" she said. "What do you want to say to me?"

"It is this," said Lucy. "I am quite determined to have my revenge on that horrid Rosamund and that odious Irene."

"I wish you wouldn't think so much about them. They are quite happy now, and don't do anybody any special harm."

"But that is just it. Rosamund ought never to have been readmitted to the school, and Irene is not the sort of girl who should have come here."

"Well, she seems a very nice sort—not that I know much about her."

"You had better not say that again in my presence, Phyllis— that is, if you wish me to remain your friend."

"Then I won't, dear," said Phyllis, "for certainly I do wish you to be my friend."

"I hate Irene," said Lucy, "and I hate Rosamund, and I hate that little sneak Agnes Frost, who tries to worm herself into everybody's good favor."

"Oh, no, she doesn't! She thinks of no one in all the world but Irene."

"I am surprised at that," said Lucy. "I imagined I had put a spoke in that wheel. I was very much amazed when I saw them thicker than ever the very next day. She is the sort of child who would tell tales out of school. I know the sort—detestable! She is a little pitcher with long ears. She is all that is vulgar and second-rate."

"Perhaps she is," said Phyllis, "although I never thought so. I thought her a pretty, sweet little creature. I think she is really fond of Irene, and Irene is sincerely devoted to her."

"Well, Phyllis, I will confide in you. A few weeks ago, when Rosamund and Irene took themselves off to The Follies to spend the afternoon, I took the opportunity of having a chat with little Miss Agnes Frost, and there and then I enlightened her with regard to certain stories which I knew for a fact to be true. I can tell you I frightened her a good bit. She is rather timid—I never knew any one more so. Her face got as white as death. Of course, I told her she was not to tell any one, but I didn't greatly care. I know for a fact she was nervous for the rest of the day, and that evening she asked poor old Frosty to let her sleep in her bed."

"But she didn't sleep with her, all the same," said Phyllis, "for I happened to see her running back to her own room quite late, after the rest of us were supposed to be in bed. And the next day she was greater friends than ever with Irene."

"What a nuisance things are!" said Lucy. "But now I am absolutely determined to punish Irene and Rosamund in the only way in which I can punish them. Rosamund is conceited enough to believe that she has made a reformation in Irene's character. I know better. I know that Irene is a perfectly horrid girl. If you could only have heard Miss Carter talk about her when she first went to the Singletons'! And we had a servant once from their house, and she told us some most ghastly tales. It is impossible to suppose for a second that Irene is a nice girl; but between Rosamund—who, I must own, is very plucky—and this mite Agnes, who is devoted to her, she is quite quiet and amenable, and she is no doubt passionately fond of that stupid, inane little Agnes. Now, I mean to get Agnes from her. You must help me, Phyllis. How are we to manage it?"

"It seems hardly worth while," said Phyllis.

"All right, Phyllis, you can please yourself. There are others who would help me—Agnes Sparkes, for instance."

"Oh! if you must have some one, I am quite as good as another," said Phyllis Flower.

"Well, you know that promise of mine that we should go to London together. My dear aunt, Mrs. Brett, is going to town, and she says that she will take me and any special friend I like as my companion, and she will show me all over the place: the Tower, the Houses of Parliament, and Westminster Abbey, and St. Paul's, and all the rest. And I mean to go to a theatre. Were you ever at a really big theatre in the whole course of your life, Phyllis?"

"Never," said Phyllis, "for you know I have lived all my life in the country."

"Well, you can't possibly imagine what it is like: the dresses and the lights, and the actors and the stage effects, as they call them, and the way the people talk—it moves you so. I went once, and I cried two handkerchiefs into wet mops, and

I could have cried into a third, only I didn't happen to have it. Oh, it was lovely!"

"It seems to be rather melancholy from your description," said Phyllis.

"Oh! it is the sort of melancholy that you can enjoy," said Lucy. "At least I enjoyed it, and I am a very matter-of-fact girl. But there, we can go to a laughing theatre. Some theatres make you laugh so much that you can scarcely stop. You get almost into hysterics. Anyhow, I mean to go, because Aunt Susan has promised to take me, either to a merry or a sad play. And then you are fond of music. I dare say I could squeeze in a concert. Think of a whole week, and not a penny to come out of your pocket; for Aunt Susan has a little sum put by, and she means to give me and whichever of my school-fellows I like best a real treat. So now you understand."

"Yes, I understand," said Phyllis.

"But you must help me to effect my object. I mean to part those two girls—that ridiculous little Agnes and that hated Irene. I mean to part them thoroughly."

"But I don't see how you can do it."

"Oh, don't you? I have thought of several ways. You know what a passion Irene has for all sorts of creatures—newts and toads and frogs. Well, I can also have a similar passion for those creatures. Anyhow, I have half-a-crown in my pocket, and I mean to—But there—the others are following us. Do let us talk in whispers. We needn't do it quite yet, but we will do it in about a week's time; and then there'll be a great rumpus, and most likely Irene will be expelled. Agnes can stay or not as she likes. She is quite a timid little thing, and I only want to separate her from Irene, and I want to prove to that horrid Rosamund that she is wrong and I am right. That's all. You can help me, and we will go to London afterwards. But please yourself."

"Let me think it over," said Phyllis. "Of course, I'd just love to go to London with you. It seems too interesting for anything; but"—

"There is generally something to be put up with when great pleasure is to be obtained," said Lucy. "I never had such a chance as this before, and I can give it to any one else. There is Annie Millar, or Agnes Sparkes—either of them would jump at it; or one of the Singleton girls. As to poor Jane Denton—but she is not at the school at present; and Laura Everett has plenty of fun of her own. I offer it to you now, provided you will help me."

"I suppose I must; but will you give me a day to think over it?"

"Yes, think it over; think what it means. You will have to be my confederate in this matter. It is just a little game I mean to play, and I think I shall play it so effectually that there will be no more friendship between pretty Agnes Frost and Irene Ashleigh."

CHAPTER XXVI

IN ROSAMUND'S BOWER

The days flew by, and apparently all was harmonious in the little school. Agnes clung more closely than ever to Irene. Irene had considerably altered. She was no longer specially wild. She was so much absorbed in watching Agnes, in seeing that no one else put in any claim with regard to this small girl, that she had no time to think of being mischievous. Besides, she had her lessons to attend to; and lessons under Miss Archer, and Mademoiselle Omont, and, still more, under the different masters who attended to the school, were of the most stimulating character. The child seemed to imbibe knowledge with a rapidity which astonished all those who watched her. She understood the meaning of a thing at a glance, and it was soon perceived that, in addition to her extraordinary and very remarkable beauty, she was also a genius, or almost that, for she had a natural talent for all sorts of things: for music, which she could already play impromptu, bringing out wild melodies on the piano to which her hearers felt they could go on listening for ever. Of course, the mistresses were supposed not to approve of this sort of playing, and tried to tie Irene down to the usual exercises and the different methods for bringing strength to the fingers. Irene did attend to these lessons, but only in a sort of half-hearted way; soon she

L. T. Meade

broke again into those wild melodies which seemed to pierce the heart and get more or less to the soul of the little performer.

The Singleton girls were often now spending a day or half a day at the Merrimans' school, and Irene and all her companions would also frequently spend an afternoon at the Rectory. People had ceased to be afraid of Irene. She was now like an ordinary child. It was quite true that those who watched her narrowly still saw that wild glance in her eyes, which could be easily excited; but then, Rosamund was near to subdue if the moment came, and little Agnes's affectionate touch on her arm had always the power to comfort and soothe her.

"Aggie," she said to the little girl one day, "I don't know how I lived without you. I used to make pets of my poor leeches."

"Leeches!" said Agnes, with a shudder.

"Yes, darling. You know that dreadful story that was told you. Well, of course it was true—quite true. But then I had no friends, and so I had Fuzz and Buzz, and Thunder and Lightning, and the little Stars. Oh! it used to be great fun to watch them, and to think how I could terrify people by them."

"But," said little Agnes, "it was very cruel, wasn't it?"

"I suppose it was, Agnes. Only I wanted the magical influence of love like yours to take the cruelty out of my heart, to smooth down all the rough edges, and to make me feel like an ordinary girl. I feel like an ordinary girl now in many ways, except that I could never give you up, Agnes."

"And I couldn't give you up, Irene. I told dear Emily so the other day."

"She didn't want you to, did she?" said Irene, with sudden fierceness.

"Oh no; but she did ask me what I found in you to make you more precious than any other girl in the school, and I said"—

"What did you say? Look me in the face, Agnes."

Agnes looked up with her melting, loving eyes.

"I said that somehow or other I loved you, and I did not love the others."

"Ah! there you struck the nail on the head," said Irene. "Look here, Agnes; if anything happened to divide us I'd get worse than ever; because, you see, I am cleverer than I used to be."

"Nothing can come to divide us," said little Agnes. "What could?"

"I am only saying that if anything did I'd be worse than ever."

"I wish you wouldn't talk like that."

"I can't help it sometimes, for I am—yes, I am—much cleverer now."

This little conversation took place in a small arbor at the Rectory; and just at this moment some one called Agnes, and Agnes, looking for permission at Irene, who nodded in reply, ran off. A moment later Miss Carter herself entered the bower, where Irene was still sitting.

L. T. Meade

"So you are not afraid of me now, Cartery dear," said Irene, speaking in the sort of tone which she supposed Maud Singleton adopted.

"No, I am not afraid of you. You are much altered. I came to say how much I admire you. In short, you are not the same girl you used to be."

"Well, it is owing to two influences," said Irene: "to Rosamund, who is so strong and brave, and took me in hand, and showed me myself, and did not express a scrap of fright, however much terror I tried to inspire her with; and it is owing also to even a stronger influence."

"And what is that?" said Miss Carter.

"Well, you see, there is that little thing—that darling—I can scarcely speak her name without trembling. I love her so much. She is like my own little child."

"Do you mean little Agnes Frost?"

"Oh yes. She is nothing to the rest of you. I do not wish her to be. She is all—all mine; and if anything happened to her, if she were taken from me, if I had to do without her, I should become worse than ever."

"But what do you mean?" said Miss Carter. "Why should little Agnes be taken from you?"

"I don't suppose anybody would dare to take her from me. Frosty wouldn't, and mother wouldn't; the school wouldn't; but there is a wicked girl who tried her very best to frighten little Agnes, only Rosamund brought her back to her senses. The darling knows that whoever else I might hurt at one time, I never could and never would hurt one hair of her head. And she loves me in return."

"Then that's all right," said Miss Carter.

Just at that moment a slight rustling was heard at the back of the little bower. Irene did not notice it, but Miss Carter did.

"I wonder if anybody is listening?" she said.

"Who cares? I don't mind if the whole world hears. There's that spy, Lucy Merriman; she is as likely as not to do mean things. But I don't mind even her."

"Oh, don't you?" thought Lucy, who had that moment come a little nearer the back of the bower.

"No, I don't mind even her," repeated Irene. "I only say that as long as Rosamund is with me I shall be a good girl, just because I can't help myself; and if any one were to take my Rosamund from me I should be worse than ever."

"You were pretty bad. I don't know how you could be worse than you used to be."

"Well, you see, I know more. I have more knowledge. I could be more refined in my acts of terrorism, or whatever you like to call them. Anyhow, people had better not try."

"People had better not try!" thought Lucy. "But, my fine Irene, somebody is going to try."

The evening passed, and the children came back again to have supper at Sunnyside. Lucy was biding her time. She disliked Irene even more than she disliked Rosamund. As to little Agnes, she was not of the smallest interest to her. She simply wished to divide her effectually from Irene, in order to punish both Irene and Rosamund; and nothing could give her greater pleasure than that Irene should burst into one of her worst frenzies. She thought she saw a way.

The family were all sitting contentedly at their supper when a telegram was brought in which was handed to Rosamund. It was from her mother, telling her that her father was seriously ill, and wanted her to come to London on the following day. Rosamund, who was intensely devoted to both her parents, was much distressed. She handed the telegram to Mrs. Merriman, who immediately gave her the necessary permission.

"You must start by the very first train to-morrow morning," said Mrs. Merriman, "and one of the governesses must go with you. Miss Frost might be the best."

"Of course, Miss Frost would be the right person," said Lucy, suddenly raising her voice, for it seemed to her that she saw the very opportunity she wished for in this unexpected absence of Rosamund.

"I shall probably only be away for a day. I cannot think there can be anything seriously wrong with dear father," said Rosamund. "But, of course, after mother's telegram I must go."

Accordingly, a reply stating the hour of Rosamund's arrival at Paddington was wired back to London, and shortly afterwards the girl went up to her own room to pack a few things. She was not depressed, for her father was subject to sudden attacks, which, although distressful, were not of a painful nature.

Presently Irene came and sat in the room with her. She sat down on the edge of the bed.

"I should almost die here," she said, "if it were not for Agnes. As it is, I feel dreadful. I feel quite frightened at the thought of your going."

"But for my sake you will do your utmost to try to be good while I am away, won't you, Irene? I shall probably only be in London one night, or two at the very most; and Frosty is coming too. You won't mind that? Miss Frost is coming back at once; she will return in time for to-morrow evening."

"Oh! I suppose it will be all right," said Irene restlessly.

Rosamund went on putting a few things into her little trunk. Then she went up to Irene, put her arm round her waist, and kissed her.

"I am proud of you, Irene," she said. "I shall always feel that I have not lived in vain when I think how different you are from the child I first saw only a few months ago."

"I feel different," said Irene. "I begin to have a sort of pleasure in being—I mean in trying to be—good. It is you, of course—you and dear little Agnes."

"Well, Agnes will be more than ever in your care now."

"Oh! I shall look after her, there's no fear of that. I shall be terribly lonely without you, darling; but she and I will be all in all to each other while you are away. If it wasn't for—for Lucy Merriman I should be quite happy, for I think the other girls are inclined to be nice; but I hate Lucy."

"Well, I must say, Irene, speaking honestly, I hate her too. But we must both make up our minds not to mind her. She cannot really hurt us."

"Hurt us?" said Irene. "I'm sure I'm not afraid of her, if that is what you mean."

"Well, that's all right. Now, let us go to bed."

"I believe I am very tired too. I will promise to be quite good while you are away, so you need not have any anxiety on my account, darling," said Irene; and she kissed Rosamund several times.

The night passed, and early the next morning Rosamund, accompanied by Miss Frost, took her departure. There was a certain loneliness felt in the school, for Rosamund was exceedingly popular with every girl in the place, with the sole exception of Lucy Merriman. Busy school-life, however, gives little time for regrets or even for loneliness. Each moment of time is carefully marked out, each hour has its appointed task, and the girls were, to all appearance, as happy as usual. Little Agnes did not in the very least miss Rosamund or her own sister Emily. Her whole soul was set upon Irene, who helped her with her lessons, walked with her, and hardly ever let her out of her sight.

In the course of the evening Lucy was seen to go up to Phyllis Flower.

"Now, Phyllis," she said, "here is your chance. I've got the very thing that will do the business. We must get Agnes to bed, and a little later, when she is asleep, you shall creep into the room and just slip this thing under the bedclothes. She won't know who has done it. She will wake out of her first sleep, and naturally think that it is Irene's doing."

As Lucy spoke she drew Phyllis towards a corner of the playground, where a large, rather ferocious-looking hedgehog was curled up in a ball.

"But that—that would almost kill the child," said Phyllis, starting back.

"We must give her a good fright; it is the only way to effect our purpose. Then one or other of us must be near, and intercept her, and tell her that we will be her friends. Then you will have your week with me in London; but you must do it."

"I almost think," said Phyllis, turning very white, "that I'd rather not have my week. You can do it yourself if you like. It seems so cruel, and they are very happy together, and she is a very timid little thing. And just when her sister is not at home!"

"That is the very time. I am going to have a chat with little Agnes this evening. I am going in a certain way to prepare her—not much. Now, don't be a goose, Phyllis. Think what a jolly time you will have in London. It will be quite impossible for us to be found out."

Lucy talked to Phyllis for some time, and finally persuaded her to act as her accomplice in the matter.

It was a rule at Sunnyside that the smaller girls, consisting of Phyllis Flower, Agnes Sparkes, and little Agnes Frost, should go to bed quite an hour before the other girls. They usually had supper of milk and a few biscuits, and went to their room not later than eight o'clock. The other girls did not go to bed until half-past nine, and had a more substantial meal at eight o'clock. Phyllis Flower, therefore, for every reason, was best able to perform the mean trick by which Lucy meant to sever the friendship between Irene and little Agnes; but the child must be slightly alarmed, otherwise the hedgehog might be put into the bed and she know nothing about it.

Consequently, just before the younger children's simple supper was brought in on a tray, Lucy came and sat down near Agnes Frost.

"You must miss your Emily," she said.

Her tone was quite caressing and gentle. Little Agnes—who did not like Lucy, but could not in her heart of hearts cherish ill-will towards any one—raised her eyes now and said gently, "Of course I miss her; but then, I have my dear Irene."

Lucy put on a smile which meant wonderful things.

"You are a very courageous little girl," she said after a pause.

Little Agnes was silent for a minute; then she said gravely, "I know exactly what you mean by that, and I think you are mistaken. You said things about my Irene which are not true."

"Oh, indeed! you accuse me of falsehood, do you?" said Lucy.

"Well, perhaps not exactly of falsehood; but I don't think it was kind of you to tell me, for Irene is changed now. She could never do cruel things now."

"She will never be changed. Don't you understand that she is not like ordinary people? She is a sort of fairy, hardly like a human being at all. I may as well tell you, now that Rosamund and Miss Frost are away, that while Rosamund slept in the next room you were practically safe. I will admit, although I have no love for Rosamund Cunliffe, that she is a very brave and plucky girl. To-night, however—But I trust it will be all right. I don't want to make you nervous. I trust it will be all right."

Lucy moved off and sat down before her books and pretended to read. By-and-by Irene, looking lovely in one of her prettiest pale-blue dresses, entered the room. Little Agnes was sipping her milk very slowly. Irene ran straight up to her. She had the power of almost divining a person's thoughts, and she was conscious that the child was troubled.

"What is it, pet?" she said. "Has anybody vexed you?"

"Oh, nobody—nobody, indeed, dear Irene."

"Well, that is all right. I wish I could go to bed with you to-night."

"I wish you could," said the child nervously.

"But I can't. I have an awfully stiff piece of work to get through before the morning, and I am determined to be first in my form, otherwise Lucy Merriman will get ahead of me, and that she shall not."

"But I sha'n't be nervous really."

"No, of course not, dear. What is there to be nervous about?"

Irene was really absorbed in an intricate calculation which she had to make with regard to a very advanced sum, and sat down at a distant table, and forgot for the time being even little Agnes. Agnes, therefore, went up to bed alone. There was no Miss Frost to help her to undress, there was no one to take any notice of her, and there were the fearful stories that Lucy kept hinting at ringing in her ears. Yes, Irene had done dreadful things. Yes, she had. But Irene to her was perfect. She had no fear with her; she was happy with her. But then,

Lucy Merriman had said that that was because little Agnes was so well protected. She had Rosamund sleeping practically in the same room, and Miss Frost, her own sister, not far away. Irene did not dare to do anything dreadful. But she had done dreadful things. She had nearly killed poor Miss Carter. She had made her own beloved sister swallow insects instead of pills. In short, she was just what Lucy had described her to be. And Lucy had said another dreadful thing to-night. She had hinted that Irene was not exactly to blame, for she was not like an ordinary girl; she was a sort of fairy girl. Now, Agnes had read several fairy-tales, and knew, supposing such a wonderful thing as a fairy really lived in the world, that she might be influenced by some other fairies, who would guide her, and help her, and force her to do things whether she liked them or not. But still she never would be unkind to little Agnes.

"It is a perfect shame of me even to think of it," said the little girl to herself. "I am ever so sleepy, but still I'll just look under the pillow. Oh, suppose Fuzz or Buzz were there, wouldn't I just scream with terror?"

But the pillow was quite innocent and harbored no obnoxious thing; the bed was smooth and white as usual; and little Agnes undressed, not quite as carefully as when Miss Frost was looking after her, and getting into bed, laid her head on the pillow, and presently fell fast asleep.

She had not been asleep more than a quarter of an hour before the room door was opened most carefully (the lock had been oiled in advance by Lucy), and Phyllis Flower, carrying the hedgehog, came in. She drew down the bedclothes and laid the hedgehog so that its prickles would just touch the child in case she moved, and then as carefully withdrew. She hated herself for having done it. All was quiet in that part of the house, which was far away from the schoolrooms, and no one heard a child give a terrible scream a few minutes later; and no one saw that same child spring out of bed, hastily put on her clothes, and rush downstairs in wild distress and despair.

Lucy had meant to be close at hand to comfort little Agnes when fright overtook her. But she had been called away to do some writing for her father. Laura Everett was busy attending to her own work. Phyllis Flower was in bed and asleep. She had earned her trip to London, and was dreaming about the delights of that time. No one heard that scream, which was at once faint and piteous. No one heard the little feet speed through the hall, and no one saw the little figure stealthily leave the house. Little Agnes was going to run away. Yes, there was no doubt whatever now in her mind: her darling Irene was a fairy, a changeling. She had done the most cruel and awful thing.

When little Agnes had seen the hedgehog in her bed she was far too terrified even to recognize the nature of the creature that had been made her bedfellow. But she felt sure that Lucy's words were right: that Irene was a wicked changeling, and that the sooner she got away from her the better. The child was too young to reason, too simple by nature to give any thought to double-dealing. All she wanted now was to get away. She could not stay another minute in the house. Her love for Irene was swallowed up altogether by her wild terror. She trembled; she shook from head to foot.

It was a bitterly cold winter's night, and the child was only half-clothed. She had forgotten to put on anything but her house-shoes, and had not even a hat on her head. But that did not matter. She was out, and there was no terrible Irene to come near her, no wicked fairy to do her damage. She would stay out all night if necessary. She would hide from Irene. She could never be her friend again.

L. T. Meade

The terror in her little heart rendered her quite unreasonable for the time being. She was, in short, past reason. By-and-by she crept into the old bower where Rosamund and Irene had spent a midsummer night—a night altogether very different from the present one, for the bower was not waterproof, and the cold sleet came in and fell upon the half-dressed child. She sank down on the seat, which was already drenched; but little she cared. She crouched there, wondering what was to be the end, and giving little cries of absolute anguish now and then.

CHAPTER XXVII

"MY OWN IRENE!"

Irene went up to bed that night in her usual spirits. She longed for the moment when she could, as usual, kiss little Agnes; but she was extra tired, for she had passed a stimulating day, and had been on her best behavior. She felt quite happy, and wondered if her mother, when her allotted time at the Merrimans' was over, would send her and little Agnes and Rosamund to another school somewhere else. She liked the excitement of school-life, and thought that if she could find a home where there was no girl like Lucy she would be perfectly happy. She little knew that in all schools there are girls of the Lucy type, who are not amiable, whose faults are far worse than those of ordinary wildness or even ordinary disobedience. But on this occasion she felt almost kindly toward Lucy, who nodded to her and said, "You and Agnes must make the most of yourselves together, for you will miss Rosamund."

"Oh! we'll be quite happy together," said Irene, with a careless nod; and then she went up to her room, opened the door gently, shut it quietly behind her, and shading the candle with one hand, went over to little Agnes's bed.

There was no Agnes there. But a huge hedgehog had curled

L. T. Meade

itself up in a ball close to the pillow where the little delicate head had been pressed. Irene was afraid of no living creature, and she recognized the hedgehog at once. She took it up and laid it on the window-sill. Then she looked round her. Her face was white as death; her teeth chattered. She suddenly left the room and went straight to Lucy's. She opened the door without knocking.

"Lucy!" she said.

"What is it?" said Lucy, who was brushing out her long fair hair.

"Did you put a hedgehog into Agnes's bed?"

"Certainly not," said Lucy.

"Well, some one did as a trick, and the child isn't there."

"The child isn't there? There's only one person who could do that sort of thing, and that is yourself, as you know very well," said Lucy. "But is the child nowhere in the room?"

"You come and look for her, will you?" said Irene. Her tone and manner had completely altered. She was forcing herself to use self-control. Had Fuzz and Buzz, and Thunder and Lightning, and the Stars been present at that moment, there is not the least doubt that Irene would have elected them to wreak their vengeance on Lucy; but she was keeping herself in for all she was worth at the present moment, for after all even Lucy did not much matter—it was little Agnes who mattered.

"Here's the hedgehog," said Irene when they entered her bedroom—"a great big one—and some one had put it into the little one's bed, and she's not there, and you know how timid she is. Where is she? You know I didn't do it. Is it likely I'd do it to one I love?"

"Oh! you're a sort of fairy—a changeling," said Lucy. "And you have done such things to other people. Why shouldn't you do it to her? Anyhow, who else in the house can be accused? Every one knows your character."

"Never mind about my character now. I know, I am positive, that you are at the bottom of this. But the thing is to find little Agnes. I must go at once to Mrs. Merriman."

"I wonder where she can be?" said Lucy, who had not expected for a moment that little Agnes would disappear. "She must have gone to one of the other girls' rooms. We will go to all the others and find out. Of course, I am sorry for you, Irene; but really you went too far when you made use of a hedgehog—such a horrid, frightening thing."

"I don't want your help. I'll go myself," said Irene.

She pushed past Lucy, and going down the corridor, entered each room. Each girl was asked where little Agnes Frost was. Each girl replied that she did not know. It was Phyllis Flower, however, who, in excitement and pallor, started from an uneasy dream.

"Little Agnes?" she said. "But she can't have gone out!"

"It seems to me you know something about this. Will you help me to find her?" said Irene.

Then, all in a minute, for some reason which she could never define, little Phyllis sprang to her feet hastily, put on her clothes, and without even glancing at Lucy, took Irene's hand.

"We'll search the house first," she said.

"Then you don't think I did such a cruel thing?" said Irene.

"Oh, don't ask me! I mean—oh, no, no! But I'll help you to find her. I'll do my best—my very best."

The whole house was awakened, and the alarm given. The Professor was not yet in bed. He was very much worried and annoyed. He directly told Irene that he believed she was guilty of giving her little companion a fright.

"You have done it so often before, you know," he said, "that people certainly do suspect you."

"Suspect me or not as you please," she answered, "but let us find little Agnes. The night is cold; there is sleet falling outside. It will turn to snow before morning. Where is the child? After all," she continued, speaking more like a grown woman than the wild sort of creature that she had been a few months ago, "she is under your charge, Professor Merriman, and you are bound to do your utmost to find her."

But nowhere in the house—not even in the cellars, which Lucy as a last resort suggested might possibly be her hiding-place—could little Agnes be found. At last a regular outdoor search was instituted. Lucy was now really frightened, although she would not own this feeling even to herself.

"Silly, tiresome child!" she kept muttering to herself.

As to Irene, not a single word passed her lips. Suddenly, in the midst of the searchers, she was missing. People wondered where she had gone to. Irene had rushed back to her own room, the room where she and little Agnes had been so happy together. She looked at the little white bed where they had lain in each other's arms. All her past, so cruel, so thoughtless, so selfish, was borne in upon her. She dropped on her knees, and in an agony of terror said aloud, "O God, help me to find her, and to be a good girl in future."

Then Irene felt a wonderful sense of calm. She went down again through the house. No one noticed her, for every one was in a great state of alarm. Those girls who were in bed were desired not to get up; but a good many had disobeyed orders, and Miss Archer, Mademoiselle Omont (gesticulating wildly), Professor Merriman, his wife, the servants, and the older girls were all searching in vain for Agnes. They were calling her name, but no one thought of the bower at the far end of the shrubbery; for what child would be likely to take refuge there?

Irene, however, all of a sudden remembered it. She remembered the night long ago when she, a wild little untamed creature, had crept into the room where Rosamund slept, had forced her to come out with her, and they had spent the night together in the bower. She would go there now. She did not know what guided her footsteps, but she felt sure some one did.

Now, the shrubbery, a delightful place in warm weather, was damp and cold as ice at this time of the year. The leaves, now falling thickly from the trees, lay sodden on the ground. Sleet continued to fall heavily from the sky. All the seekers were chilled to the very bone, and the bower, so charming in summer, so perfect a resort, so happy a hiding-place, was now the very essence of desolation. But Irene cared nothing for that. She cared nothing for the fact that her thin shoes were soaked through and through, that her dress hung closely round her, that her hat was bent forward over her eyes. She only wanted to find little Agnes, and to have her love again. In the bower Irene did find the child crouched up in one

L. T. Meade

corner, terrified, an almost unseeing expression in her eyes. Irene rushed to her with a glad cry.

"My darling! my darling! Oh, my own sweet little darling, come to your own Irene!"

But Agnes gave a shriek of terror when she saw her.

"No, no! Keep away! It's you who did it! You don't love me! No, no, I won't come to you!"

The piercing shrieks that came from the poor little girl's lips brought the rest of the party to the scene. When they appeared, Professor Merriman holding a lantern, they saw Agnes crouched in the farthest corner of the bower, her eyes semi-conscious, her face deadly white with terror, while Irene stood a little way off.

"Some one has turned her brain. Take her; do what you can with her," said Irene; and she walked away, not caring where she went.

They brought little Agnes back, and of course they sent for the doctor. The doctor stayed all night, for he said the child had received some very severe and terrible shock. Mrs. Merriman nursed her, and the next day, as soon as possible, Miss Frost returned.

But neither Miss Frost, nor the doctor, nor any one else could ease the terrors which had laid hold of the brain of little Agnes. She believed Miss Frost to be a sort of magnified Irene. The very name of Irene was enough to set her screaming again. She called Irene a fairy, a changeling, and nothing could soothe her or comfort her.

At last one day the doctor spoke to Mrs. Merriman.

"The case is quite a serious one," he said. "I cannot imagine what has happened to the child. You ought to find out who put that hedgehog in her bed. Hedgehogs are quite harmless in their way; but they would give a timid child a very nasty fright, which she evidently got."

"What we fear is that Irene did it. She has done all sorts of tricks of that kind before now. You remember how poor Miss Frost went to you on a certain occasion."

"Alas! that is true. But compared to this, her sin against poor Miss Frost was innocence itself. Such a timid, gentle, confiding little creature as this! And then report says that she was so devoted to Irene, and that Irene was so changed."

Yes, indeed, Irene was changed, and the great change lay now in the fact that she did not say a word or admit her suffering to any one; but sat moody and silent, scarcely attending to her lessons, indifferent to bad marks, without the least vestige of spirit, with no desire to injure any one. Even Lucy could not provoke a retort from her lips. Whenever she was allowed to, she stole outside little Agnes's door to listen to her mutterings, and to wonder and wonder if the child was to die.

"If she dies I shall go mad," thought the miserable girl, "for she has not only been frightened, but she has been turned against me. Who could have done it?"

Miss Frost had returned; Rosamund had also come back (her father was better); but the key to the mystery was still missing. Irene declared positively to Rosamund that she had nothing to do with the fright that little Agnes had received; but no one could explain how the hedgehog had got into the child's bed. Some one suggested that it had crawled in by itself, but this was repudiated as absolutely impossible.

Somebody had put it there, and no doubt with evil intent. Rosamund thought a good deal over the matter. She thought so much that at last she came to a certain conclusion.

Little Agnes still lay between life and death, and death came nearer and nearer to the little, weakened frame each moment and each hour. Then Rosamund determined to take the doctor into her confidence. She waylaid him as he came downstairs.

"Dr. Marshall," she said, "may I speak to you for a minute?"

"Certainly, Miss Cunliffe," he replied.

Rosamund took him into one of the sitting-rooms. She closed the door behind them and bolted it.

"Why do you do that?" he said.

"Because I am not sure of things. I want to take you into my confidence, and I don't want any one to hear."

"Well, Miss Cunliffe, you must be brief."

"First of all, may I ask you what you think of little Agnes? Is she in danger?"

"Undoubtedly she is in danger."

"Is she so much in danger that she is likely to die?"

"Unless she gets better soon, unless the strange pressure on her brain is removed, she will die," said the doctor. "The shock has been much more severe than any one could have believed possible, even from such an ugly thing occurring. But, be that as it may, she is in extreme danger of her life."

"Thank you," said Rosamund.

"Then you don't want to say anything more?"

"I don't think I do."

"I will come in again to-night. The child's case is interesting. She is a dear little creature."

The doctor went away, and Rosamund entered the school-room. The girls were trying to perform their usual tasks. Irene was bending over a history-book. There was such a sadness now pervading the house, such a necessary stillness, that all life seemed to have gone out of it. The wintry weather continued, and it was as gloomy outside as in. Miss Archer was in vain explaining a rather interesting point in English history, to which no one was attending much, when Rosamund entered the room. All the girls seemed to feel that she had news.

She had. She marched up to the top of the room and stood there. Irene only raised her head; but Lucy, who was pale and had black shadows under her eyes, and Phyllis Flower, who had certainly looked far from well for the last fortnight, glanced at her with considerable interest.

"I have something to say," said Rosamund.

There was a dead silence for a moment; then Miss Archer said, "I am giving my history lecture, my dear."

"You will postpone it, for life—human life—is more precious than facts in old history," said Rosamund.

"Certainly, my dear," said Miss Archer in quite a meek voice; and she sat down and prepared to listen with as much

L. T. Meade

interest as the others.

"It is this," said Rosamund. "Little Agnes Frost—I have just seen the doctor—is most dangerously ill." Phyllis Flower gave a gasp. "I won't go into the particulars of her illness; but the doctor says that unless a certain load of terror can be immediately removed from her mind she will die. Yes, she will die. Now, girls, it is quite plain to me, as it is doubtless to all of you, that a most cruel practical joke was played on little Agnes. Some people can stand practical jokes; some people cannot. But those who are cruel enough to exercise them upon little children are really too contemptible even to be spoken about. I wish this girl or that girl joy who knows that she may be the cause of the death of so sweet a child as Agnes Frost."

Irene lifted a face of agony. She struggled to speak, but no words came.

"You most of you think," continued Rosamund, who had watched Irene, and saw the look on her face, "that my friend Irene Ashleigh is the guilty person; but I am quite as certain as I am standing here that she is not. I have watched Irene for some time; and although she did all kinds of naughty things—very naughty things—months ago, she has abstained from anything of the kind for some time. In short, I believe her to be innocent, and I am going to ask her a direct question to that effect. Now, I shall believe her word, for with all her sins she never told a lie yet. Irene, were you the cause of Agnes Frost's terrible shock?"

"I was not," said Irene stoutly. She stood up as she spoke, and Rosamund went up and took her hand.

"Then some one else has done it. I believe Irene's word."

"And so do I," said Laura Everett.

"And so do I," said Annie Millar.

"And I also," exclaimed Agnes Sparkes.

But Phyllis Flower and Lucy Merriman were silent.

"Phyllis, what is your opinion?" said Rosamund suddenly. "Don't hesitate now. If you or any one else in this school has been tempted to commit a dastardly and wicked deed, don't let the thought that you may have caused a child to die rest on your conscience for all your days. You will be miserable. Had you or had you not anything to do with the fright which little Agnes received?"

"Oh!" said Phyllis; and she suddenly left her seat and fell on her knees. She covered her face with her hands; she swayed backwards and forwards. "Oh, I know—I know! I can't help myself. I did it."

"You did it—you?" said Rosamund sternly.

"Phyllis!" cried Lucy.

"Phyllis, you must speak up. The child's life is at stake. You must speak out and tell the truth."

"Then I will," said Lucy in a defiant tone. "I didn't know you were such a coward, Phyllis."

"Yes, I was a coward," said Phyllis. "I will tell my part of it. I did want a week in London, and I was tempted, and I put the hedgehog into Agnes's bed."

"You yourself did that? You did that yourself—alone?"

"That is all I am going to tell."

"Then I will tell the rest," exclaimed Lucy. "I made her do it. I was jealous of you, Rosamund, and I always hated you, and I was even more jealous of that horrid Irene and her love for Agnes. I only thought that I would punish her and you by taking Agnes away from her, and I think I have succeeded; but I never thought it would make Agnes ill. I am very, very, very sorry for that;" and, to the surprise of everybody, Lucy, the proud, the haughty, the reserved, burst into tears.

No one took much notice of her tears, for all eyes were fixed on Irene and the strange look which was filling her face. After a pause she went straight up to Lucy and took her hand.

"Lucy, will you come with me upstairs?"

"What do you want me to do?" said Lucy, in great astonishment.

"I want you to come with me, that is all."

"But why?"

"If you are at all sorry, will you come? There isn't a minute to lose."

"Yes, go with her—go for heaven's sake!" said Rosamund; and Lucy found herself going.

They went up the softly carpeted stairs and down the silent corridor, and then the two girls paused before a door which was partly ajar. The room was darkened, and Miss Frost was sitting by a little bed, and a little voice kept on crying suddenly, "Oh, there never was any Irene, there never was any Irene, and I loved her so! I loved her so! But she was a fairy, and the fairies took her back again, and—and—oh, I want to die! I want to die!"

The little hot hands were stretched outside the bedclothes, the beautiful dark eyes were open wide, and just at that moment Irene, very pale, still holding Lucy's hand, entered the room. Miss Frost stood up in speechless horror.

"Do sit down again, Miss Frost," said Irene; and she went straight up to little Agnes, who, to the astonishment of every one, no longer shrank from her, but, on the contrary, allowed her to hold one of her hands. Irene then turned to Lucy.

"Lucy," she said, "speak the truth now this minute, and I will forgive you."

"It was I who did it," said Lucy. "Go to sleep, and forget all about it. Irene isn't a changeling at all, and she never had anything to do with the fairies. I was jealous because you loved her and only her, and I wanted you to hate her, and I got Phyllis Flower to help me, and we put the hedgehog into your bed; but we didn't guess—we couldn't guess—that it would make you so ill."

Little Agnes looked with wide eyes at the speaker.

"Go away now," said Irene. "I think she understands. You go away also, Frosty. Please, please go!"

Miss Frost and Lucy found themselves impelled to leave the room, while Irene lay down on the bed beside the little girl, and taking both her hands, held them fast and whispered softly in the little ear:

"I am no changeling, but your own Irene, and I would rather

die than injure one hair of your head. Come close, darling; come close. It wasn't I, but another, and I am no changeling."

"Oh, my own Irene! My own, own Irene!" whispered the little voice; and then it grew fainter, and there came a smile on the tiny face, and in a few minutes' time the tired bright eyes closed, and the child slept.

When the doctor came that evening little Agnes was still sleeping, and Irene was still holding her hands. The fever was going down moment by moment. The doctor came in and said "Hush!" and whispered to Irene that she must on no account stir. She must be close to little Agnes, when she woke, and he himself would stay in the room, for the child would be very weak; but doubtless the fever would have left her. He was much puzzled to account for the change; but Rosamund was the one to enlighten him. She just told him that some very mischievous girls had played a trick, but she mentioned no names. For Lucy seemed really broken-hearted; and as to Phyllis Flower, she had cried so hard that her eyes were scarcely visible.

About midnight little Agnes woke in her right mind. She saw Irene, and lifting a tiny white hand, she stroked her cheek.

"I have had a very bad dream; but I don't seem to remember anything," she said.

"Only that you are with me," said Irene; "and you will be with me all my life—won't you, little darling?"

By slow degrees little Agnes got well, and when she was well enough she and Irene and Rosamund left the school; and from that day, as far as I can tell, Irene has been a changed character: thoughtful though spirited, beautiful, talented, but with much consideration for others, and the comfort and joy of her mother's heart. But the one she loves best on earth is the one whom she calls her own little Agnes.

THE END

L. T. Meade

Choose from Thousands of 1stWorldLibrary Classics By

A. M. Barnard
Ada Leverson
Adolphus William Ward
Aesop
Agatha Christie
Alexander Aaronsohn
Alexander Kielland
Alexandre Dumas
Alfred Gatty
Alfred Ollivant
Alice Duer Miller
Alice Turner Curtis
Alice Dunbar
Allen Chapman
Alleyne Ireland
Ambrose Bierce
Amelia E. Barr
Amory H. Bradford
Andrew Lang
Andrew McFarland Davis
Andy Adams
Angela Brazil
Anna Alice Chapin
Anna Sewell
Annie Besant
Annie Hamilton Donnell
Annie Payson Call
Annie Roe Carr
Annonaymous
Anton Chekhov
Archibald Lee Fletcher
Arnold Bennett
Arthur C. Benson
Arthur Conan Doyle
Arthur M. Winfield
Arthur Ransome
Arthur Schnitzler
Arthur Train
Atticus
B.H. Baden-Powell
B. M. Bower
B. C. Chatterjee
Baroness Emmuska Orczy
Baroness Orczy
Basil King
Bayard Taylor
Ben Macomber
Bertha Muzzy Bower
Bjornstjerne Bjornson

Booth Tarkington
Boyd Cable
Bram Stoker
C. Collodi
C. E. Orr
C. M. Ingleby
Carolyn Wells
Catherine Parr Traill
Charles A. Eastman
Charles Amory Beach
Charles Dickens
Charles Dudley Warner
Charles Farrar Browne
Charles Ives
Charles Kingsley
Charles Klein
Charles Hanson Towne
Charles Lathrop Pack
Charles Romyn Dake
Charles Whibley
Charles Willing Beale
Charlotte M. Braeme
Charlotte M. Yonge
Charlotte Perkins Stetson
Clair W. Hayes
Clarence Day Jr.
Clarence E. Mulford
Clemence Housman
Confucius
Coningsby Dawson
Cornelis DeWitt Wilcox
Cyril Burleigh
D. H. Lawrence
Daniel Defoe
David Garnett
Dinah Craik
Don Carlos Janes
Donald Keyhoe
Dorothy Kilner
Dougan Clark
Douglas Fairbanks
E. Nesbit
E. P. Roe
E. Phillips Oppenheim
E. S. Brooks
Earl Barnes
Edgar Rice Burroughs
Edith Van Dyne
Edith Wharton

Edward Everett Hale
Edward J. O'Biren
Edward S. Ellis
Edwin L. Arnold
Eleanor Atkins
Eleanor Hallowell Abbott
Eliot Gregory
Elizabeth Gaskell
Elizabeth McCracken
Elizabeth Von Arnim
Ellem Key
Emerson Hough
Emilie F. Carlen
Emily Bronte
Emily Dickinson
Enid Bagnold
Enilor Macartney Lane
Erasmus W. Jones
Ernie Howard Pie
Ethel May Dell
Ethel Turner
Ethel Watts Mumford
Eugene Sue
Eugenie Foa
Eugene Wood
Eustace Hale Ball
Evelyn Everett-green
Everard Cotes
F. H. Cheley
F. J. Cross
F. Marion Crawford
Fannie E. Newberry
Federick Austin Ogg
Ferdinand Ossendowski
Fergus Hume
Florence A. Kilpatrick
Fremont B. Deering
Francis Bacon
Francis Darwin
Frances Hodgson Burnett
Frances Parkinson Keyes
Frank Gee Patchin
Frank Harris
Frank Jewett Mather
Frank L. Packard
Frank V. Webster
Frederic Stewart Isham
Frederick Trevor Hill
Frederick Winslow Taylor

Friedrich Kerst
Friedrich Nietzsche
Fyodor Dostoyevsky
G.A. Henty
G.K. Chesterton
Gabrielle E. Jackson
Garrett P. Serviss
Gaston Leroux
George A. Warren
George Ade
Geroge Bernard Shaw
George Cary Eggleston
George Durston
George Ebers
George Eliot
George Gissing
George MacDonald
George Meredith
George Orwell
George Sylvester Viereck
George Tucker
George W. Cable
George Wharton James
Gertrude Atherton
Gordon Casserly
Grace E. King
Grace Gallatin
Grace Greenwood
Grant Allen
Guillermo A. Sherwell
Gulielma Zollinger
Gustav Flaubert
H. A. Cody
H. B. Irving
H. C. Bailey
H. G. Wells
H. H. Munro
H. Irving Hancock
H. R. Naylor
H. Rider Haggard
H. W. C. Davis
Haldeman Julius
Hall Caine
Hamilton Wright Mabie
Hans Christian Andersen
Harold Avery
Harold McGrath
Harriet Beecher Stowe
Harry Castlemon
Harry Coghill
Harry Houidini

Hayden Carruth
Helent Hunt Jackson
Helen Nicolay
Hendrik Conscience
Hendy David Thoreau
Henri Barbusse
Henrik Ibsen
Henry Adams
Henry Ford
Henry Frost
Henry James
Henry Jones Ford
Henry Seton Merriman
Henry W Longfellow
Herbert A. Giles
Herbert Carter
Herbert N. Casson
Herman Hesse
Hildegard G. Frey
Homer
Honore De Balzac
Horace B. Day
Horace Walpole
Horatio Alger Jr.
Howard Pyle
Howard R. Garis
Hugh Lofting
Hugh Walpole
Humphry Ward
Ian Maclaren
Inez Haynes Gillmore
Irving Bacheller
Isabel Cecilia Williams
Isabel Hornibrook
Israel Abrahams
Ivan Turgenev
J. G.Austin
J. Henri Fabre
J. M. Barrie
J. M. Walsh
J. Macdonald Oxley
J. R. Miller
J. S. Fletcher
J. S. Knowles
J. Storer Clouston
J. W. Duffield
Jack London
Jacob Abbott
James Allen
James Andrews
James Baldwin

James Branch Cabell
James DeMille
James Joyce
James Lane Allen
James Lane Allen
James Oliver Curwood
James Oppenheim
James Otis
James R. Driscoll
Jane Abbott
Jane Austen
Jane L. Stewart
Janet Aldridge
Jens Peter Jacobsen
Jerome K. Jerome
Jessie Graham Flower
John Buchan
John Burroughs
John Cournos
John F. Kennedy
John Gay
John Glasworthy
John Habberton
John Joy Bell
John Kendrick Bangs
John Milton
John Philip Sousa
John Taintor Foote
Jonas Lauritz Idemil Lie
Jonathan Swift
Joseph A. Altsheler
Joseph Carey
Joseph Conrad
Joseph E. Badger Jr
Joseph Hergesheimer
Joseph Jacobs
Jules Vernes
Julian Hawthrone
Julie A Lippmann
Justin Huntly McCarthy
Kakuzo Okakura
Karle Wilson Baker
Kate Chopin
Kenneth Grahame
Kenneth McGaffey
Kate Langley Bosher
Kate Langley Bosher
Katherine Cecil Thurston
Katherine Stokes
L. A. Abbot
L. T. Meade

L. Frank Baum
Latta Griswold
Laura Dent Crane
Laura Lee Hope
Laurence Housman
Lawrence Beasley
Leo Tolstoy
Leonid Andreyev
Lewis Carroll
Lewis Sperry Chafer
Lilian Bell
Lloyd Osbourne
Louis Hughes
Louis Joseph Vance
Louis Tracy
Louisa May Alcott
Lucy Fitch Perkins
Lucy Maud Montgomery
Luther Benson
Lydia Miller Middleton
Lyndon Orr
M. Corvus
M. H. Adams
Margaret E. Sangster
Margret Howth
Margaret Vandercook
Margaret W. Hungerford
Margret Penrose
Maria Edgeworth
Maria Thompson Daviess
Mariano Azuela
Marion Polk Angellotti
Mark Overton
Mark Twain
Mary Austin
Mary Catherine Crowley
Mary Cole
Mary Hastings Bradley
Mary Roberts Rinehart
Mary Rowlandson
M. Wollstonecraft Shelley
Maud Lindsay
Max Beerbohm
Myra Kelly
Nathaniel Hawthrone
Nicolo Machiavelli
O. F. Walton
Oscar Wilde
Owen Johnson
P.G. Wodehouse
Paul and Mabel Thorne

Paul G. Tomlinson
Paul Severing
Percy Brebner
Percy Keese Fitzhugh
Peter B. Kyne
Plato
Quincy Allen
R. Derby Holmes
R. L. Stevenson
R. S. Ball
Rabindranath Tagore
Rahul Alvares
Ralph Bonehill
Ralph Henry Barbour
Ralph Victor
Ralph Waldo Emmerson
Rene Descartes
Ray Cummings
Rex Beach
Rex E. Beach
Richard Harding Davis
Richard Jefferies
Richard Le Gallienne
Robert Barr
Robert Frost
Robert Gordon Anderson
Robert L. Drake
Robert Lansing
Robert Lynd
Robert Michael Ballantyne
Robert W. Chambers
Rosa Nouchette Carey
Rudyard Kipling
Saint Augustine
Samuel B. Allison
Samuel Hopkins Adams
Sarah Bernhardt
Sarah C. Hallowell
Selma Lagerlof
Sherwood Anderson
Sigmund Freud
Standish O'Grady
Stanley Weyman
Stella Benson
Stella M. Francis
Stephen Crane
Stewart Edward White
Stijn Streuvels
Swami Abhedananda
Swami Parmananda
T. S. Ackland

T. S. Arthur
The Princess Der Ling
Thomas A. Janvier
Thomas A Kempis
Thomas Anderton
Thomas Bailey Aldrich
Thomas Bulfinch
Thomas De Quincey
Thomas Dixon
Thomas H. Huxley
Thomas Hardy
Thomas More
Thornton W. Burgess
U. S. Grant
Upton Sinclair
Valentine Williams
Various Authors
Vaughan Kester
Victor Appleton
Victor G. Durham
Victoria Cross
Virginia Woolf
Wadsworth Camp
Walter Camp
Walter Scott
Washington Irving
Wilbur Lawton
Wilkie Collins
Willa Cather
Willard F. Baker
William Dean Howells
William le Queux
W. Makepeace Thackeray
William W. Walter
William Shakespeare
Winston Churchill
Yei Theodora Ozaki
Yogi Ramacharaka
Young E. Allison
Zane Grey